16LIVES

ROGER CASEMENT

ANGUS MITCHELL – AUTHOR OF 16LIVES: ROGER CASEMENT

Dr Angus Mitchell has published extensively on the life and legacy of Roger Casement and his significance to the history of human rights. He edited *The Amazon Journal of Roger Casement* (1997) and *Sir Roger Casement's Heart of Darkness* (2003). His work has appeared in the *Field Day Review*, *Irish Economic and Social History* and *Dublin Review of Books*. He has lectured at universities in Ireland, Britain, Brazil and the USA. He is on the editorial board of *History Ireland*.

LORCAN COLLINS – SERIES EDITOR

Lorcan Collins was born and raised in Dublin. A lifelong interest in Irish history led to the foundation of his hugely-popular 1916 Walking Tour in 1996. He co-authored *The Easter Rising: A Guide to Dublin in 1916* (O'Brien Press, 2000) with Conor Kostick. His biography of James Connolly was published in the *16 Lives* series in 2012. He is also a regular contributor to radio, television and historical journals. *16 Lives* is Lorcan's concept and he is co-editor of the series.

DR RUÁN O'DONNELL – SERIES EDITOR

Dr Ruán O'Donnell is a senior lecturer at the University of Limerick. A graduate of University College Dublin and the Australian National University, O'Donnell has published extensively on Irish Republicanism. Titles include *Robert Emmet and the Rising of 1803*, *The Impact of 1916* (editor), *Special Category, The IRA in English prisons 1968–1978* and *The O'Brien Pocket History of the Irish Famine*. He is a director of the Irish Manuscript Commission and a frequent contributor to the national and international media on the subject of Irish revolutionary history.

16LIVES
ROGER CASEMENT

Angus Mitchell

THE O'BRIEN PRESS
DUBLIN

First published 2013 by
The O'Brien Press Ltd,
12 Terenure Road East, Rathgar,
Dublin 6, Ireland.
Tel: +353 1 4923333; Fax: +353 1 4922777
E-mail: books@obrien.ie.
Website: www.obrien.ie

ISBN: 978-1-84717-264-8

PICTURE CREDITS

The author and publisher thank the following for permission to use photographs and
illustrative material: front cover image: Courtesy of the National Library of Ireland; inside
front cover: 'High Treason – The Trial of Sir Roger Casement', by Sir John Lavery, the
UK Government Art Collection, on permanent loan to the Honorable Society of King's
Inns; back cover: Author's collection. National Library of Ireland: section 1, p1 top and
bottom, p2 top left, p5 top, p6 top and bottom; section 2, p2 bottom, p3 bottom. Milligan
Family and Catherine Morris, author *Alice Milligan and the Irish Cultural Revival*: section
2, p2. Lorcan Collins: section 2, p5 top and bottom. Welcome Library, London: section
1, p3 top. National Portrait Gallery, London: section 1, p4 top. Cambridge University
Library: section 1, p2 bottom. Author's collection: section 1, p3 bottom left and right, p4
bottom, p5 bottom, p7 top and bottom, p8; section 2, p1, p2 top left, p3 top, p4 top and
bottom, p6 top and bottom, p7, p8 top and bottom. If any involuntary infringement of
copyright has occurred, sincere apologies are offered and the owners of such copyright
are requested to contact the publisher.

Back cover photograph: The earliest known photograph of Roger Casement in the
Congo alongside senior colonial officers. Casement is third from left in the back row.

1 2 3 4 5 6 7 8 9 10
13 14 15 16 17 18 19

Printed and bound by CPI Group (UK) Ltd, Croydon, CR0 4YY
The paper in this book is produced using pulp from managed forests

DEDICATION

This biography is dedicated to the communities living near the waterways of the Congo and Amazon: their suffering is central to this story.

ACKNOWLEDGEMENTS

My greatest debt of thanks extends to Caoilfhionn Ní Bheacháin. Her constancy and belief have sustained me during the writing of this book and our beautiful daughter, Isla Maeve, is the result of our long friendship and deep love.

In Limerick: Brian Murphy OSB, Tom Toomey and Pattie Punch.

In Spain: Eduardo Riestra of Ediciones del Viento and Sonia Fernández Ordás, as well as Justin, Carmen and Beibhinn Harman, Sinéad Ryan, Ann Marie Murphy and the staff of the Irish embassy.

In Brazil: Laura PD de Izarra at the University of São Paulo, Mariana Bolfarine, Ambassador Frank Sheridan, Sharon Lennon, Tom Hennigan, Fernando Nogueira, Aurélio Michilis, Milton Hatoum, Elizabeth MacGregor, Filomena Madeiros, Liana de Camargo Leão, Beatriz Kopschitz X Bastos, Munira H Mutran, Juan Alvaro Echeverri (Colombia) and María Graciela Eliggi (Universidad Nacional de La Pampa, Argentina).

In Ireland: Jim Cronin and Rebecca Hussey. In Tralee: Seán Seosamh O Conchubhair and Dawn Uí Chonchubhair, and Donal J O'Sullivan, Padraig MacFhearghusa, Brian Caball, and Bryan O'Daly. In Dublin: Tommy Graham, Brigid, Malachy, Alexander and Nina. The staff of the National Library of Ireland, especially Colette O'Flaherty, Tom Desmond, Gerry Long, Gerard Lyne and the late and much lamented Maura Scannell. At the USAC summer school programme at NUI Galway: Mark Quigley, Méabh Ní Fhuartháin, Anne Corbett and Deaglán Ó Donghaile.

Thanks should also extend to Mairéad Wilson, Frank Callanan, Declan Kiberd, Deirdre McMahon, Catherine Morris, Paula Nolan, Luke Gibbons, Seamus Deane, Kevin Whelan, Tom Bartlett, Martin Mansergh, Stephen Rea, Tanya Kiang and Trish Lambe at the Gallery of Photography, Tadhg Foley and Maureen O'Connor, Maureen Murphy, Jordan Goodman, Mary Jane Smith, Amy Hauber, David P Kelly, Ronan Sheehan, Pierrot Ngadi of the Congolese Anti-Poverty Network, Dorothee and Michael Snoek, Moira Durdin Robertson, John O'Brennan, Pat Punch, Michael McCaughan, Leo Keohane, Eoin McMahon, Sinead McCoole, Brock Lagan, Radek Cerny, Stephen Powell and Inigo Batterham.

My editors at The O'Brien Press – Ide ní Laoghaire, Jonathan Rossney, Lorcan Collins and Ruan O'Donnell – applied the pressure when pressure was needed. I did my best!

Finally, I must acknowledge the unfaltering support of my wonderful mother, Susan Mitchell OBE, my brother Lorne, Susie, Yolanda, Torin, Rory and Oscar, my sister Colina, and my daughter Hazel: you are in my heart forever.

16LIVES Timeline

1845–51. The Great Hunger in Ireland. One million people die and over the next decades millions more emigrate.

1858, March 17. The Irish Republican Brotherhood, or Fenians, are formed with the express intention of overthrowing British rule in Ireland by whatever means necessary.

1867, February and March. Fenian Uprising.

1870, May. Home Rule movement founded by Isaac Butt, who had previously campaigned for amnesty for Fenian prisoners.

1879–81. The Land War. Violent agrarian agitation against English landlords.

1884, November 1. The Gaelic Athletic Association founded – immediately infiltrated by the Irish Republican Brotherhood (IRB).

1893, July 31. Gaelic League founded by Douglas Hyde and Eoin MacNeill. The *Gaelic Revival*, a period of Irish Nationalism, pride in the language, history, culture and sport.

1900, September. *Cumann na nGaedheal* (Irish Council) founded by Arthur Griffith.

1905–07. *Cumann na nGaedheal*, the Dungannon Clubs and the National Council are amalgamated to form *Sinn Féin* (We Ourselves).

1909, August. Countess Markievicz and Bulmer Hobson organise nationalist youths into *Na Fianna Éireann* (Warriors of Ireland) a kind of boy scout brigade.

1912, April. Asquith introduces the Third Home Rule Bill to the British Parliament. Passed by the Commons and rejected by the Lords, the Bill would have to become law due to the Parliament Act. Home Rule expected to be introduced for Ireland by autumn 1914.

1913, January. Sir Edward Carson and James Craig set up Ulster Volunteer Force (UVF) with the intention of defending Ulster against Home Rule.

1913. Jim Larkin, founder of the Irish Transport and General Workers' Union (ITGWU) calls for a workers' strike for better pay and conditions.

1913, August 31. Jim Larkin speaks at a banned rally on Sackville (O'Connell) Street; Bloody Sunday.

1913, November 23. James Connolly, Jack White and Jim Larkin establish the Irish Citizen Army (ICA) in order to protect strikers.

1913, November 25. The Irish Volunteers founded in Dublin to 'secure the rights and liberties common to all the people of Ireland'.

1914, March 20. Resignations of British officers force British government not to use British army to enforce Home Rule, an event known as the 'Curragh Mutiny'.

1914, April 2. In Dublin, Agnes O'Farrelly, Mary MacSwiney, Countess Markievicz and others establish Cumann na mBan as a women's volunteer force dedicated to establishing Irish freedom and assisting the Irish Volunteers.

1914, April 24. A shipment of 35,000 rifles and five million rounds of ammunition is landed at Larne for the UVF.

1914, July 26. Irish Volunteers unload a shipment of 900 rifles and 45,000 rounds of ammunition shipped from Germany aboard Erskine Childers' yacht, the *Asgard*. British troops fire on crowd on Bachelors Walk, Dublin. Three citizens are killed.

1914, August 4. Britain declares war on Germany. Home Rule for Ireland shelved for the duration of the First World War.

1914, September 9. Meeting held at Gaelic League headquarters between IRB and other extreme republicans. Initial decision made to stage an uprising while Britain is at war.

1914, September. 170,000 leave the Volunteers and form the National Volunteers or Redmondites. Only 11,000 remain as the Irish Volunteers under Eoin MacNeill.

1915, May–September. Military Council of the IRB is formed.

1915, August 1. Pearse gives fiery oration at the funeral of Jeremiah O'Donovan Rossa.

1916, January 19–22. James Connolly joins the IRB Military Council, thus ensuring that the ICA shall be involved in the Rising. Rising date confirmed for Easter.

1916, April 20, 4.15pm. *The Aud* arrives at Tralee Bay, laden with 20,000 German rifles for the Rising. Captain Karl Spindler waits in vain for a signal from shore.

1916, April 21, 2.15am. Roger Casement and his two companions go ashore from U-19 and land on Banna Strand. Casement is arrested at McKenna's Fort.

6.30pm. *The Aud* is captured by the British navy and forced to sail towards Cork Harbour.

22 April, 9.30am. *The Aud* is scuttled by her captain off Daunt's Rock.

10pm. Eóin MacNeill as chief-of-staff of the Irish Volunteers issues the countermanding order in Dublin to try to stop the Rising.

1916, April 23, 9am, Easter Sunday. The Military Council meets to discuss the situation, considering MacNeill has placed an advertisement in a Sunday newspaper halting all Volunteer operations. The Rising is put on hold for twenty-four hours. Hundreds of copies of *The Proclamation of the Republic* are printed in Liberty Hall.

1916, April 24, 12 noon, Easter Monday. The Rising begins in Dublin.

South America

Caribbean Sea

Atlantic Ocean

Caracas

Bogota

COLOMBIA

Belém do Para

Quito

Putumayo

Amazon

Iquitos

Manaus

Madeira-Mamoré Railway

BRAZIL

Lima

Salvador

PERU

BOLIVIA

Petrópolis

São Paulo

Rio de Janeiro

Pacific Ocean

ARGENTINA

Santiago

Buenos Aires

Montevideo

Mar del Plata

Atlantic Ocean

The Congo Free State (1903)

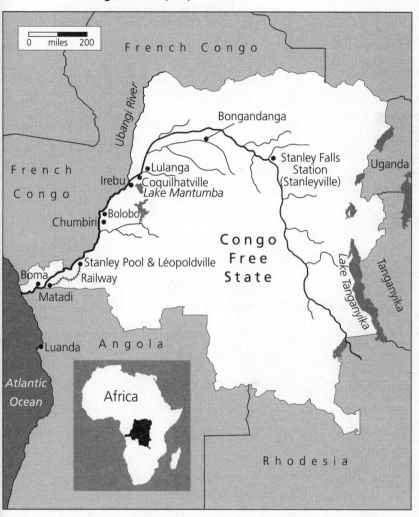

16LIVES – Series Introduction

This book is part of a series called *16 LIVES*, conceived with the objective of recording for posterity the lives of the sixteen men who were executed after the 1916 Easter Rising. Who were these people and what drove them to commit themselves to violent revolution?

The rank and file as well as the leadership were all from diverse backgrounds. Some were privileged and some had no material wealth. Some were highly educated writers, poets or teachers and others had little formal schooling. Their common desire, to set Ireland on the road to national freedom, united them under the one banner of the army of the Irish Republic. They occupied key buildings in Dublin and around Ireland for one week before they were forced to surrender. The leaders were singled out for harsh treatment and all sixteen men were executed for their role in the Rising.

Meticulously researched yet written in an accessible fashion, the *16 LIVES* biographies can be read as individual volumes but together they make a highly collectible series.

Lorcan Collins & Dr Ruán O'Donnell,
16 Lives *Series Editors*

CONTENTS

Introduction

The death of Roger Casement after a lengthy trial for treason closed the tragic events of the 1916 Easter Rising. In the eyes of the British authorities, Casement's revolutionary turn was particularly loathsome because of his long and distinguished career as British consul in Africa and South America. For his service to the Crown, and his courage and integrity while carrying out investigations into crimes against humanity, he received a knighthood in 1911. During the course of his career he had corresponded with and influenced many of the leading statesmen of his age. For many years he operated inside the system and tried to bring about reform from within; when that failed, he emerged as its fiercest critic.

Casement's extraordinary and somewhat enigmatic life has intrigued a succession of journalists, authors and historians. His meaning has never been easy to discern because, as both Foreign Office trouble-shooter and Irish revolutionary nationalist, he operated between two diametrically-opposed spaces of secrecy. Although he left behind an extensive and at times labyrinthine paper-trail, in which the paradoxes underlying his dual existence as government official and revolutionary can be perceived, the 'truth' about Roger Casement remains deeply contested. But truth and history are not always compatible.

One early chronicler of the War of Independence, Shaw Desmond, wrote of Casement: 'Look well upon this man, because he carried in himself the whole story of Ireland. Learn the secret of this man and you have learnt the secret of Ireland.'[1] What secret about both the man and Ireland did he mean? Was it what Éamon de Valera alluded to in 1934 when he commented: 'No writer outside Ireland, however competent, who had not the closest contact with events in this country during the years preceding and following the Rising of 1916 could hope to do justice to the character and achievements of this great man … a further period of time must elapse before the full extent of Casement's sacrifice can be understood and appreciated outside Ireland.'[2]

This biography attempts to unpick and explain the achievements of Casement by probing some of the interlinking secrets and conspiracies that have made him perplexing to historians. A century has elapsed since he openly turned from British official into Irish rebel leader, and we can now assess Casement in the light of much new evidence, including a box of material released as recently as 22 December 2012 by the National Library of Ireland. The veil of mystery has been lifted as far as it is ever likely to be, especially on the clandestine dimension of British state secrecy and Casement's role as a consular representative of the Foreign Office.

In the last sixty years, much of the scholarship and journalism about Casement has been framed by the controversy over the authenticity of the Black Diaries. These shadowy documents, purportedly written by Casement and containing explicit evidence of homosexuality, were used during his trial by the British secret services as part of a coordinated campaign to discredit him and deter his allies from seeking a reprieve from the death sentence. After 1916, their very existence was denied until they were published in 1959 in Paris (at that time publication in Britain would have contravened the Official Secrets Act).

While there is a fascinating sexual dimension to Casement's interpretation, there has been a reluctance to assess the Black Diaries within their proper historical context: either as valid sources for analysing his investigation of crimes against humanity, or as components in a bitter propaganda attempt to undermine his moral authority as a whistle-blower and to demean his intervention in the struggle for Irish independence. In the century since his death, an often violent war of words has been fought over these documents, with various political and academic reputations resting on the question of their authenticity. Casement's wider concerns about the fate of humanity and his relevance to modern Ireland have been conveniently obscured by an enduring and ultimately pointless anxiety about his sexuality. My own scholarship preceding the publication of this book has argued that the Black

Diaries are indeed forgeries and with this biography I build on that over-arching argument.

The ongoing debate over Casement's meaning (the subject of the last chapter of this book) offers insight into why history matters and why the stakes involved in some aspects of historical representation are necessarily high. Casement's life and death requires us to ask searching questions about the 1916 Rising and the last hundred years of Anglo-Irish relations. However, his legacy also obliges us to think about the ethics of international trade, slavery and his relevance to the modern discourse of human rights. More problematically, his flight to Germany in 1914 and the justification of his self-confessed treason sets us off down the thorny path of discussion on the causes of the First World War. Was Britain justified in declaring war in August 1914 (Casement did not think so) and what did Ireland's sacrifice achieve? The historian Desmond Greaves alluded to these unsettling questions when he wrote:

> So we must ask ourselves, what is it that makes the powers that be so determined that this mystery shall not be probed? Why are they so determined to discourage enquiry that would settle matters once and for all? Is it possible that we are all underestimating Casement's importance and the part he played on the stage of history?[3]

Since this comment was written in 1975, at the height of

the Troubles in Northern Ireland, Casement has been the subject of a series of revisionist biographies that have placed undue emphasis on his sexuality, downplayed his relevance to his age and presented his contribution to the Easter Rising as peripheral and ultimately incoherent.[4] Sixteen years later in 1991, when Ireland commemorated the seventy-fifth anniversary of the 1916 Rising, Casement's name and meaning had been largely written out of the canon of modern Irish history. In 2012, the Irish novelist John Banville claimed Casement as 'not only one of the greatest Irishmen who ever lived but also a considerable figure on the world stage' and asked: 'Why then is he largely forgotten, or ignored, in Ireland and elsewhere?'[5] In a country where history and politics mix uneasily, the reasons are not hard to see.

Casement does not belong as wholly to Ireland as, say, the lives of Patrick Pearse or Thomas MacDonagh. His years in sub-Saharan Africa and Brazil are very much part of Britain's imperial past. More than that, as this biography will argue, Casement represented a cosmopolitan nationalism and internationalism that cut against the grain of the image of the post-Treaty state. He had a definite sense of the future of Europe and Ireland's place within the community of European nation states. While he may have turned decisively against the British Empire and returned to Ireland on the eve of the Rising to try and stop the rebellion, his reasons contained their own logic and integrity. In the narrating of

1916, Casement was himself betrayed, isolated and his intellectual contribution obscured.

His presiding sense of Irish nationalism was rooted in his love for the province of Ulster. It is symbolically revealing that the largest GAA stadium in Northern Ireland is Casement Park in West Belfast, and that Casement expressed a desire to be buried in Murlough Bay in Antrim and not Glasnevin Cemetery, where his bones currently reside. He claimed Ulster as the critical constituent in the making of a stable and prosperous Ireland, a view that has never suited the history of two nations of the last century. His historical meaning has therefore required sustained manipulation in the histories of modern Ireland and Great Britain. Understanding the management of his historical legacy is now central to appreciating his revolutionary turn, and the irreconcilable contradictions and differences encoded into his interpretation.

Angus Mitchell
Limerick, 2013

Chapter One

• • • • • •

1864–1883

Nomadic Upbringing

The plaque commemorating his birth is still visible above the front door of Doyle's Cottage in a quiet street of Sandycove, where Roger Casement entered the world on 1 September 1864. It is a simple house in a respectable neighbourhood of Dublin, renowned as the area of the city where the Martello tower in James Joyce's masterpiece *Ulysses* is located. This coincidence is highly apposite, as Casement's life has fascinating connections with the modernist epic of the 20th century; indeed, his name is referenced in the 'Cyclops' chapter:

> Did you read that report by a man what's this his name is?
> —Casement, says the citizen. He's an Irishman.
> —Yes, that's the man, says J.J.

On 16 June 1904, the date *Ulysses* made famous as Bloomsday, Casement's name was circulating not merely through the pubs of Dublin but in conversations across the globe, from the heart of central Africa to the outposts of the British Empire in India, Australia and Canada. But despite being born in Dublin, Casement spent a comparatively small amount of time residing in his native city; like Stephen Dedalus, he became a citizen of the world. Nevertheless, Dublin would eventually become the site for the rebellion in which he played such a defining part and where his bones would finally come to rest.

Recent genealogical research has shown how the Casements moved from the Isle of Man to Antrim in the early eighteenth century. Different branches of the family held lands in both Wicklow and Antrim, and produced sons who generally went into either trade or the armed forces, and daughters who married into their own social class. Although Casement is inevitably categorised as 'Anglo-Irish', this is in some ways misleading. The extended Casement family might have had the airs and graces associated with the ascendancy class in terms of land, a big house and privilege, but for Roger Casement's own family money was always scarce, and in references to his upbringing there is not the usual sense of either entitlement or advantage.

Roger's father, also named Roger (1819-77), served in the British army in India with the Third Light Dragoons. In 1848 he sold his commission and returned to Europe to take part in the Louis Kossuth-led liberation of Hungary. Stories relate of how he held strong Fenian sympathies, identified with the Paris communards, and expressed beliefs in the principles of universal republicanism.[1] He also dabbled in more esoteric interests, like Sikh mysticism; although, in line with Victorian parenting, he was quite a disciplinarian with his children. In 1855 he married Anne Jephson (1834–73), who was fifteen years his junior.

The background of Casement's mother Anne is harder to establish with much certainty. In later life, Casement tried to research her connection to an old landed family, the Jephson-Norreys from Mallow in north Cork, but the information he uncovered was sketchy. It appears that she was baptised a Catholic, but quite possibly became an Anglican on marriage. Baptismal records show how she had Roger and his three elder siblings, Agnes, Charles and Tom, all secretly baptised as Catholics in Rhyl in north Wales. In Ireland, where religious difference is so accentuated, this unusual Protestant-Catholic duality is noteworthy, which might help to explain Casement's early identification with the aspirations of the United Irishmen and his life-long desire to unite Catholic, Protestant and Dissenter.

The little that is known about the circumstances of the family derives from personal reminiscences written by his cousins Gertrude and Elizabeth and his sister Agnes, or 'Nina', as she was affectionately called. According to these, the family moved around the European continent, living briefly in France, Italy, London, the Channel Islands and Ireland, although it is not known why they moved so frequently. This state of nomadism would come to define Casement's life, as he was destined never to settle in any place for any length of time. He lived in a constant state of motion: staying with friends and relatives, living briefly in rented accommodation, moving across the world by steamship and railways, or sleeping rough on his journeys into the African and South American interiors. But in the midst of all this endless travelling, Casement came to develop a particularly deep attachment to Ireland, and this love maintained him wherever he found himself.

The death of both parents by the time Roger was thirteen created a strong bond between him and his three siblings that would last for the rest of their lives. Roger's relationship with his sister Nina was particularly close and in her memoir she lovingly described how from a very early age her little brother enjoyed the great outdoors. He learned to swim well and developed an exceptionally kind and empathetic nature, along with a hatred of injustice.[2] She recalled, too, how he was an avid reader. Among his favourite books was James Fenimore Cooper's *The Last of the Mohicans*, a tale of the demise of Native American culture during the Seven Years' War (1756–63), when France and Great Britain fought for control of North America.

The family home still directly associated with Casement is

Magherintemple, a large and rather austere big house adjoining a lovingly-tended walled garden on the hills outside Ballycastle in County Antrim. This belonged to his uncle John, who took the orphaned Casement children in as his wards after the death of their parents. In his youth, Roger – or Roddie, as he was called by his immediate family – spent significant amounts of time at Magherintemple, and he returned there regularly to visit his relations throughout his life. To this day, the drafty rooms contain pieces of African furniture carved from tropical hardwoods, and a cabinet of ethnic curios that he presented like trophies to relations after returning from his African and Brazilian postings. But Magherintemple was not the only Antrim home where he was welcomed, and in several other ascendancy households, as well as the more humble abodes of local families, Roger was always made to feel at home.

He attended the Ballymena Diocesan School, where the principal, the Rev. Robert King, was one of the greatest Irish language scholars of the day, and Casement's love for the Irish language appears to have been nurtured from a very young age in this environment. In notes written to the scholar and revolutionary Eoin MacNeill (1867–1945), he recalled:

My very old Master, the late Revd Robert King, of Bally-mena, spoke and knew Irish well and often preached in Irish in his Protestant church of the Six Towns up in the Derry hills above Maghera and Magherafelt in the 1840s.[3] ... The

first Irish I heard was in Ulster, in Co. Down in 1869, when
I remember well often hearing the market people talk in it
altho' I was a tiny child then – also the boatmen from the
Omeath Shore.[4]

By all accounts he was a diligent, quick-witted and intelligent pupil at school, and won several prizes for Classics.
He enjoyed acting and singing, building up a repertoire of
songs that included *The Wearing of the Green* and *Silent O
Moyle*. According to Nina, he always stood firmly on the
side of truth and integrity, while developing a strong sense
of history. He read widely about the 1798 rebellion and how
Presbyterian Antrim rose against English oppression. The
nine Glens of Antrim, that stunning expanse of countryside
within walking distance of Magherintemple, became the
formative landscape for his youthful imagination. He took
pleasure in linking the histories he studied to the surrounding environment. Nina remembered how he would walk
around Donegore Hill, the site of a mass hanging of United
Irishmen in 1798, and by connecting the landscape and local
memory of sites of resistance to British rule in Ireland, he
quickly cultivated a deep identification with the land and
its people. 'He learned much of the history of our country
during those years. Long walks and visits to historic remains
of antiquity, talking to the kindly Ulster folk who could tell
many a tale of '98 and the horrors perpetrated by the brutal
soldiery of George III,' Nina recalled.[5]

By his late teens he was writing poetry related to the history of Ulster, influenced by the melodies of Thomas Moore and the poetry of James Clarence Mangan and Florence McCarthy. Another inspiration was the late nineteenth century fashion for epic rhyme, while a familiarity with the Romantic tradition of Byron, Shelley, Keats and Tennyson was also evident. Metaphorically, this poetry was punctuated with the Celticist iconography and Gothic symbolism typical of the time: the silent harp, the mysterious ruined abbey, prophetic and spectral presences, and plenty of violence in the description of battles.[6]

O'Donoghue's Daughter[7]

'Twas a calm Autumn evening, from hunting returning
  I wearily spurred my poor steed thro' the glade—
And on thro' the glen past the Abbey lights burning,
  Beneath its tall oaks and their far spreading shade—
And as nearer I drew to the lake I sent pealing
  My bugle's wild notes o'er the mist-shrouded water
When, oh! Like the voice of an Angel came stealing
  From distance the song of O'Donoghue's daughter.

Around 1880 Casement developed an interest in the politics of the Irish National Land League and the two principal figures involved in agitation for land redistribution and the protection of tenant farmers: the leader of the Irish Parliamentary Party, Charles Stewart Parnell, and the more radical MP, Michael Davitt. The politics of land became the determining issue of Casement's life. 'The land is at the bottom of all human progress and health of body and mind – and the land must be kept for the people,' he wrote in 1911.[8] This comment, made at the very height of his fame as a British government official, was shaped by his own observation of the Irish Land War and a belief that land should be utilised for the benefit of the nation and its citizenry and not exploited for the profits of the few. His intuitive analysis of the relationship between land, freedom, rights and national identity always informed his politics. In a speech he made about the Irish language during a tour of Antrim in 1905, he adopted geographical metaphors to explain his view of Irish nationality as inclusive, fluid and spiritually located:

> [R]emember that a nation is a very complex thing – it never does consist, it never has consisted solely of one blood or of one simple race. It is like a river, which rises far off in the hills and has many sources, many converging streams before it becomes one great stream. But just as each river has its peculiar character, its own individual charm of clearness of water, strength of current, picturesqueness of scenery, or commercial importance in the highways of the world – so every nation has its own peculiar attributes, its prevailing characteristics, its subtle spiritual atmosphere – and these it must retain if it is to be itself.[9]

Casement's upbringing coincided with the golden age of Victorian natural history and the belief that its study contributed to good health. His deep empathy for Ireland was developed as much by extensive walks and direct experience of the land and people as it was by reading newspapers and keeping abreast of events. The Victorians were obsessed with collecting, taxonomising and classifying the natural world and exotic cultures, and in this respect Casement was a product of his age. The Natural History Museum in Dublin contains a collection of butterflies he obtained when travelling through the Amazon. The anthropology collection in the National Museum of Ireland holds many artefacts – musical instruments, fabrics, basket weaving, fetishes and drums – which he gathered during his trips to Africa and South America. His official reports back to the Foreign Office contain references to issues like economic botany (the study of the commercial potential of plants), forestry, and environmental depletion. Much of his interest in the new sciences was learnt not only in the formal atmosphere of the classroom but as a naturally curious and energetic lad exploring the great outdoors. Later in life he would befriend and correspond with the most eminent Irish plant collector and forester of the age, Augustine Henry.

Many of the defining friendships of his life were made with people from the Glens of Antrim. During his late teens he spent much time with Ada MacNeill, a woman a few years older than him from a family near Cushendun. She too left a memoir of her formative years with Casement:

> We were both great walkers and strode over the hills and up the Glens and we both discovered we could talk without ceasing about Ireland … Roger had the history of Ireland at his fingers' ends.[10]

Over the next thirty years, Ada would become a tireless grassroots organiser for different nationalist causes in Ulster and a particularly active supporter of the Irish language movement. She remained a devoted friend of Casement's. Her recollection of him, written shortly after his death, provides insight into less well-known aspects of Casement's personality, including his spiritual and religious development. In his late teens, Casement was confirmed into the Anglican faith at the church of St Anne's in the Liverpool suburb of Stanley while staying with relatives there. Although part of his faith merely conformed to the social expectations of the time, Casement was also moved by the deep religious fervour of late Victorian Britain and a more proselytising influence evident in Ulster since the Great Awakening of 1859, when evangelical preachers encouraged a religious enthusiasm that sparked widespread missionary endeavour. 'He talked eloquently and earnestly against scoffing at religion,' Ada remembered.

If by his late teens Ulster rather than Dublin had become

his home, it would be Liverpool, the hub of Britain's oceanic commercial power, that became the launch pad for his career. Known as the second city of the Empire, and long associated with both the slave trade and antislavery activism, Liverpool had deep connections to both West African trade and Ireland. Over the course of his life, Casement would build a lasting attachment to Liverpool, and much of the support he later garnered for his campaign to bring about Congo reform derived from his core of friends, fellow activists and philanthropists. In 1964, while canvassing during the general election as an MP for Liverpool, the future Prime Minister Harold Wilson invoked the memory of Casement during his campaign to win over the large Irish vote in his constituency with the promise that Casement's body would be returned to Ireland in the event of a victory by the Labour Party.

Throughout his teenage years Liverpool served as a second home, largely due to his close contact with and many visits to his cousins, the Bannisters. His mother's sister Grace had married Edward Bannister, then a prosperous trader with extensive interests in West Africa. The Bannisters provided Casement and his siblings with support and encouragement as they prepared to go out into the world. By all accounts, Edward Bannister was another important influence on Casement. In 1893, after eight years of sporadic service as Honorary Consul in Angola, Bannister was appointed Vice-Consul in Boma, a port town on the Congo river. His time there proved brief and controversial, as he personally stood up to the increasing levels of oppression by the Belgian authorities in the region, which contravened the humanitarian promises justifying European colonial activity in Africa. Casement's early career in Africa was both facilitated and influenced by Bannister. The two shared a concern for the basic rights of the African, and Casement's straight-forward and unaffected language, as well as his measured and methodical approach to the compilation of evidence, were skills apparently developed early in his relations with his uncle.

The Bannisters lived in the suburb of Anfield and Casement was given a room in the attic of their house. For the rest of his life he was particularly close to his two cousins Elizabeth and Gertrude, and carried out the longest and most intimate correspondence of his life with the latter, who stood devotedly by him until the bitter end and beyond. In her introduction to *Some Poems of Roger Casement*, published in 1918, Gertrude wrote of her cousin's extraordinary level of empathy, evident since his childhood:

> Even as a little boy he turned with horror and revulsion
> from cruelty of every description; he would tenderly nurse
> a wounded bird to life, and stop to pity an overloaded horse.
> This gentleness and tender-heartedness was one of his most
> marked characteristics; it led him to champion the cause
> of the Congo native and the Putumayo Indian, and to
> spend his slender means in later life in trying to relieve the

wretched fever-stricken inhabitants in Connemara when typhus was raging amongst them, or to provide a mid-day meal for children in the Gaeltacht.[11]

For Casement, Liverpool became as much a place of departure as it was a place for family comfort and support. In 1880 he stood with his cousins on Waterloo Dock to bid farewell to his elder brothers Charlie and Tom as they set out for Australia to seek their fortunes. He would never see Charlie again. A few months later he found employment through family connections with a powerful Liverpool-based trading company, the Elder Dempster Shipping Company, one of several such companies shifting cargo throughout the Atlantic region and facilitating trade between Europe, Africa and the Americas. For two years he worked in a clerical capacity, keeping the books and familiarising himself with accounting and trading practices. However, it soon became clear to his managers that his temperament did not suit the regular hours and monotonous work of an office clerk. After initial voyages to West Africa to test the water, Casement applied and obtained a job with the International African Association, the name of the organisation established by King Leopold II of Belgium to implement his colonial interests in the vast territories in central Africa to which he laid claim.

When Casement embarked from Liverpool in 1884 bound for a career in sub-Saharan Africa, no one could have imagined that twenty years later he would be both reviled and revered in the very city of his departure for launching a movement that is today upheld as precursory to that phenomenon of globalisation: the international non-governmental organisation.

Chapter Two

• • • • • •

1884-1898

African Roots

Roger Casement's arrival in Africa coincided with the two events that did most to shape the continent during his lifetime: Britain's unilateral occupation of Egypt in 1882 and the Berlin West Africa Conference (1884-85). The broad imperative determining British commitment to Africa was security of the Suez Canal; the safety of the routes to India in particular motivated political and economic strategy more than some master plan to carve out a new world.

After a period of intense exploration by European adventurers and missionaries, the natural resources and the enormous potential of the interior of Africa had been roughly measured. At the Berlin Conference, convened by the German chancellor Otto von Bismarck, European diplomats tried to stabilise domestic rivalries by stimulating trade and turning their attention towards the colonial frontier of Africa. Following the signing of the General Act of the Berlin Conference (1885) a new relationship between Europe and Africa was initiated on European terms. This triggered a rapid division of the African sub-continent into spheres of influence as colonial powers scrambled for control of uncharted land. Exploration gave way to the signing of bilateral treaties with local chiefs and elders, the occupation of territorial claims through the agents of commerce and Christianity, and the imposition of structures of local administration. To pay for colonial government it was deemed necessary to develop the territories and make them economically viable. The dominant diplomatic player at the Berlin conference was the ambitious King Leopold II of Belgium, a man on a mission to build an empire. Through skilful negotiation he managed to persuade the other powers to recognise his rights to almost two million square miles of territory in central Africa.

For the years following the Berlin Conference, diplomats from Britain, France, Germany and Belgium were locked into a struggle for regional control. There were grand strategies at play: the French desired to connect their west African territories to the Nile; Britons dreamed of building a railway across Africa from Cape Town to Cairo; Germany wished to compete as an imperial power and join its colonies in southwest Africa (Namibia) to the Indian Ocean; while Portugal's colonial settlements were in a state of stagnation and decline.

The language used to achieve these ends was one of humanity. The justification and moral legitimacy for what might now be understood as an act of 'conquest' was built on various discourses, which fused ideas of racial supremacy with the philanthropic concept of rights. The white man was bringing what he considered to be the values and advantages of western civilisation to the 'savages' of Africa. The rhetoric of empire was primarily inspired by a sense of mission, both social and religious, and a belief that power brought responsibilities. At Berlin, King Leopold preached philanthropy, promoting the idea of liberating Africans from slavery and implementing law and justice as building blocks towards a civilised future. But such idealistic notions needed to be underpinned by economic success. Ambitious young men were encouraged to see Africa as a land of opportunity and set forth to discover it for themselves. But whatever ideals might have driven them to leave their lives in the metropolitan centres of Europe, what they arrived in was a harsh new world driven by the trinity of imperialism, racism and militarism.

In 1884 in the town of Banana, at the delta mouth of the Congo river, Roger Casement offered his services to the International African Association 'as a volunteer ... to aid in what was then represented as a philanthropic international enterprise, having only humanitarian aims'.[1] There he became one of the pioneer officers in what was soon to be known as the Congo Free State, that vast tract of land ruled by the absentee authority of King Leopold II.

The geographical enormity of the Congo defies straight-forward description; it is equally difficult for the reader to imagine. Comprised of thousands of miles of inland waterways dissected by immense regions of unmapped, hardwood forests, it was quite the heart of the African continent. The reaches of the lower Congo region, extending from the nine-miles-wide river mouth to the settlement at Matadi, (a distance of around sixty kilometres by boat) was the area that was accessible to Atlantic steamship traffic and was initially colonised by European missionaries. Here Leopold claimed territorial rights to both sides of the river and two administrative settlements at Boma and Matadi expanded as colonial administration was extended. From Matadi, however, a series of cataracts and whitewater rapids cut off the lower or Bas-Congo from the upper Congo.

The upper Congo was in many ways another country: a vast basin of river systems and inland lakes hemmed in by tropical highlands and rainforest. Over centuries, communities had settled along the waterways, and boats were the most practical (and more often than not the only) form of transportation. But it was in the upper Congo where extensive, almost limitless resources in rubber, hardwoods, minerals and precious stones might be exploited. For the European, the problem remained one of access and logistics: how to transport the resources into their market economy as efficiently and discreetly as possible.

Abuses were inevitable. Until the building of the railway from Matadi to Léopoldville (Kinshasa), the base camp and hub for Belgian administration on the upper Congo, everything was fuelled by the blood and sweat of African forced labour. In 1898 a railway between Matadi and Léopoldville was opened. This engineering project was integral to Casement's long involvement with the Congo. As goods moved in and out more freely, the Congo river became a commercial highway, but traditional settlements were decimated and communities ravaged. Commercial expansion necessitated ever-increasing levels of exploitation of the local people,

Casement's initial duties for the International African Association appear to have been managing a local supply store and building up local trading networks. He appears in a photograph, dated 1886, beside several senior officers involved in pioneering work in the Congo.[2] This included Sir Francis de Winton and Camille Janssen, the highest-ranking administrators on the Congo. Casement is visible at the back of the group, informally dressed compared to the others and wearing a straw hat instead of a pith helmet. The photograph acknowledges his early proximity to that exclusive administrative circle of white men who would ultimately wield huge influence in determining European policy in Africa. But while some of the men, such as Adolphe de Cuvelier, would go on to hold high office in Belgium, Casement would emerge twenty years later as the most energetic and outspoken witness and opponent to King Leopold II's administration in the Congo Free State.

In 1886 and 1887, as an agent of the Sanford Exploring Expedition, led by the US diplomat and entrepreneur 'General' Henry Sanford, Casement helped to organise the transportation of a steamer, the *Florida*, overland beyond the cataracts to the navigable waters of the upper Congo river. This was followed by several months exploring the tributaries and villages of the upper Congo region and an extended journey through the rain-forested area that he would subsequently revisit in an official capacity in 1903.

This up-river voyage included a sixteen-day riverboat ride with the vicious Belgian Captain Guillaume van Kerckhoven, an officer in the *Force Publique*, the name of King Leopold's military police force in the Congo. This officer is often cited as the inspiration for Joseph Conrad's Mr Kurtz in his novel *Heart of Darkness* – the book that did more than any other to shape European views of Africa in the twentieth century. In 1887 Casement made his first personal complaint to the judicial authorities at Boma about brutality against the local people, only to be told bluntly that he had 'no right of intervention'.[3]

The few surviving fragments of evidence relevant to Casement's pioneering years in Africa indicate that his sense of youthful idealism was quite quickly tempered by disillusionment with what he witnessed. Perhaps this was the reason he chose to decline the offer made by the most heralded explorer of the age, Henry M Stanley, to join him on the Emin Pasha relief expedition, an opportunity that several of Casement's closest friends opted for. This was the last exploration led by Stanley to cross central Africa with the somewhat spurious intention of relieving Emin Pasha, a German natural scientist who had been appointed governor of Equatoria (now part of the Sudan) and was being threatened by Mahdist forces. The expedition was a debacle and mushroomed into a vast controversy, with accusations of disloyalty, cannibalism, deceit and a series of conflicting eyewitness accounts by several of the officers involved.

One explorer who did join the venture was Casement's Irish cousin, James Mountney-Jephson, whose diary contains the earliest published impression of Casement in Africa. It is an image of the conventional white explorer, adhering to the prevailing trends of colonial behaviour and, by this account, enjoying the African interior in some degree of style. The description contrasts distinctly with the ascetic existence that distinguished Casement in later life.

April 14 1887 … After I had been in camp about a couple of hours Casement of the Sanford Expedition came up & camped by me. We bathed & he gave me a very good dinner – he is travelling most comfortably & has a large tent & plenty of servants. It was delightful sitting down to a real dinner at a real table with a table cloth & dinner napkins &

plenty to eat with Burgundy to drink & cocoa & cigarettes
after dinner – & this in the middle of the wilds – it will
be a long time before I pass such a pleasant evening again.[4]

The image of Casement's generous hospitality in the African interior is augmented a week later when a further entry in the diary describes how Casement saved his cousin's life, nursing him through a near fatal attack of fever while personally administering quinine from his own supply and letting him sleep in his bed until recovered. The sense from Jephson's narrative, partly reinforced by his own dislike of Stanley, is that Casement was a much better 'type' than the arch-explorer, knew his own mind, and had a special affinity with Africa rare amongst white men of his ilk.

Casement resigned from the Sanford Exploring Expedition in February 1888 and found new employment with the Etudes du Chemin de Fer, the advance expedition surveying the route for the proposed railway linking Matadi to Stanley Pool, on the upper Congo. In August 1888 he reported from the N'Kissi (Kasai) river valley that progress was 'rapid' and that Stanley Pool should be reached by November.[5] But his resignation towards the end of that year to join the Baptist Missionary Society (BMS) as a lay helper at their mission station of Wathen on the lower Congo would indicate further concerns with Leopold's enterprise and the recognition of a deepening spiritual dimension to his life. Casement's own religious convictions were strengthened by his regular contact with the missionary world. The development of his spirituality would form a critical part of his intellectual formation. As an Irishman christened into the churches of the two main Christian faiths, he ultimately came to embrace basic Christian doctrines uncomplicated by schism and dissent. Throughout his life he nurtured close friendships with missionaries, divines and priests, and there was always a sense of missionary zeal in both his political and humanitarian actions.

Missionary work in central Africa had been pioneered by Mr & Mrs Henry Grattan Guinness. Henry Grattan Guinness (1835-1910) was a grandson of the brewer and philanthropist Arthur Guinness and one of the prominent evangelical preachers of the age. With his wife, he had established the East London Missionary Training Institute in the East End of London in 1874, which would despatch almost 1,400 missionaries to the uttermost ends of the earth until it closed its doors in 1914. In 1877 the Grattan Guinnesses founded the Livingstone Inland Mission society and established the first mission stations on the lower Congo, which became vital staging posts for later administrative development of the region. In 1884 they handed over the control of the Livingstone Inland Mission to the American Baptist Missionary Union and shortly afterwards went on to set up a chain of mission stations on the upper Congo, named the Congo-Balolo Mission. Casement's work in the Congo was deeply entangled with the politics of this group and several of the missionaries educated in the East London Missionary Training Institute would later supply evidence of atrocities to Casement in his case against the Congo Free State.

Casement volunteered at the Wathen Mission from December 1888 to April 1889 where he was liked and considered 'a successful experimentation in lay assistance'.[6] In letters back to the Mission's headquarters in London, he was described as a 'fit and likely specimen,' who was 'very good to the native, too good, too generous, too ready to give away,' adding that 'he would never make money as a trader,' although he 'kept the books well'.[7]

In 1890, after a short lecture tour in America to speak about the Congo with his friend Herbert Ward, who would later establish himself as a sculptor of distinction, Casement spent several months in London. Various letters from this period are addressed from a house in Bedford Park, the fashionable suburb of West London where the poet WB Yeats lived among a number of Bohemian artists and writers, including the actor and feminist Florence Farr, and several practitioners involved with the Theosophical movement and the Golden Dawn. Whether Casement fraternised with this group is not known.

In early May, shortly before leaving for the Congo, he went to St James's Hall to hear Stanley speak in the presence of various members of the royal family, including the

Prince of Wales.[8] A recently discovered collection of letters he wrote to the founder of a global pharmaceutical empire, Henry Wellcome, demonstrated the influential company he now kept.[9] The letters detail his meetings in London with both Wellcome and Stanley in 1890, and indicate that Casement was working as an 'agent' for the pharmaceutical entrepreneur, and discreetly informing him about colonial affairs in central Africa and passing on any knowledge relevant to medical research.

Part of the friendship of Casement and Wellcome was no doubt rooted in a mutual respect for native life. Wellcome had presented Casement with a copy of his book *The Story of Metlakahtla* (1887), describing the evangelising efforts of William Duncan amongst the Tsimshean (Native Americans of British Columbia) and expressing his own sympathies for Native American traditions.

Before returning to Africa in 1890, Casement requested 'useful medicines' from Wellcome, who presented Casement with a medicine case containing quinine, trianol (used for lung infections) and *cascara sagrada*, a strong laxative developed by Native Americans. This medicine case remained an essential item in Casement's luggage and he was still requesting pills and remedies from the Wellcome laboratory over a decade later.

He kept in touch with both Stanley and Wellcome after returning to Africa. Soon after arriving back in the Congo he wrote a long letter to Stanley praising the trading potential of the river, although clearly concerned about rising tariffs on ivory and crude rubber.[10] He scribbled another long missive to Wellcome from Manyanga on the Congo river on 2 August 1890, lambasting the Congo Free State administration. He described in detail the vicious murder of two boys in the lower Congo, victims of the paranoid, alcohol-induced hallucinations of a state official who, believing his tea had been laced with *nkasa*, a poison used in local witchcraft rituals, ordered that his two servants be flogged to death. To add insult to injury, after a show trial and light fine by the Congo Free State authorities, the official was later reinstated to a post in the same vicinity. Casement implored Wellcome to 'make this story public'.[11]

Another individual who crossed Casement's path during these months on the Congo was Józef Korzeniowski, a young Ukrainian-born sea captain who would soon find fame writing under the name Joseph Conrad. The link between Conrad and Casement has an enduring fascination and prompts plenty of speculative questions as to how they influenced one another. Was it Casement who told Conrad the stories that would inspire him in 1899 to write his best-known novel, *Heart of Darkness*? Did Casement structure his own voyages into the upper Congo in 1903 and into the Amazon in 1910 and 1911 like the journey of Marlow in search of Mr Kurtz? Might Casement's own transformation from a decorated agent of empire into unrepentant republican revolutionary mirror Mr Kurtz's own rejection of the empty spectacle of civilisation?

The fact that the friendship between Casement and Conrad began on such a positive note in such exceptional circumstances, before either man had achieved any kind of public fame, is significant. It is interesting that over the years Conrad came to revise his view of Casement in line with public perceptions of the man. Conrad's *Congo Diary* recorded their initial meeting:

> 13 June 1890 ... Made the acquaintance of Mr. Roger Casement, which I should consider as a great pleasure under any circumstances and now it becomes a positive piece of luck. Thinks, speaks well, most intelligent and very sympathetic.[12]

From this simply observed initial impression, however, Conrad's view of Casement gradually transformed. In 1903, when writing a letter to the Scottish nationalist and historian-adventurer, RB Cunninghame Graham, he referred back to their original meeting but embellished it with a revealing series of inserted details:

> I send you two letters I had from a man called Casement, premising that I knew him first in the Congo just 12 years ago. Perhaps you've heard or seen in print his name. He's a Protestant Irishman, pious too. But so was Pizarro. For the

rest I can assure you that he is a limpid personality. There is a touch of the Conquistador in him too; for I've seen him start off into an unspeakable wilderness swinging a crook-handled stick for all weapons, with two bull-dogs: Paddy (white) and Biddy (brindle) at his heels and a Luanda boy carrying a bundle for all company. A few months afterwards it so happened that I saw him come out again, a little leaner, a little browner, with his stick, dogs, and Luanda boy, and quietly serene as though he had been for a stroll in a park. Then we lost sight of each other.[13]

In 1916, as Casement languished in Pentonville prison, Conrad wrote a third version to the Irish-American art collector John Quinn, who was a generous patron to Conrad and a friend to Casement during his journey to the US in 1914. To Quinn, Conrad re-orientated that initial encounter, but the 1890s Casement, who 'thinks, speaks well' and was 'most intelligent' had now become 'a man, properly-speaking, of no mind at all. I don't mean stupid. I mean that he was all emotion ... But in the Congo it was not yet visible':

I met Casement for the first time in the Congo in 1890. For some three weeks he lived in the same room in the Matadi Station of the Belgian Société du Haut Congo. He was rather reticent as to the exact character of his connection with it: but the work he was busy about then was recruiting labour. He knew the coast languages well. I went with him several times on short expeditions to hold 'palavers' with neighbouring village-chiefs. The object of them was procuring porters for the Company's caravans from Matadi to Léopoldville – or rather to Kinchassa (on Stanley Pool). Then I went up into the interior to take up my command of the stern-wheeler "Roi des Belges" and he, apparently, remained on the coast.[14]

The 'limpid personality' had become a labour recruiter to conform, perhaps, to the image of the disgraced 'traitor' Casement of 1916. Conrad's evolving view of Casement reveals the complex politics of remembering him, and the instability of memory that took some quite dramatic turns once his revolutionary sympathies were revealed. Conrad's deteriorating sympathy for Casement was influenced too by his loyalty to Britain during the war and the fact that he lost a son on the Western Front.

Casement was conscious that his first seven years in Africa were relevant to his understanding of the scramble for territorial control, which he had witnessed first hand. In 1905 he wrote to ED Morel: 'I am thinking of writing a brief account of my entire connection with the Congo from the date of my volunteering in 1884 … up to my final leaving the Congo in May 1891'.[15] The book never materialised, but those seven years had uniquely prepared him for his official posting as consul to the region in 1898, by which time he was positioned to prepare a devastating case exposing King

Leopold II's rule in central Africa. Over the years a principal criticism of Casement has suggested that his close association with the Congo Free State administration somehow compromised his later condemnation of Leopold II's system, but this argument ignores how Casement's inside knowledge of the Congo Free State and European power in Africa made his rejection even more convincing, damning and conclusive.

In 1892 Casement was spotted by the British Foreign Office and recruited into the colonial service as a customs officer. From 1892 to 1895 he helped to establish British administrative authority in the Niger Coast Protectorate (modern Nigeria's Niger Delta region). The initiative was led by Sir Claude Macdonald, an able intelligence officer seconded from the staff of Evelyn Baring, the British Pro-Consul in Egypt, who was the most powerful British colonial official in Africa at that time. Macdonald's brief was to build up British administrative power in the region and to achieve this outcome he recruited a number of Irishmen and Scotsmen onto his staff. He established his headquarters at a new purpose-built residence in Old Calabar, a port in the estuary of the Cross river in south-eastern Nigeria, a location deeply implicated in Britain's lucrative slave trade with Africa in the eighteenth century.

Casement's three years in the Niger Coast Protectorate connects him to a struggle which in more recent times has been defined by the insurgency waged by local communities against social and environmental violations committed by international oil companies in another resource-rich region. The trial and execution of the intellectual and activist, Ken Saro-Wiwa in Port Harcourt in 1995 for his organisation of opposition to multinational power (most notably, Shell Oil), has powerful similarities with Casement's own revolutionary trajectory and treatment by powerful vested interests.

The most revealing documents from these formative years are the reports Casement produced for the Foreign Office and the accompanying maps printed by the Intelligence Department of the War Office describing his surveying journeys into the delta region.[16] By now Casement had mastered the technical skills of exploration. He could navigate by the stars and take accurate astronomical readings with chronometers. Both his maps and the description of his journeys bore testimony to his physical and moral courage, tempered by a deep sensitivity towards local custom. His keen eye for both ethnographic and anthropological detail embellish his reports with information on local currency, traditional farming methods, resources, botany, and the cultural impact of European trade on indigenous customs.

Although Casement was well informed on humanitarian issues and had tried to intervene on behalf of victims of colonial violence as early as 1887, his earliest surviving correspondence on issues to do with such abuses dates from 1894. Soon after returning from his surveillance trip along the border separating the Niger Coast Protectorate from the German colony of Cameroon, he wrote a letter to the acting secretary of the Aborigines' Protection Society, HR Fox Bourne, a man who had been at the forefront of humanitarian discussion in Britain for over a decade. In 1890 Fox Bourne had started to speak out against alleged atrocities being committed in the Congo Free State, and the following year he attacked Stanley in *The Other Side of the Emin Pasha Expedition* (1891) emerging as a fierce public critic to European territorial claims in sub-Saharan Africa. One consequence of opening up communication with Fox Bourne was that Casement effectively closed the door on his connection with Stanley and Wellcome.

Casement's letter described the severe retaliation of the German authorities in Cameroon against insurgents after a rebellion.[17] He detailed how the insurgents were mainly 'natives of Dahomey' who had originally been purchased as slaves from the king of that country before being recruited as colonial policemen. The mutiny, he stated, had been sparked by the cruelty of the acting governor of Cameroon. Trouble began when the wives of these soldiers were flogged for disobedience. That night the mutineers seized the magazine and stormed Government House, where they killed some senior officials. Terrified, the German colonists fled onto two steamers, the *Soden* and *Nachtigal*, giving the rebels complete possession of Cameroon. Although the mutineers wrecked government buildings, other property was left alone and Casement carefully noted how they 'touched nothing' belonging to the English trading community. After several days of fighting, they surrendered and were promptly hanged, 'men and women alike'. Casement admitted that 'there may be slight discrepancies, here and there, as always in a second-hand tale – but the main facts, I know, are absolutely true.' He asked Fox Bourne 'to raise a protesting voice in England against the atrocious conduct of the Germans', adding that the 'opinion of every Englishman in this part of the world ... is strongly in favour of the soldiers and dead against the German government.'[18]

In the light of the significance that atrocities would later play in Casement's official denunciations of King Leopold II's regime and of international interests in the Atlantic rubber trade, this letter is highly revealing. First of all, it demonstrates that Casement was supplying humanitarian initiatives with information a full decade in advance of the founding of the Congo Reform Association. Secondly, it suggests that from the earliest stage of his career he was defining an exceptional official role for himself by disseminating information to non-governmental agencies. Thirdly, it is significant for what it says about his view on the rights of resistance and how the control of outbreaks of resistance prompted distortions of facts. Finally, he divulges his own awareness of the politics of atrocities in international relations. Each of these points would resonate in Casement's later life and even sway his ultimate commitment to Ireland.

The most remarkable individual to enter Casement's orbit during his time at Old Calabar was the determined figure of Mary Kingsley (1862-1900). During her brief exposure to Africa in the closing decade of the nineteenth century, Kingsley assumed an unrivalled position in shaping British attitudes and ideas on Africa. Her two published works, *Travels in West Africa* (1897) and *West African Studies* (1899), had an extraordinary influence on the colonial thinking of her time and greatly influenced the form of government known as 'indirect rule' which would define British policy towards its colonies in the early twentieth century. This was the system of governance whereby the day-to-day running of government was left in the hands of local elites, but control of matters (including external affairs and fiscal issues) was taken with the collaboration of colonial administrators and advisors. Popular fascination for Kingsley also stemmed from how a respectable Victorian woman was able to enter the male-dominated world of African exploration and succeed.

Kingsley's voyages in west Africa, including her stay in the residence at Old Calabar over the New Year of 1894-95, coincided with Casement's time there. Sadly, their correspondence has not survived. In the earliest biography of Kingsley, written by Stephen Gwynn, a prominent author and adherent of constitutional nationalism in Ireland, he noted how a significant part of her correspondence had disappeared after her death. From a few brief surviving fragments in other correspondence it is apparent that Casement and Kingsley were well acquainted and he advised her on her ascent of Mount Cameroon and conversed with her on a number of aspects of African life and culture.

Another connection with Casement was Liverpool. Kingsley's main support base was among the cohort of Liverpool merchants who had enjoyed trade with west Africa over many decades. As the 1890s brought a rapid change in west African trade relations, the decades of unobstructed free trade enjoyed by mainly Liverpool companies (especially the ship-owner and philanthropist John Holt) was shifting. By 1890 the decades of 'informal empire' and *laissez-faire* dealings with coastal middlemen, free from the burdens of direct administration, were drawing to a close. Kingsley lamented the decline of this unregulated commercial interaction, based upon fair dealing and mutual respect, and defended it in preference to the emerging system of monopolies enjoyed by concessionaire and chartered companies supported by colonial administration. Kingsley's life and legacy would motivate the two people who formed the closest alliance with Casement in his campaign in Africa: ED Morel and Alice Stopford Green.

In the spring of 1895 Casement returned to England in the company of the missionary TH Hoste. The June elections had seen the defeat of the Liberal Party and the return of a Conservative/Unionist majority. Lord Salisbury once more took on the onus of leadership as both Prime Minister and Foreign Secretary. The Liberals would spend more than a decade in opposition. Casement passed the summer in Ireland and entered into correspondence with Louisa Jephson-Norreys regarding his mother's background and family papers. He also made a trip to Rathlin, the small Irish-speaking island off Ballycastle, and for a few weeks enjoyed the freedom of the Antrim glens. But his services were soon in demand. In June he was informed that he had been fast-tracked into a new posting and the normal requirement for him to sit the consular exams had been waived. He was to proceed immediately to the old Portuguese settlement of Lorenzo Marques in Delagoa Bay, Portuguese East Africa (now Maputo, the capital of modern-day Mozambique) to act as consul there.

The mechanics of his appointment remain unclear. He would later insist that it was the out-going Liberal Foreign Secretary, Lord Kimberley, who informed him by telegram.[19] But it seems probable that the permanent staff at the Foreign Office, who were now well aware of Casement's proven abilities serving under Macdonald, may have had a hand in his appointment. Good men in Africa – capable 'men on the spot' – were difficult to recruit. Casement was becoming one of a select group of individuals indispensable to British imperial rule in Africa, and his various postings over the next eight years indicate his value.

In the summer of 1895 Africa was about to enter a new cycle of interference. The unstoppable ambition of the arch-imperialist Cecil Rhodes, combined with the aggressive vision of the new Colonial Secretary Joseph Chamberlain, would prove a potent combination in escalating tensions. Prime Minister Salisbury sought a path that would maintain stability between the European powers. Casement's new posting was intricately and often covertly entangled with the build-up to the second Boer War; a conflict that split British public opinion and inspired a new generation of resistance to the British Empire.

Although Lorenzo Marques had long been coveted as one of the finest natural harbours on the eastern coast of Africa, by 1895 its strategic importance was critical to European power politics. Against Salisbury's wishes, Cecil Rhodes had been scheming to annex the port to enable access to the sea for his expanding territorial gains north of Cape Colony (today part of the Republic of South Africa). The landlocked Boer republics – the Transvaal and Orange Free State – also saw it as their most direct route to the coast and an exit that was not under direct British authority. The Germans, while fostering their alliance with the Boers, similarly had their eyes fixed on its strategic potential. The Portuguese, as the hereditary colonisers, were reluctant to let go, and their declining presence in Africa did not ease the tension. In 1895 a new factor was added: the railway line connecting Pretoria, in the Transvaal and Delagoa Bay was finally opened.

Since 1875, when the British and Portuguese had settled rival claims over Delagoa Bay, the Boers had worked to connect the Transvaal to the coast along a line that was outside British jurisdiction. British annexation of the Transvaal in 1877 had led to the First South African War of 1880 and the humiliating defeat of the British forces at Majuba Hill, which ended with a negotiated settlement. In the Convention of Pretoria of March 1881, the Transvaal was given self-government, although Britain retained charge over foreign and 'native' affairs.

British policy was also shaped by the German factor. Since 1884, when Germany had declared a protectorate in south-west Africa between the Orange river and southern Angola, Britain had feared that German intentions would move eastwards. German investment into the Transvaal had been significant and Transvaal President Paul Kruger used the 'German card' in his negotiations with Britain, but otherwise British fears about German designs were exaggerated. However, the discovery of gold in Witwatersrand in 1886 turned the Transvaal into the largest goldmine in the world over the next decade. This alteration in the balance of economic forces in the region, mixed with the political and financial ambitions of Rhodes, proved an explosive combination.

Casement's appointment was partly determined by his

expertise in railway construction. The Foreign Office needed discreet and accurate information about the line and what it was carrying, especially information on the movement of arms into Boer territory. While on the surface Casement's appointment was about the protection of the community of the 169 British citizens in Delagoa Bay and the defense of British interests, there was much going on beneath the surface.

His arrival in Delagoa Bay was part of an effort to affirm British presence in southern Africa and place the administration there on firmer foundations. In the light of what happened over the next months in the build-up to the Jameson Raid, it is hard not to speculate that Casement's posting was part of a deliberate plan to organise intelligence operations on the ground.

Much of what is known about Casement's time in Lorenzo Marques is based upon the detailed reports and memoranda he sent back to the British Foreign Office. What they document is quite matter-of-fact.[20] He details, often at great length, day-to-day consular business: trade disputes involving British subjects, economic issues, and shipping news. On several occasions he was occupied with extensive court hearings involving claims by British subjects whose interests had been affected by the deliberate harassment of Portuguese officials and corrupt local practices. The experience made him highly critical of the efficacy of Portuguese justice.

Further information on life in Portuguese East Africa

is forthcoming from Casement's private correspondence. While in Lorenzo Marques, Casement fraternised closely with a group of German-speaking officials, businessmen and white hunters. These included the Austrian nobleman Count Richard Coudenhove, the Germans Fritz Pincus and Count Gebhard von Blücher (the grandson of the famous field-marshal who played such a decisive role in Wellington's victory at Waterloo) as well as the American writer and adventurer, Poultney Bigelow, a good friend of Kaiser Wilhelm II. All of these individuals remained close to Casement and became lifelong correspondents.[21]

On 29 December 1895 political tensions were brought to a head with the Jameson Raid, an effort by Cecil Rhodes to trigger a revolt among foreign workers in Johannesburg, in the Transvaal and overthrow Kruger's political hold on the region. The venture was a fiasco. Dr Leander Starr Jameson, who led the attack, was captured along with his raiders, mainly white police officers recruited in Rhodesia and Bechuanaland. The news was received with alarm in London. Rhodes was forced to resign as Prime Minister of the Cape Colony and was temporarily relieved of the director's chair of the British South African Company. Although Kruger used the situation to great propaganda advantage, the political landscape of southern Africa was changed and Boer fears that their independence was under threat were confirmed. Preparations for war began.

In the months after the raid, Casement was kept busy learning what he could about the movement of arms into the area while reporting on German activities. The Kaiser had reacted to the Jameson Raid bullishly and had sent a letter of sympathy to Kruger, which aroused fierce reaction in England.

In early March of 1896 Casement submitted his *Report on the Port and Railway of Lorenzo Marques*.[22] Having recovered from a bout of fever, he travelled at the end of March via Pretoria to Johannesburg and in early April sent a chatty and informal letter to Henry Foley, a colleague at the Foreign Office, full of insider gossip and on-the-spot advice.[23] Despite his request at the end of the missive to 'tear this up', the letter passed from Foley into the hands of Joseph Chamberlain. While expressing support for British policy towards southern Africa, it built up to a very forceful proposition as to how the Boers should be handled in the current political crisis. His comments included some revealing thoughts about the conduct of the trial of the Jameson raiders:

> I am certain the trial and sentence were part of the put up game to enable Mr. Kruger to again display his "generous forbearance and magnanimity" in the eyes of the world. An imported judge from the Free State was got in on the plea of impartiality, but really because the Transvaal judges would not have passed the death sentence; then the solemn lecture from the bench was delivered, the charge of high

treason was trotted out at length, and the five guilty chiefs
of the Reformers [Jameson Raiders] were commended to
the hangman and the Almighty – while the rest were sent
to banishment, fines, and imprisonment.[24]

By the time of his return to Lorenzo Marques in early May,
tensions were running high, and on one evening Casement
reported how stones were thrown at the British Consulate
by anti-British protesters. Casement continued his investigations into the scale of gun-running into the Transvaal. On
6 June he informed the Foreign Office that large quantities
of arms had recently entered the region through Delagoa
Bay, although it was difficult to assess quantities accurately as
the materials were often labelled in English as 'Government
Goods'. It was apparent, however, that the Boers were now
in possession of large stores. On 16 June he sent a cypher
containing exact figures taken from an examination of the
dispatch manifests for the freight: 104 cases of Maxim guns,
sixty-five cases of rifles and four million cartridges (with
another four million awaiting dispatch).[25]

Casement was an exceptional example of the 'man on
the spot' and his activities on the frontier directly shaped
decision-making in London. He had established himself as
a highly capable troubleshooter. His abilities as an explorer-
administrator with a reputation for dedication, honesty and
initiative were unquestioned. He had shown himself adroit
at carrying out difficult and sensitive operations on behalf of

the government: map-making expeditions, data collection, economic information gathering, surveillance on the movement of arms and ships – in short, espionage. His reports and memoranda were written in a clear, direct style and, above all, were possessed with that most important quality of good administration: integrity. He experienced Africa as few men of his time had, he had lived among the tribes and, more importantly, he had survived to tell the tale.

The roving American journalist Poultney Bigelow (1855-1927), who knew Casement well during this time, and was partial himself to a bit of spying on behalf of the US government, described Casement as follows:

> He would wander away for weeks and months with merely a black attendant or two, trekking along the Swazi frontier, studying the language and the customs of the natives, establishing relations with the chiefs, and sounding them as to their feelings in matters interesting in Downing Street …
> It is not saying more than the truth when I testify that Mr. Casement knew more of the natives between Basutoland and the shores of Mozambique than any other white man.[26]

On 6 January 1898 Casement arrived back in England on sick leave and went to stay with Herbert Ward, who was now working as a sculptor and had rented a large Tudor mansion, Lambourn Place in Berkshire. Casement had requested four months' leave to recover, which the Foreign Office granted, as long as he kept them supplied with information as and when it filtered through from his informants in Lorenzo Marques. Over the following months he moved between England and Ireland, addressing letters from various locations including Baronstown House in County Meath, and rooms in Lower Baggot Street, Dublin. In a letter to his cousin Gertrude he confided that 'I have been writing a great deal of late and never seem to get time to write letters I want to people I like – hence these silences'.[27]

At the end of May he wrote to the Foreign Office from Antrim requesting an extension of leave, and he was granted a further six weeks from 6 June. But in July, as he prepared to return to Lorenzo Marques, the Foreign Office decided instead to send Casement to the extensive consular district of Portuguese West Africa, based at Luanda (the capital of Angola). The consular jurisdiction there included the extensive territorial claims of Portuguese West Africa including Angola and Cabinda as well as the Congo Free State and the French Congo.

Chapter Three

• • • • • • •

1899-1902

Congo Consulate

Casement's new consular appointment was indicative of a refocusing of attention in Africa away from mounting pressures in southern Africa and towards deepening tensions further north. In September 1898, the geo-political significance of linking the Congo river system to the upper Nile came to a head. Major-General Horatio Kitchener's victory over the Mahdists at the battle of Omdurman and the retreat of the French from the British at Fashoda in the Sudan put an end to French dreams of carving out a trans-African colony connecting their west African territories to the Nile. But if the French had been brought to heel, Lord Salisbury now faced a more ambitious diplomatic contender in King Leopold II. Since the Brussels conference of 1890, when European powers again discussed the issue of African slavery, Leopold II had increased his activity in the economic and administrative development of the Congo Free State. In order to avoid financial ruin due to overspending on various lavish private and civic building projects, he reneged on his diplomatic promises. The free trade guarantees enshrined in the Berlin Act (1885) were disregarded as new decrees brought all sectors of the Congo economy more tightly under his control and the control of Belgian companies. From 1891 all rubber and ivory had to be sold directly to the Congo Free State administration. Land was appropriated using increased levels of violence. Even Belgian competitors of the king were intimidated. Despite having never visited his vast African fiefdom, King Leopold II aspired to joining his Congo territories to the upper Nile and appears to have harboured some fantasy of attaining the status of a latter-day pharaoh.

The symbol of Leopold's ambition was the inauguration of building work on his Versailles-like palace at Tervuren on the outskirts of Brussels. Today this same building houses the African Museum and the largest collection of sub-Saharan African art in the world. In 1898, the opening of the railway between Matadi and Léopoldville, linking the lower and upper Congo, enabled the efficient and less labour-intensive transportation of natural resources. Increasingly, the most lucrative resource was rubber.

Until the plantation rubber economy of southeast Asia became competitive from around 1908, most rubber was extracted as latex rubber from the tropical forests of sub-Saharan Africa and tropical South and Central America. The technological harnessing of rubber to a range of innovations in the manufacturing sector inaugurated a new generation of industrial development and made it into an extraordinarily valuable material. In addition to being used as a waterproofing agent and an insulator for electrical and communication cables, rubber was central to the reinvention of the wheel by a Belfast-based Scottish vet, John Dunlop, who patented his homemade prototype of the pneumatic tyre. This in particular turned rubber into the most prized commodity on the stock exchanges of New York and London.

At the close of the nineteenth century, the mass production of the bicycle and the motor vehicle revolutionised transport. Thousands of migrant workers travelled into the tropical interiors of the Amazon and sub-Saharan Africa to attempt to profit from the extraction of this invaluable resource and a vast and highly lucrative sector of global commerce was deeply intertwined with the political economy of extractive rubber.

But to many Africans, rubber meant death. As the demand increased, the supply chain became more and more merciless. Stories began to reach Europe and America of the reign of terror committed against the native inhabitants by

King Leopold II's regime in the Congo Free State. Until the outbreak of war in Europe in 1914, rubber was the most prominent resource in the broadening discussion on colonial relations and ethical issues of empire. No other product epitomised the excesses of the age quite as graphically. It helped to build and sustain some of the largest private fortunes in the world at the time, not least for Leopold II himself, but the human cost was devastating. From the late 1890s onward, missionaries, travellers and administrators reported on the widespread nature of abuses committed in pursuit of rubber quotas: torture, violence, indentured slavery and mass killings. Many public intellectuals and philanthropists would engage with the tragedy produced by this appalling resource war, but it was Roger Casement who became its chief official witness.

From the moment he arrived in his consular office in Luanda in 1898, Casement began to report back to the Foreign Office on every subject of interest, from stationery needs to news about the shipments of arms. In February 1899, Casement journeyed to the lower Congo to assess the situation. Over the following weeks, much information was gathered from the private testimony of missionaries, who spoke of deepening tensions and an increase in the number of uprisings against the Congo Free State administration. Beside confidential reports on the increase of French armaments, he detailed the deepening levels of violence against the local population and met with a British intelligence officer undertaking an independent assessment of the Congo region. Casement realised that a more permanent consular presence was required to deal with the Congo Free State.

On 1 September, his thirty-fifth birthday, Casement transmitted his trade report on Portuguese West Africa.[1] A listing of the various latex-bearing plants of west Africa was supplemented with a description of recent efforts to start planting trees, in particular, imported saplings from the Amazon river basin, including the most prized rubber-bearing plant of all, the *Hevea brasiliensis*. In drawing the report to a close, Casement aggravated diplomatic anxieties in Whitehall by observing how German efficiency was starting to push Britain out of its previously unchallenged trade in this district, leading him to conclude that German traders were better than their British counterparts. With railway construction and improved communications opening up new territories, British business had plenty of room for improvement.

Casement's work in the Congo was interrupted towards the end of the year with news from southern Africa, where tensions were running high in anticipation of war between Britain and the Boers. Casement was immediately ordered by Lord Salisbury to return to the region and play his part in the rapidly unfolding conflict. His role in the first months of the South African war remains something of a mystery. In evidence he gave in May 1914 he recalled how:

Lord Salisbury employed me in South Africa during the

Boer War for nearly a year in a political capacity which had nothing to do with my being consul at St Paul de Luanda, but had some relation to my previous experiences at Delagoa Bay.[2]

A 'political capacity' might be understood as a veiled reference to intelligence work. His initial task was to return to Lorenzo Marques to report on alleged Portuguese infractions of neutrality, including smuggling operations, and to provide a situation report on security. The British military command was convinced that government agents and corrupt local officials were allowing the passage of arms, war materials and recruits into the Boer republics. Casement met with the High Commissioner for southern Africa, Lord Alfred Milner, at Government House in Cape Town in December. During this encounter he suggested his derring-do plan to blow up the bridgehead at Komatipoort on the railway from Delagoa Bay to Pretoria, thereby disrupting the Boers' main supply route with the coast. The plan, however, was vetoed by the commander-in-chief of the British expeditionary force, General Redvers Buller, for reasons that were never made clear.

Casement travelled to Delagoa Bay on 8 January 1900 and remained there for the next seven weeks as a 'special commissioner' ordered to work 'in secret harmony with the Portuguese authorities'.[3] The appointment was otherwise kept secret and he was instructed 'to act as though he were visiting Lorenzo Marques privately'.[4] It took him just seven weeks to report back to Whitehall that he was unable to uncover sufficient evidence of corruption amongst the local authorities to justify international denouncement of Portuguese neutrality. He was better able to make an astute analysis of the efficacy of British field intelligence and how it could be improved. On the last day of February 1900, as he boarded the *HMS Raccoon* bound for Cape Town, he wrote a twenty-four page memorandum outlining a series of suggestions as to how British presence could be strategically improved.[5] His principal recommendation was that if the customs and railway administration could not be brought under 'veiled control', then a 'more able intelligence department' should be organised.[6]

> The intelligence work there should be placed in the hands of a skilled man, of experience in such matters, having under him a staff of expert men – some in the customs, some at the railway, and others up and down the coast, or on ship board.[7]

The remark suggests that he was making a pitch for the post himself. But matters now took a new turn that briefly placed Casement at the centre of British military covert operations in southern Africa.

In Cape Town, during his absence, interest had revived at the highest level for his idea to attack the Boer railway supply route. Casement's plan was to send a force of around five hundred cavalry armed with cannon. Roughly half the party would march cross-country through Zululand to Komatipoort into a position well suited for the attack. The rest of the taskforce would make their way by boat to Kosi Bay and from there march to the Swaziland frontier. On 6 April, Joseph Chamberlain, now the Secretary of State for the Colonies, sent a cypher to Lord Milner:

> Casement reports that the danger of war material passing to the Transvaal through Portuguese territory must continue to exist, whatever measures we may take at Lorenzo Marques and however loyal the Portuguese may be. The only satisfactory way to stop it is in his opinion to destroy the Railway, of course on the Transvaal side, and, despite adverse opinion of Buller and others, he maintains his view based on local knowledge of the country and its resources that the thing can be done. It is the wish of H.M. Govt. that you and Lord Roberts will consider this question most seriously and fully report your views.[8]

Milner now entered into the finer details of the plan with senior officers: Lord Roberts, General Forestier-Walker, Colonel Trotter and Admiral Harris. On 25 April he sent a message through to Chamberlain:

> I have taken upon myself to detain Casement, who is here on his way back to Luanda, for a week or two, as Lord Roberts is seriously considering details of scheme to send

small expedition through Swaziland to seize Komatiiport, and C'.s local knowledge is valuable. I hope Foreign Office will approve my action in keeping him. Scheme is being kept very secret.[9]

Copies of Chamberlain's telegram and Milner's reply were passed to the Prime Minister, Lord Salisbury, and planning the raid was now prioritised.

At the end of May, 540 men of a Canadian cavalry regiment, known as Lord Strathcona's Horse, were separated into two groups and prepared for departure. Casement boarded a naval vessel with two hundred members of the assault party. However, on their arrival at Kosi Bay, news came through that the mission had been aborted. Casement's efforts to keep the momentum of the expedition going were ineffective. The plans had apparently leaked out, and the Boers took defensive measures against such an attack. The vital element of surprise had been lost.

For Casement it was bitterly disappointing. However, the acceptance of his plan at the highest level of military command demonstrates a level of influence he now wielded over field intelligence operations in Africa. His South African activities link him to the often unfathomable world of British military intelligence and an embryonic secret intelligence service. Since 1892, when his official duties as a survey officer for the Foreign Office began under Claude Macdonald in the Niger Coast Protectorate, Casement had entered into this known–unknown world of official secrecy.

Casement's plan was indicative of a shift in the way wars were fought; not on the open field of battle but in response to localised skirmishes and commando-like operations mounted by the Boer. Britain responded to the guerrilla campaign with a bitter scorched earth policy, burning Boer farmsteads and imprisoning thousands of civilians, including women and children, in concentration camps. Although the Boers were eventually defeated in 1902, British authority was deeply scarred by the experience. The Boer War changed popular views of the British Empire and in many ways it also changed Casement. In Britain it aggravated a radical anti-imperial voice which over the forthcoming decade would shape issues to do with neutrality, pacifism and secret diplomacy. What Casement had experienced and witnessed started to sow doubts in his mind. Sixteen years later, as he languished in the Tower of London, he reflected on the change stimulated within him:

> I arrived home in July 1900 and I was then becoming a pro-Boer as a result of what I had seen in South Africa. I went home to Ballycastle and this visit and the lessons of the Transvaal brought my thoughts back to Ireland, for although always a strong nationalist I had lost interest when Mr Parnell died and had come to look upon myself as an African, until my stay in the Cape and closer touch with "Imperial" ideals.[10]

Casement left Cape Town on 7 July and arrived back in England on 26 July, staying briefly in Notting Hill at the house of Count von Blücher. After eighteen months of active service, he was suffering from jaundice and physical exhaustion. He yearned for the countryside and, after a few days in London, left to stay at the beautiful medieval farmhouse in Buckinghamshire owned by his friend Richard Morten. Over the next few weeks the main issue was his health. He was clearly unwell. His doctor told him that a minor operation to deal with a problem in his bowel was necessary and that a long spell of good climate, food and rest was needed for his recovery. But Casement was in no doubt that when he was better he would be returning to Africa.

From southern Africa, Casement had maintained pressure on the Foreign Office over reform in the Congo. At the end of April 1900 he had forwarded a letter to a senior British diplomat, Sir Martin Gosselin, a key negotiator of British interests at the conferences of Berlin and Brussels. Casement suggested that after the end of the war in South Africa, Britain should ally with Germany to 'deal with Belgian brutality on the Congo' and put 'an end to the veritable reign of terror which exists'.[11] He quoted at length from two letters he had received from unnamed Baptist missionaries describing horrors committed by the soldiers of the *Force Publique*. Evidence of a widespread rebellion in the upper Congo was supplied by another informant. The end of the letter described in lurid detail some of the punishments meted out by the state authorities in the name of civilisation. Casement concluded:

> The root of the evil, to my mind, lies in the fact that the Congo Government is first of all a trading concern – that everything else is subordinated to the lust of gain – and that, only when its claims in this respect are attended to, does it become an instrument of reform ... It is not the white men on the Congo who are so bad, as that the system under which they serve is evil – their first duty is to show a profitable balance-sheet, and a well-governed district in all other respects may be anywhere they please at the end of their annual statement.[12]

Casement travelled between London and Antrim over the summer, recovering his strength and seeing friends and family. In the second week of October 1900, on the orders of Lord Salisbury, he journeyed to Brussels to speak directly with King Leopold II, as his recommendation for the redrawing of the British consular districts and the establishment of a specific British consul dealing with the Congo Free State required official approval from the King of Belgium.

He arrived in Brussels off the train from Antwerp early in the morning of 10 October and called initially upon Constantine Phipps (1840-1911), the British ambassador and the official responsible for arranging the meeting in the hope of mending differences. Instead, the discussion only emphasised an unbridgeable clash of viewpoints: Leopold defended his imperial interests while claiming humanitarian intentions, while Casement demanded greater levels of protection for the Congolese. The king was now struggling to hang on to private control of the Congo Free State in the face of both national and international calls that it should be annexed to the Belgian parliament. While Casement was certainly of the mind that this could help improve the situation, Leopold was extremely reluctant to let go.[13] The meetings continued over two days and ended with Leopold II approving Casement's consular appointment.

On 17 October, with the news that Salisbury's government had been re-elected by a clear majority, Casement wrote to the Prime Minister suggesting a further division within the consular districts of the French and Belgian Congo. He argued that the inland districts of the French Congo could be more efficiently administered if they fell under the jurisdiction of the new consulate at Léopoldville, while the coastal districts should remain within the jurisdiction of Luanda.[14] He also informed Salisbury that he was taking a significant part of the Luanda archives with him to form the foundation for a new archive at the Congo consular office. Lord Salisbury was in the process of handing over the reins of the Foreign Office to his trusted Minister for War, Lord Henry Petty-Fitzmaurice, Marquess of Lansdowne, an Anglo-Irish peer with extensive landed interests in County Kerry.

Casement departed for Africa at the end of October, taking a few weeks' holiday in Sicily and Italy before continuing via Barcelona across Iberia to Lisbon. Although his stay was brief, he was charmed by the British consul there, FH Cowper, who became a valuable ally and confidant over the next four years. After various last-minute changes in plan and missing a boat, he eventually caught the Portuguese steamer *SS Cazengo* from Lisbon on 21 November, and finally reached Luanda after brief stopovers in the Cape Verde archipelago and the island of Principe in the Bight of Biafra.

Over the next few months his tiring routine of travel and administration continued as he worked to reorganise the consular district based on his suggestions to Lord Salisbury earlier in the year and establish a network of vice-consuls. In March 1901, while on a visit to Léopoldville, news reached him of the death of Queen Victoria. He telegraphed the Foreign Office his condolences and in private correspondence expressed his 'heartfelt sorrow'.[15] Over the following weeks, out of respect for the departed queen, he held a series of memorial services, the first in Léopoldville. His correspondence makes frequent reference to the news. He wrote privately to Cowper in Lisbon that it was an 'irreparable loss' and he felt it hard to 'think of an England without "the Queen"'.[16] As a show of respect to the departed monarch, he organised a Queen Victoria National Memorial Fund and convened a meeting in June at Matadi of labourers from British West African colonies of the Gold Coast, Sierra Leone and the Gambia, in order to raise funds for the memorial.[17]

In April he journeyed to Luanda to undertake a 300km journey on foot into the Angolan interior to inspect work on a railway line before returning to the Congo on 25 April. During this period, any lingering confidence in the ability of the Congo Free State authorities to reform the administration in the Congo had diminished to nothing. He had adopted a more confrontational position and had no doubt that the Congo Free State must be wrested from the monarch's private control:

> [T]he only hope for the Congo, should it continue to be governed by the Belgians, is that it should be subject to a European authority responsible to public opinion, and not to the unquestioned rule of an autocrat, whose chief preoccupation is that this autocracy should be profitable.[18]

Casement arrived back in Liverpool on 12 October with his health clearly impaired, and went initially to London to seek medical opinions as to his condition. Intestinal problems, fever and depleted energy levels had left his immune system vulnerable. He caught a cold almost immediately and after a brief visit to the Foreign Office he fled to Portrush in Antrim to recuperate. On 13 November he sent on to the Foreign Office a letter from Dr Percy Dean saying that as a consequence of 'a weak and irritable state of the mucous membrane of the lower bowel' he should reside in 'a temperate climate for at least six months'.[19] The following day he left for a fortnight in Paris to stay with Herbert Ward at his new studio. On his return, at the end of the month, he was granted an extension of leave for four months from 12 December. This, at least, would take him beyond the hottest and most humid period in the Congo, to the season when the temperatures subsided. But if he escaped the uncomfortable heat of west Africa, he had the harsh European winter to endure. In late January he travelled to Naples for some winter sun, returning in the third week of February to his various responsibilities.

Casement was back in Africa by the end of April 1902. On board the SS *Anversville*, off the coast of Sierra Leone, he wrote a long letter to Sir Eric Barrington, a senior official at the Foreign Office, reinforcing his agenda to expose King Leopold II.[20] He expressed no confidence in the idea, suggested by the Aborigines' Protection Society, of convening another international conference among the European powers to discuss the Congo question. Such multilateral pow-wows, he felt, 'generally end in agreements which it is nobody's business to see maintained'. Instead he recommended assertive action to force reform and the need to keep compiling evidence exposing the authorities and the 'organised system of plunder'. At the end of the letter Casement confided that nothing would give me more sincere pleasure than to see the Congo State called to account for its unjust stewardship – and I trust the matter may be taken up very seriously and pushed to its legitimate conclusion ... I do hope that before I may be forced to give it up I shall see its rotten system of administration either mended or ended'.[21]

Over the forthcoming months he supplied a stream of reports about aspects of the administration, including its judicial system, postal service and the *Force Publique*. In various ways his actions exceeded the responsibilities expected of a British consular official and he adopted at times the position of sociologist and anthropologist more than colonial officer. He undertook inspections of prisons and hospitals, analysed the impact of the colonial economy on the customary life of the Congolese, and assessed aspects of resistance to the regime. Although his official reason was to defend the interests of mistreated British West African workers, this was the entry point for a much broader analysis of the colonial system and labour relations.

A recurring subtext in much of his official analysis during this period is the tension between power and resistance. While not directly condoning resistance, Casement argued that brutal administrative failures were provoking rebellions. His analysis of resistance was later articulated in his speech from the dock in June 1916:

> If there be no right of rebellion against a state of things that
> no savage tribe would endure without resistance, then I am
> sure that it is better for men to fight and die without right
> than to live in such a state of right as this.[22]

In the Congo Free State, where rights were neither
respected nor protected, the colonial powers had implemented such an oppressive system of government that resistance was often justified. In a letter to Barrington written in
April, Casement had predicted the inevitability of trouble
if the administration was not reformed. It would, he said,
'result in a widespread upheaval some day, of the native African against his European despoiler ... [a consequence that]
... all men of white race in tropical Africa may be made to
pay for.'[23] Casement realised that the African would not tolerate forever the strategy of corporal and cultural oppression
imposed by the white man's world.

Wars of resistance against the authority of the Congo Free
State were quite widespread. Leopold II's forces had, in fact,
been fighting interior wars throughout the 1890s. After the
fight against the Arab slavers (one of the reasons that Leopold used to justified his intervention in central Africa), was
nominally brought to a close in 1895, there remained many
trouble spots, notably in the Ubangi, Welle and Equateur districts in the upper Congo. A number of notorious Belgian
generals (Francis Dhanis and Louis Napoleon Chaltin in
particular) had been occupied in the intervening seven years

with suppressing rebel outbreaks and their violent acts of retaliation had become part of the Congo Free State's history of atrocity. Increasingly, however, the concession companies, who profited from the trade of rubber and other commodities, were entering into unethical alliances with the military authorities, which encouraged their excesses.

Casement targeted the *Force Publique* as the main culprit for brutality: 'it would be useless to tell the local authorities that their cannibal army is a disgrace to civilisation' he informed Lansdowne.[24] In an interview with the Vice-Governor-General Emile Wangermée, the senior Belgian official in the Congo Free State, Casement demanded to know their terms of engagement and sought a 'clear definition of the limits within which the police may exercise their obvious right of search and arrest.'[25]

Rebellion was not confined to the Congo. At the end of June of 1902, reports reached Casement from Luanda of serious revolts in the Angolan interior.[26] Forced labour 'sanctioned by the Portuguese government under the term of "contracted labour" had led to a significant trade in slaves from Angola to the islands of San Tomé & Principe.'[27] Both these islands – Portuguese colonial possessions in the Bight of Africa – were important cocoa producing regions, but a shortage of labour and increased global demand for cocoa had resulted in cross-border slave raids into the Congo Free State and the transportation of slaves from other central

African regions. Casement appears to have been the first voice to awaken concerns about this new slave trade.

Over the next few years, the issue would escalate into yet another public scandal and bring Casement into contact with two public figures sympathetic with his beliefs: the crusading journalist HW Nevinson and the philanthropist William A Cadbury. In 1904-05, Nevinson set out for Angola to investigate this slave trade and the following year his book, *A Modern Slavery*, placed a large share of the blame on 'the world-wide issue of capital'. The question of West African labour was also taken up by Cadbury, part of the Quaker dynasty, whose chocolate-making business stood most to lose from these highly damaging allegations.

Between 1906 and 1909 this slavery scandal was exacerbated further as a result of a sensational libel trial between Cadbury Bros. Ltd and Standard Newspapers, who had accused the Cadburys of running their profitable chocolate business on human misery. The *Standard* was represented by the Ulster Unionist, Sir Edward Carson, best known for his prosecution of Oscar Wilde, while the Cadbury's interests were defended by the ambitious Liberal barrister, Sir Rufus Isaacs, a future Viceroy of India, who, as Lord Chief Justice, would pronounce Casement's death sentence in 1916. The jury found in favour of the Cadburys but only 'one farthing' was awarded in damages, a sum so trifling that it was considered contemptuous.[28]

The stories of revolt in the upper Congo and Angola persuaded Casement of the urgency to extend his investigations deeper into the interior of central Africa so as to determine the truth behind the rumours. Permission was finally granted by the Foreign Office and Casement was ordered back to London to be briefed and to prepare for the journey. On 19 November 1902, after an arduous trip lasting forty-three days, he arrived into Plymouth.

Britain had undergone significant changes with the ushering in of the new century. The question of Africa was a live issue following the end of the Boer War, with a deepening concern about the conflict of European interests in the region. The dynamic for this was partly catalysed by the formidable Irish-born intellectual, Alice Stopford Green, the widow of social historian John Richard Green. During the 1890s, Stopford Green had nurtured a close friendship with the explorer Mary Kingsley and the two had corresponded closely. Both women had bitterly opposed the Boer War, believing that it was largely driven by vested economic interests. Kingsley had felt so strongly about the matter that she volunteered to look after the Boer women and children held in British concentration camps. However, her good intentions were cut short when she died from enteric fever in a refugee camp in Simonstown near Cape Town in 1900. Stopford Green was so distraught by Kingsley's death that she undertook a trip to southern Africa to investigate the circumstances surrounding it, and to discover the facts behind the disturbing rumours circulating about the treatment of Boers held in prison camps.

Having investigated the condition of British-run concentration camps on the island of St Helena, Stopford Green returned to London and founded the Mary Kingsley Society of West Africa with the stated intention of drawing together expertise on Africa from various fields. Her committee included some formidable public figures, including future Prime Minister Herbert Asquith and historian-statesman John Morley. She also transgressed the patriarchal and racist boundaries of the time by inviting both women and Africans to be part of the organisational structure. Stopford Green gathered influential industrialists, politicians, churchmen, explorers, academics, anthropologists and medical researchers to discuss cultural, political and social aspects of Africa. She was also the founding editor of the *Journal of the African Society*.

Around this time, Stopford Green extended her support for the endeavours of a young crusading journalist with a French and Quaker background, ED Morel. Like Casement, Morel had started his working life as an employee of the Elder Dempster Shipping Company in Liverpool, working on the Congo desk. To supplement his income, Morel submitted articles to local newspapers on West African affairs. Initially, these were quite positive, but as Morel came to doubt the efficacy of colonial government, he became increasingly critical of the political economy of sub-Saharan Africa and, in particular, King Leopold II's regime. Using Stopford Green's influential network of contacts, Morel established a newspaper, *The West African Mail*, and advocated reform.

There is no evidence that Morel and Green were in communication with Casement before he left for his journey to the upper Congo in 1903. But when the three entered into close contact in 1904, after Casement had returned from his perilous investigation, they would together create one of the most progressive alliances in early twentieth-century British politics. Their union proved to be a critical influence on the destiny of not just Ireland and Africa, but on the future directions of a socialist foreign policy and the recalibration of colonial relations.

Over the next decade, Stopford Green, Morel, Nevinson and Casement, with the backing of William Cadbury, emerged as the central public figures involved in a series of interlinking investigations into what are now defined as the 'new slaveries' of the early twentieth century. After a century of history, it is apparent that their dialogue helped with the emergence of many progressive, representative and participatory discourses to do with rights: rights of self-determination, indigenous rights, resource rights and, ultimately, human rights.

Chapter Four

• • • • • • •

1903–1904

Heart of Darkness

The image of Africa in the European imagination is even today largely defined by the myths of nineteenth-century exploration and conquest of the interior. The expeditions of Richard Burton and John Hanning Speke to find the source of the Nile, the famous meeting on the banks of Lake Tanganyika between Henry M Stanley and Dr David Livingstone ('I presume') in 1871, and the work of Carl Peters in pioneering German colonies in Africa are the more familiar ones. But the history of European travel writing is largely a narrative of invasion and subjugation driven by a breed of white, hyper-masculine explorers, who set forth to bring light and civilisation to the so-called 'Dark Continent'. African savagery is inevitably upheld in a debasing contrast to the civilising mission of European modernity.

If Casement's early years in Africa to some extent configured with the norms of African discovery narratives, his journey into the interior of central Africa in 1903 may be upheld as a voyage of a completely different type. It would paradigmatically shift western views on Africa. Rather than describe in order to dominate, his intention was to assess the efficacy of colonial government. It was a journey that bore none of the normal signs of heroism. Instead it empathised with those who had suffered the consequences of power. It was not exploration, but investigation of the system and of colonial power relations. It was a counter-narrative to the self-justifying narratives produced by colonial authors.

Casement arrived by train into Liverpool on 20 February 1903 and departed the following day on board the *SS Jebba*. A week later, after a rough crossing, he disembarked with his West African manservant into the fashionable resort-port of Funchal, capital of the Portuguese island of Madeira off the north-west coast of Africa, one of several hubs of transatlantic shipping passing between Europe, Africa and the Americas.

Why Casement remained in Funchal for almost three weeks is open to speculation. Certainly it was a good place to acclimatise and prepare for the arduous journey ahead, but was there another agenda at play? On 3 March, two days after his arrival, the local papers announced the departure of the British Navy's Canal Fleet from Funchal to take part in a naval exercise between Madeira and Porto Santo. A week later, Joseph Chamberlain, on his return from a tour of South Africa, arrived at Funchal and came ashore for an official lunch party amidst much Portuguese pomp and ceremony. On St Patrick's Day, King Edward VII arrived in Lisbon for a brief state visit and an important secret convention of Anglo-Portuguese diplomats to discuss the future of Portuguese possessions in West Africa. It is possible that Casement's presence was required in a covert advisory capacity. But the official record does not relate. Casement's narrative briefly disappears off the radar during these days.

Casement left Madeira on 19 March and spent a month travelling to Boma on the lower Congo. On his way he reported back to Westminster on various sensitive matters; specifically, the continued movement of armaments into the region on board French and Belgian boats. During the two months after his arrival, he dealt with pressing consular matters and developed building plans for the new consulate. In a number of official missives back to the Foreign Office, he expressed concerns about how the Congo Free State authorities were increasingly suspicious of his presence, especially after his inspection of the prison in Matadi. This type of action lay beyond the normal brief expected of an official consul, and was quite possibly motivated by many independent inquiries carried out by Quakers whose brethren conducted regular prison visits and advocated for better conditions for prisoners.

Matters back in London were now starting to create their own dynamic. A debate about the Congo Free State in the House of Commons on 20 May had obliged Lord Lansdowne to act. At the start of June he sent a more urgent telegram ordering Casement to proceed to the upper Congo river to collect 'authentic information'.[1] Within forty-eight hours he had departed Matadi on the railway, and on the afternoon of 5 June he arrived in Léopoldville, where he would remain until 22 June.

Léopoldville served as an administrative barracks and was inhabited by some three thousand government workers, most of them Africans, with only about one hundred and thirty resident Europeans. The workforce was primarily engaged in the management of trading vessels on the upper Congo river. Every day steamers from the fleet of forty-eight government-owned riverboats pulled up alongside the wharf at Léopoldville. From these, bales of rubber, tusks of ivory, bushmeat, animal pelts and other produce was off-loaded onto freight cars and taken by rail to Matadi for shipment to Antwerp and elsewhere in Europe.

Casement immediately reconnected with his closest allies in the region: the Protestant and Evangelical missionaries. The Congo-Balolo Mission, the organisation founded and run by the Grattan Guinness family, with outposts through-out the upper Congo, was particularly forthcoming. Over the following weeks his investigation was hugely facilitated by this cooperation. Missionaries would become key allies in compiling his case and provided vital evidence in terms of stories, testaments and photographs exposing the violent excess of the colonial regime and the *Force Publique*.

He continued to report secretly to the Foreign Office on the movement of arms shipments. On 11 June he sent a detailed dispatch about two different consignments. One batch had arrived on a steamer from Antwerp, while another was transported overland from Angola:

> these weapons, chiefly the kind termed Albini, are in the hands of the large, loosely organised masses of natives who compose the public force [*Force Publique*] of the Congo State, and doubtless have often passed beyond the control of their European officers into the hands of revolted soldiery and others.[2]

In light of his later gun-running efforts into Ireland in 1914, it is evident that his intelligence gathering on armament movements into Africa helped prepare him for this later even-tuality. However, Casement's reports to the Foreign Office were highly critical of the unregulated passage of armaments into sub-Saharan Africa, and despite the widely-held image of Casement as a gun-runner, his later political writings and correspondence articulate deepening concerns about the irresponsible trafficking of modern arms. 'Ever increasing armaments but insured ever increasing animosities', he later wrote in his analysis of the causes of the First World War.[3]

His efforts to move on up-river were initially obstructed by the authorities. Not until 4 July was a boarding permit granted, enabling him to embark as a guest on the *Brugmann*, a river steamer of the main company trading on the upper Congo, the *Société Anonyme Belge pour le Commerce du Haut-Congo*. Two days later he arrived at the riverside settlement of Chumbiri. From his visit in August 1887, Casement remembered Chumbiri as a bustling fishing village of around five thousand people. Such a description no longer applied. Over the next four days he witnessed the quite drastic changes that had occurred during sixteen years of colonial rule. To the credit of the authorities, he noted how slave-dealing was nowhere in evidence, but along with it had gone the fishing boats and other local industries that were formerly its lifeblood. The reduced population of around five hundred people was now employed in producing food for the government staff at Léopoldville.

During his days at Chumbiri, Casement was the guest of an old friend, the Rev. Arthur Billington of the American Baptist Missionary Union (ABMU). His priority was to organise some form of independent transport into the upper Congo so that his investigation would not be jeopardised by government interference. Billington was clearly sympathetic to Casement's plans and agreed that he could use the mission's riverboat, the *Henry Reed*, for his intended purpose, once some necessary repairs had been undertaken. The *Henry Reed* had been the first steam-powered boat to work the waters of the upper Congo. Paid for by the Congo Balolo Mission, it had been sequestered by Henry M Stanley for his infamous Emin Pasha relief expedition. Although the boat had seen sixteen years of service, it was still in good working order. Billington's generosity in lending the vessel was matched by a Danish missionary, DJ Danielson, who volunteered his services as an experienced navigator of the upper Congo waterways and who had indispensible skills as a riverboat mechanic.

On 10 July Casement continued on from Chumbiri with Billington and Danielson. At Bolobo, lying nearly two hundred miles above Léopoldville, the *Henry Reed* was put ashore while necessary repairs were undertaken. Casement stayed as a guest of the Baptist Missionary Society (BMS) and used the days to send extensive correspondence back to London.

The *Henry Reed* departed Bolobo on 20 July. Over the next week, Casement, Danielson and the crew of two Congolese snaked their way up-stream, crisscrossing between the Belgian and French banks of the river, gathering intelligence and testimony where and when they could. In those first days, Casement was fortunate to locate and speak to

George Grenfell, the legendary missionary-explorer, whose detailed map of the Congo waterways, recently published by the Royal Geographical Society, was an essential tool for navigating their way through the region.

The two men spoke at length. Grenfell unloaded his concerns about the difficulties that the Baptist Mission and other non-Catholic denominations were facing in obtaining licenses to expand their operations. Increasingly Leopold II was privileging Catholic missions. Grenfell was highly dismissive of the Commission for the Protection of the Natives, an initiative set up by Leopold II in 1896, confiding that it had met only twice and 'then only to transmit formal business, and no inspector has ever been appointed by it'.[4] Leopold II's stated intentions to 'protect the natives' rang empty.

At Irebu, on 28 July, the *Henry Reed* entered the mouth of the channel connecting the Congo with Lake Mantumba. Casement later recalled in his report how when he had visited this same township in the autumn of 1887 'scores of men had put off in canoes to greet us with invitations that we should spend the night in the village'.[5] But there was no such welcoming party this time. The village had all but disappeared and was now replaced by a military training camp housing around eight hundred recruits.

The *Henry Reed* remained on Lake Mantumba for the next two weeks, gathering extensive testimony from both missionaries and the victims of exploitation. The most distressing stories were told by a group of young African women, referred to in Casement's report as 'female scholars', who graphically described their experiences. Bikela told how she had been driven from her village by the soldiers and watched as her mother and grandmother were slaughtered in front of her. Sekolo described how her town had been burnt to the ground and, after the massacring of her people, she had been forced to carry a basket containing their severed limbs before witnessing the murder of her sister. Elima gave a deeply disturbing account of cannibalism and how her mother had been murdered by soldiers. As a consequence, her father lost the will to live and killed himself, leaving her orphaned. Bonsondo remembered that as a small child she had watched her village of around fifty people murdered by soldiers. Finally, Ncongo related how shortly after her family was forced to flee their village, her mother and father had died. Subsequently she had witnessed the decapitation of a child.

From Lake Mantumba the *Henry Reed* returned to the Congo river, stopping briefly in Coquilhatville, the regional capital of L'Equateur, a highly productive rubber district, before entering the Lulongo river. After noting the considerable number of 'armed men' in the territories of the La Lulanga Company, who operated in the lower reaches of the Lulongo, Casement started to interrogate the managers of the company. He was keen to establish the methods employed in the extraction of rubber and the 'impositions' forced upon the people, 'but there was no explanation offered to me that was not at once contradicted by the next'.[6] At a small collection of dwellings named Bolongo, visited by Casement on 22 August, three forest guards were quartered to force the villagers to collect rubber in a district that was quite exhausted of extractive supplies. Equally disturbing, he noticed, was the total absence of livestock.

On 29 August the *Henry Reed* reached the mission station and rubber depot at Bongandanga, where Casement concentrated his investigation for the next week. Here he made detailed investigation of the working practices of the rubber station and also walked into the outlying districts and spoke to the locals, whose lives had been most directly affected by the extractive rubber economy. Further gruelling testimonies described the violence that had plagued the region for so many years: punishment beatings, revenge killings, the slaughtering of innocents, slavery, and cannibalism.

The stories collected by Casement are an extraordinary indictment of a careless regime functioning beyond the rule of law for years and inflicting devastating damage on the indigenous people. He amassed an extensive portfolio of statements from both the African victims and the missionaries who were no longer prepared to turn a blind eye to the outrages. The cumulative effect of this evidence was to arouse in Casement an extraordinary level of outrage and disgust. But how could he meaningfully respond?

As the *Henry Reed* steamed back downstream, Casement drafted a series of dispatches to the Foreign Office expressing his indignation at what he had seen and heard. The moment can be described as an epiphany, when the flame of anti-imperial revolt was first ignited within Casement's spirit. Reflecting on it a few years later, he wrote to Alice Stopford Green:

> I knew well that if I told the truth about the devilish Congo conspiracy of robbers I should pay for it in my own future, but when I made up my mind to tell, at all costs, it was the image of my poor old country stood first before my eyes. The whole thing had been done once to her – down to every detail – she too, had been "flung reward to human hands" and I felt that, as an Irish man, come what might to myself, I should tell the truth. I burned my boats deliberately, and forced the Foreign Office either to repudiate me, or back my report. And yet I knew quite well, in the end, I should have to go overboard, and I wrote that in my diary on Sept. 4th 1903, the day I wrote to the Governor-General at Boma denouncing the whole infamous system, and so committing myself to no compromise.[7]

Unfortunately the diary recording these feelings has not survived, but much associated correspondence illuminates the transformation in Casement's thinking. It took two weeks for the *Henry Reed* to return to Léopoldville and after ten days there, he caught the train back to Matadi on the lower Congo.

On the way he persisted with his investigation, writing to the Foreign Office and to senior Congo Free State officials to reveal 'the truth about the devilish Congo conspiracy'. He confessed that the experience had 'left me in bewilderment as to what my duty as a civilised man should be'.

On reaching the Portuguese enclave of Cabinda, at the mouth of the Congo river, he wrote to Lansdowne and admitted that in his frank condemnation of the regime he had departed from the 'friendly intercourse' expected of his consular position. He acknowledged that he had to ignore consular protocols 'even at the risk of incurring your Lordship's displeasure', admitting that his higher 'duty was to serve the persecuted beings who had far and wide appealed to me for help'.[8]

> I am amazed and confounded at what I have both seen and heard; and if I, in the enjoyment of all the resources and privileges of civilised existence, know not where to turn to, or to whom to make appeal on behalf of these unhappy people whose sufferings I have witnessed, and whose wrongs have burnt into my heart, how can they, poor, panic-stricken fugitives, in their own forest homes, turn for justice to their oppressors. The one dreadful, dreary cry that has been ringing in my ears for the last six weeks has been, "Protect us from our protectors."[9]

One suggestion he made was that an extensive investigation should now be undertaken by an 'International Commission' with a brief to deal with 'the monstrous and altogether extraordinary invasion of the rights of humanity'. Over the next few weeks Casement's analysis of the situation necessitated a different type of language about rights and responsibilities, as the people of the Congo had no rights to speak of and were vulnerable to a state administration that clearly seemed not to care.

From Cabinda, Casement steamed on to Luanda. Shortly after his arrival, the Imperial German consul, Paul Dorbritz, who had also recently returned from a journey to Léopoldville, contacted him. Dorbritz was keen to know Casement's views and the two men talked at length about aspects of colonial administration. Casement reported the conversation in a dispatch. He wrote that while Dorbritz also found the Congo authorities 'bad in the extreme', he felt that the atrocities were 'universal and inevitable incidents of European colonisation in Africa'.

> shocking barbarities are an essential item in the programme of civilised dealings with the blackman [that] he [Dorbritz] asserts everyone with knowledge of Colonial African affairs must accept without question. Wholesale butcheries accompanied by mutilations as disgusting as any related of Congolese officials, he assured me, were by no means unknown in Cameroon — and he presumed were equally frequent (and pardonable) incidents in our

own West African Colonial Enterprises.[10]

Casement spent a month in Luanda, tidying up details in his report. He scribbled a hasty note to ED Morel and suggested that Morel contact Joseph Conrad:

> the author of some excellent English — a Pole, a seaman, an ex-Congo traveller. I knew him well — and he knows something of the Congo — indeed one or two of his short stories — such as "The Heart of Darkness" [sic] deal with his own view of Upper Congo life.[11]

Casement left Luanda on 6 November on board the *SS Zaire*. During a brief stop in São Tomé he met the American journalist May French-Sheldon, who told him that she was visiting the Congo Free State with the approval of King Leopold II and Alfred Jones, the Liverpool shipping magnate, who had employed Casement in a clerical capacity back in 1882. French-Sheldon — a close friend of Sir Henry Wellcome — proved to be the first of a series of journalists paid by King Leopold II and his defenders to file positive copy about the Congo Free State in the wake of Casement's revelations.

A photograph of Casement and May French Sheldon standing together on the waterfront at São Tomé would indicate the poor state of Casement's health at the end of his deeply exacting investigation. He is a gaunt, almost ghostly figure, dressed in a white homespun Irish linen suit, his eyes ringed by dark circles, pointing his stick at some object or person in the distance.

Chapter Five

● ● ● ● ● ●

1904–1913

The Congo Reform Association

A fearful row is brewing I fear over my recent Congo journey. I saw some revolting things and I mean to speak the truth straight out from the heart. The result will be Hades, and I shall come in for a tide of the most relentless personal abuse from Brussels. Of that I have been sure from the first—when I turned my face up country on the Congo in May last I knew I was letting myself in for the most displeasing and ungracious task of my life and that for me, personally, there could come only bitter days, much keen regret at breaking friendships and in the end perhaps ruin – *if I told the truth.*

There are two ways of seeing the interior of the Congo State – either blindfolded or looking for the facts affecting the social condition of the natives underlying the veneer of European officialdom which had imposed itself upon them.

I chose to look for the facts. I said: he who goes to a foreign country to see the people of it and form a just conclusion of their mode of life does not confine his investigation to museums, picture galleries and public buildings, or to the barracks and reviews of soldiers or State conducted enterprises: he goes also into the villages of the people, he speaks with the peasant and the shopkeeper and enters sometimes the dwellings of the very poor: he watches the growth of crops and how the fields are tilled and seeks from the country producer to understand how his agricultural industry rewards him. He does not confine himself, for all the information he desires, to the statistics published in official bulletins – or seek for the main springs of national economy in the routine statistics of Government offices. If he wants to see how a people live and how they are affected by the laws they must obey and the taxes they must pay he goes, if he goes for truth, to the homes of the people themselves.

… The easiest way to refute the truth of my observations or diminish their significance is to vilify the individual and the Congolese authorities are past masters in the art of innuendo and the basest forms of *tu quoque*. [to attack your critic with accusations of hypocrisy and inconsistency].

… [T]here's a good Yoruba proverb I came across two days ago which the people in the hinterland of Lagos employ – "A man doesn't go among thorns unless a snake's after him – or he's after a snake". I'm after a snake and please God I'll scotch it. If I go under in the tide of abuse I shall not sink in vain – for I feel an undying certainty that truth will win in this campaign and that the freedom and happiness which may yet come to the poor, persecuted beings I saw on the Upper Congo will in some measure be due to me.[1]

So Casement wrote candidly to his friend Poultney Bigelow shortly after arriving in England in December 1903. With this comment, he acknowledged how his perception of the 'truth' would lead him into a diplomatic row that might ultimately result in personal ruin. Casement's 'truth', as it would develop over the next twelve years, was one that Western power was (and still is) reluctant to acknowledge. It was a 'truth' intended to unmask the very lie and deceptive practices at the heart of the imperial 'civilising' mission and the oppressive system of governance imposed by the powerful upon the weak and vulnerable. His journey into the upper Congo armed him with the necessary evidence to start formulating a direct challenge to that system.

Casement's report was presented to the Houses of Parliament on 11 February 1904. It would cause an extraordinary and long-lasting diplomatic sensation. On an initial reading it is not obviously influenced by any revolutionary or ideological commitment. As befits a government report, the narrative gives little away about the author and is couched in the language of officialdom. The style is putatively detached, objective, factual, and all personal sentiments largely hidden from view. However, it is still a terse condemnation of the system, exposing the betrayal of the humanitarian principles and promises laid down by Western powers in the Articles of the Berlin and Brussels Acts.

Domination of the moral high ground was critical to Casement's investigative approach and made him a stickler for truth. He was determined that there would be no grounds for undermining the legitimacy of his findings. In a letter to the missionary explorer George Grenfell, he stressed: '[I]t is essential that I should attribute nothing to you [that] you did not actually state to me.'[2] Communicating with the Foreign Office shortly after his arrival in England, he wrote: 'I must be quite sure of my ground before I intervene officially – it would never do to lay myself open to the charge of acting on insufficient or inadequate grounds.'[3] In a further official missive sent after the publication of the report, he explained about his determination from the outset to establish 'internal evidences of truth'.[4]

What is clearly visible is Casement's indignation at the cruelty and barbarism of the regime. But this is based upon observation, not dogma, and the evidence is allowed to speak for itself. The report recommends that reform through the implementation of measures capable of improving the treatment of Africans and lessening the barbarism imposed from the outside would be enough. What is ultimately demanded is fair trade and improved administration through the impartial rule of law bound by international guarantees.

In the report, he adopted the tone of an anthropologist coaxing stories sensitively from the victims; in a measured and dispassionate manner he mediated coherent testimony from the various witnesses of a widespread crime against humanity. But the report should not be considered in isolation. It reached beyond an account of the immediate findings from his journey and might be located in the much broader context of his on-going investigation over the previous seven years into the colonial administration of the Congo Free State. In this regard it served as an over-arching conclusion and judicial summing-up to a vast body of interlinking, on-the-spot evidence and analysis exposing the failures of the regime.

But Casement's intention to disrupt the cosy civility of existing diplomatic protocols and the embedded prejudices structuring imperial power relations was only part of his plan. He was highly circumspect about the reforming abilities of international diplomacy and had little belief in any genuine official determination to change the situation in favour of the colonised African. Diplomacy was primarily about the protection of national interest, not human rights. It was essential, he believed, for the Congo question to be put to the people and to catalyse a popular campaign, similar to the campaign that had galvanised British public opinion against the transatlantic slave trade a century earlier. A heightened awareness of the outrages stimulated by a campaign from below might, he felt, deliver meaningful reform. Nevertheless, he was sceptical of the ability of Britain's two principal humanitarian organisations – the Anti-Slavery Society and the Aborigines' Protection Society – to achieve this end. Both societies were over-burdened with campaigns on so many different fronts tackling slavery and working to expose colonial atrocities that they could not exert the necessary pressure required to bring rapid and effective reform to the Congo. What was required was an organisation able to target the problem directly and operate between diplomatic and popular levels in order to deliver solutions. For this reason, Casement was the prime mover in the founding of the Congo Reform Association (CRA).

Within days of returning to England in December 1903, Casement met ED Morel for the first time in a private house in Chelsea, London. Morel recalled his first impression of Casement:

> I saw before me a man my own height, very lithe and sinewy, chest thrown out, head held high – suggestive of one who had lived in the vast open spaces. Black hair and beard covering cheeks hallowed by the tropical sun. Strongly marked features. A dark blue penetrating eye sunken in the socket. A long, lean, swarthy Vandyck type of face, graven with power and withal of great gentleness. An extraordinary handsome

and arresting face. From the moment our hands gripped and our eyes met, mutual trust and confidence were bred and the feeling of isolation slipped from me like a mantle. Here was a man, indeed. One who could convince those in high places of the foulness of the crime committed upon a helpless race, who would move the bowels of popular compassion as no one else could do … if he were unmuzzled.[5]

From that first meeting Morel and Casement collaborated on what is now widely regarded as a seminal development in the emergence of the contemporary discourse of human rights. They formulated a challenge to the very working practices of international diplomacy, and in particular the anti-democratic apparatus of secrecy determining so much foreign policy.

They were determined to change the system, not merely to record its injustices. The word 'system' appears with increasing frequency in the writings of both Casement and Morel from this time. 'I do not accuse an individual: I accuse a system,' Casement wrote boldly to the Congo Free State authorities as he exited the river in 1903. The 'system' was really an umbrella-term for the political economy of colonial administration. It included the violent exploitation of the people and the complete disregard for their rights; the appropriation of the land by concessionaire companies who had a semi-official role in the running of the country; the corrupt economic model which allowed for vast amounts of natural resources to hemorrhage from sub-Saharan Africa in exchange for guns and liquor. Above all it indicted a system that failed to protect the most basic rights and freedoms of the people.

Casement and Morel met again to discuss the CRA at the Slieve Donard Hotel in County Down on 24 January 1904. The choice of an Irish venue for this first meeting was a deliberate act by Casement to symbolically connect the CRA to the Irish question. In time he would compare Morel's work banishing King Leopold's regime from the Congo as comparable to St Patrick ridding Ireland of all snakes. The following day, Casement wrote to Morel, enclosing a cheque for £100 – the seed capital for the organisation. The single organising principle at this early stage was to make it an inclusive initiative, to unite people in common purpose and cut through religious, national and class differences:

> We must unite in an organised association having one clear sole aim – namely to enlighten systematically and continuously public opinion in this country and abroad upon the actual condition of the Congo people … [S]poradic meetings and occasional lectures, articles in the press from time to time are not sufficient. They do good, of course, but they are not systematic. The defenders of the monstrous regime we are each individually attacking in our separate paths are all banded together in one powerful and wealthy league with a sovereign state for executive and a King for Chair-

man. They are systematic – and only systematised effort can get the better of them.[6]

If the existing system was to be replaced, this could only be achieved through promotion of an alternative and the co-operation of the leading organisations in Britain working for colonial reform. In an effort to create a united front, Casement wrote letters to leading figures involved in anti-slavery and humanitarian action, including HR Fox Bourne of the Aborigines' Protection Society and Dr. Harry Grattan Guinness, the son of Henry Grattan Guinness. In a letter to Liberal politician and reformist, Sir Charles Dilke, he wrote:

It is this aspect of the Congo question – its abnormal injustice and extraordinary invasion, at this stage of civilised life, of fundamental human rights, which to my mind calls for the formation of a special body and the formulation of a very special appeal to the humanity of England.[7]

But his innovative adoption of the concept of human rights drew from other associated struggles. Some of the organising principles of the CRA were appropriated from the strategies of resistance of the Irish Land League. Indeed, the term 'Plan of Campaign' was knowingly adopted in the Casement-Morel correspondence, thereby connecting Ireland's nineteenth-century agitation for rent reduction to their Congo campaign. Casement adhered firmly to the belief that the cause of Irish freedom should not be exclusive to Ireland but should be a fight for freedom wherever oppression was to be found. This sentiment was expressed concisely a decade later in a letter to the poet and anti-imperialist agitator Wilfrid Scawen Blunt, when he spoke fondly of a time 'when Irishmen preached not freedom for themselves alone but freedom for all others.'[8] This was the essence of his own blend of cosmopolitan Irish nationalism. His determination to banish Leopold's regime from the Congo was as tenaciously held to as the vehement struggle of Irish republicans to liberate Ireland from centuries of British military occupation.

The next priority was to build a network of support. In early 1904, Casement travelled to Kent to stay with Joseph Conrad in the hope that he could be persuaded to contribute to the cause. Although Conrad was not prepared to lend his name directly, he wrote a series of letters to Casement with supportive comments expressing his outrage at King Leopold's enterprise. 'It is an extraordinary thing that the conscience of Europe, which seventy years ago put down the slave trade on humanitarian grounds, tolerates the Congo State to-day. It is as if the moral clock had been put back many hours.'[9]

Over the next months, Casement worked hard to attract a firm foundation of Irish support for his Congo cause. This included prominent Irish peers and supporters of Irish Home Rule. Two of Gladstone's closest advisers, Liberal statesman-historian John Morley and John Hamilton-Gordon (Lord

Aberdeen), the soon-to-be re-appointed Lord Lieutenant of Ireland, headed the list. However, Casement's hope for support from the Irish nationalist MPs, notably John Redmond, was not forthcoming, as they excused themselves on religious grounds and allied instead with King Leopold II. During this time he opened his correspondence with the historian Alice Stopford Green, at the time acting secretary of the African Society, whose house on Millbank, a few minutes from the Houses of Parliament, became a regular haunt. Green was already a firm supporter of and mentor to Morel but her friendship with Casement would prove to be one of the determining relationships in the build-up to 1916.

A strong Anglican element to the CRA was evident in the support of seven bishops and various leading clergymen. The Evangelical voice was represented by Harry Grattan Guinness and another leading Congo missionary, John Harris, who was soon to be appointed as Acting Secretary of the amalgamated Antislavery and Aborigines Protection Society. In the early years of Congo reform from 1904-08, the Grattan Guinnesses and other evangelical missionaries made a critical contribution to popularising the cause of the CRA, using their local support networks to arrange mass meetings and lectures, where graphically shocking lantern-slides of disfigured African bodies were used to stir up popular outrage. But as Casement and Morel were dependent upon the Evangelicals' organisational input, they remained sceptical of introducing too much religious fervour into the campaign. Differences erupted over the running of the organisation and its political rather than religious trajectory that would eventually lead to a split.

Beyond seeking the support from existing humanitarian campaign groups, Morel and Casement sought approval from the families long associated with humanitarian work. Representatives from the Wilberforce, Cadbury, Gladstone and Kingsley family dynasties were all present on the masthead of the programme from the CRA's inaugural meeting. So, too, were the names of two leading shipping magnates representing Liverpool's trading interests: Alfred Booth and John Holt.

Every available seat at the inaugural meeting of the Congo Reform Association on 23 March 1904, at the Philharmonic Hall in Liverpool, was occupied. The event generated widespread publicity. There were two stated objectives: restoration of land rights to the people of the Congo, and the implementation of 'humane administration' and 'individual freedom'. Casement stayed away from the event, as his mind was pre-occupied with other matters. Brussels had responded to his report.

On 13 March, the British ambassador in Brussels, Sir Constantine Phipps, was handed Belgium's response by one of King Leopold II's most senior secretaries dealing with Congo affairs, M. Adolphe de Cuvelier, *Notes on the Report of Mr. Casement,* and passed it on immediately to the Foreign Office.[10] De Cuvelier was an ex-Congo administrator who had been introduced to Casement soon after his arrival in Africa in 1884; the two men appear in a group photograph taken in 1886. The response from Brussels was both defensive in the face of criticism and aggressively censuring towards the methods of the inquiry. Casement was broadly criticised for his investigative approach. The main points of reproach were incorrect representation of the facts and the liberal use of 'native evidence'.[11] In the opinion of de Cuvelier, the voice of the African, integral to Casement's investigation, was inadmissible, as the African could not be trusted in the white man's eyes.

Just as Casement predicted, a campaign of vilification now swung into operation. Its intention was to subvert the credibility of his word and thereby discredit his report. However, one indication of the integrity of his case was how it held up under the inspection of international commentators. The majority of opinion-makers, journalists and public intellectuals endorsed the findings.

In the months following the launch of the Congo Reform Association, Casement and Morel communicated regularly in a correspondence that continued uninterrupted for a decade. Casement addressed Morel as 'Bulldog' and signed his letters 'Tiger'. Morel shouldered the responsibility of collating, verifying, publishing and popularising the many stories that now circulated about the Congo Free State. He produced an extensive documentary record and published a stream of pamphlets, newspaper and journal articles and books that explained the rapid development of the narrative at both an official and unofficial level. Casement operated behind the scenes: spreading the story through his various Atlantic networks, maintaining informal pressure at a diplomatic level and always generous with advice.

From the outset, matters of confidentiality and official secrecy became an issue, as Casement occasionally conveyed information of a classified and official nature. Morel's newspaper *The West African Mail* and his other published writings make regular references to unnamed sources and information supplied by 'a personal friend'; this referred more often than not to Casement. Conscious that he was stepping across the official line of discretion expected of public servants, Casement occasionally asked Morel to 'burn' a letter once he had digested the contents. From an early stage in their collaboration, Morel and Casement transgressed the limits of state secrecy. This became an issue for them both as their collaboration deepened and they realised the burgeoning role secrecy played in European and imperial power politics. In 1911, the year Britain passed its comprehensively amended Official Secrets Act, Morel and Casement would reconfigure the framework of their activism to encompass a direct attack on the 'secret diplomacy' central to Western power relations in Africa and which they both felt was propelling Europe towards a desperately destructive war.

Towards the end of 1904, Morel stepped up this subtle challenge to secrecy in his book *King Leopold's Rule in Africa*. This was a comprehensive, well-illustrated volume that brought a considerable amount of textual and photographic information into the public domain.[12] Although Morel's name appeared on the cover, the work included substantial input from Casement. The book gave as much space to exposing the mistreatment of the Africans as it did to lambasting King Leopold II for subverting the humanitarian principles justifying his initial intervention. To make his case, Morel published a large selection of government documents: transcripts from debates held in both the British and Belgian parliaments, witness statements, and reports. His analysis exposed the games of distortion and verisimilitude played with the truth in the efforts made by the Belgian monarch to cover up his activities. The over-arching narrative detailed twenty years of oppression exacted against the native population. It began with the diplomatic promises made at Berlin and ended with the birth of the campaign for Congo reform. Casement's report 'on the spot' was upheld as foundational to the movement:

> It remains to be said that Mr. Casement, whose reputation already stood high, performed the difficult and unpleasant task entrusted to him with extraordinary ability, and that

his report might have been written by a machine – a painfully eloquent machine – so judicious, and free from bias or
prejudice is its tone.[13]

The book also included some of the deeply upsetting
images that would remain central to the propaganda war
between supporters of Casement and those of Leopold II
for many years afterwards, including a powerful and deeply
symbolic photograph of severed hands.

Over the coming months and years, Casement provided
Morel with a steady supply of opinions, advice, suggestions
and secrets. The enemies of the CRA reached well beyond
Brussels. King Leopold bankrolled lavish PR exercises on
both sides of the Atlantic to justify his activities in the Congo.
By now Catholic missionaries supported by King Leopold II
were making significant inroads into the Congo Free State,
which caused antagonism amongst the Protestant and Evangelical mission groups, who had built many of the first mission stations on the upper and lower reaches of the Congo.
Leopold's defenders identified the Congo Reform Association with the grievances of these missionary organisations,
and the propaganda war was partly divided by the politics of
faith. Casement and Morel were portrayed as the biased and
untrustworthy defenders of the interests of Protestant and
Evangelical missions. Casement parodied the situation in a
letter to Morel:

In Rome, the air of things is to regard the Congo State as a little garden of Eden! A delightful paradise truly – the only serpent in it being either "Casement" or "Morel the Multimillionaire" seeking to corrupt the Belgian Adam – until Archangel Leopold with the flaming sword of *La Justice Congolaise* drives the sinning pair out.[14]

The question of Casement's future remained a matter of concern all year. He had hoped to be selected for the post of British consul in Portugal, which had been mooted by the Foreign Office for several months, and travelled out to Lisbon twice in the latter half of 1904 with the intention of taking up a post there, but both times ill-health intervened. Twenty years of service in the tropics had taken a huge physical toll. After much soul-searching, Casement decided to temporarily retire from active duty from 1 January 1905. During his eighteen-month sabbatical, he devoted substantial energy towards building up the CRA. He was heavily involved in the organisation of a meeting at Holborn Town Hall on 7 June 1905 and collaborated with Morel and the Belgian socialist and parliamentarian Emil Vandervelde, the leader of the Belgian Workers' Party and a fierce critic of Leopold II, on 'the Belgium solution': a policy document that would lead in 1908 to the transfer of power over the Congo Free State from Leopold II to the Belgium Parliament.

The CRA also achieved something of a publicity coup by persuading literary luminaries to identify with their cause.

The author Arthur Conan Doyle weighed in behind the cause with his book *The Crime of the Congo* (1908). Henry Wilcox, the rich protagonist of EM Forster's novel *Howards End* (1910), lives from a fortune built from rubber trading interests in west Africa. America's most eminent man of letters and an outspoken critic of empire, Mark Twain, wrote a scathing satirical pamphlet, *King Leopold's Soliloquy*, denouncing the European monarch's colonial policy. The satire, written from the perspective of King Leopold II, included a fictitious reference to Casement's use of a 'private diary' as part of his body of evidence:

> [T]hey spy and spy, and run into print with every foolish trifle. And that British consul, Mr. Casement, is just like them. He gets hold of a diary which had been kept by one of my government officers, and, although it is a private diary and intended for no eye but its owner's, Mr. Casement is so lacking in delicacy and refinement as to print passages from it.[15]

With this comment, Mark Twain introduced the politics of the 'private diary' into the propaganda mix and unwittingly inaugurated an enduring controversy of twentieth-century history. Although Twain's reference to Casement's use of a private diary was an invention, the comment has bizarre later ramifications in Casement's trial and the scandals surrounding the Black Diaries.

Since 1904, King Leopold II spared no cost and ignored no strategy to protect the integrity of his violent enterprise. However, the fourteen-man official commission of inquiry set up to investigate the accusations of Casement's report did not deliver the whitewash the king had hoped for. His Congo administration was found not merely wanting, but there was no forthright effort to deal with widespread cruelties and abuse. The King was furious, and had no option but ramp up his public relations campaign in both Europe and the US in an effort to undermine the credibility of his critics. An American Congo Lobby was funded to influence Congress. Journalists were paid handsomely to defend the king's colonial interests. The publicity agent Henry Wack wrote *The Story of the Congo Free State*, a fawning celebration of King Leopold's work on the Congo. Casement came in for a sustained campaign of criticism and accusations of forgery, exaggeration and partiality were levelled against him.

In a letter to the Foreign Secretary, Lord Lansdowne, on 9 October 1905, he wrote to denounce the attacks made upon him 'either directly or indirectly by the Congolese administration':

> I have seen myself referred to in untruthful and disparaging terms by the Congolese Secretary of State in an international document; and I have been the object of highly improper attacks by Belgian officials who have no representative authority ... In addition to official action of

this reprehensible kind I have been subjected to a lengthy course of personal attack carried on by private individuals or inspired and subsidised press agencies who have alike drawn their inspiration and financial sustenance from the same official quarter – the headquarters of the Congo State government in Brussels ...[16]

In another letter to Lansdowne's Private Secretary, Sir Eric Barrington, he confided that 'the methods of Congolese diplomacy were beneath my notice ... the *suppressio veri suggestio falsi* [suppression of the truth is the suggestion of falsehood] have always found adept handlers at the headquarters of that State.' He made reference to the 'diplomacy of innuendo' and how the 'real facts of the Congo questions would have been still further obscured by a press battle, waged with all weapons of deceit, over my "corpse"'.[17]

During a decade of demanding operations until the CRA was wound up in 1913, the cause of Congo reform endured as an extraordinary platform for an alternative discussion on empire and colonial policy. In the background to the battle in the public sphere there remains an immense paper trail in the official government archives held in London, Brussels and Washington. Historians now recognise the Congo controversy as the great colonial issue of its time: it functioned as a prism through which a spectrum of debates on imperial power, 'native' rights and the ethics of free trade were refracted and rethought.

The work of the Congo Reform Association became a broad church for those prepared to challenge imperial power and its support-base spread into mainland Europe and North America. Morel travelled to the US to raise the profile of the cause and the American Baptist Missionary Society galvanised support through its congregations. The campaign helped to build solidarities of activism on a scale that had not been seen since the antislavery campaigning of the nineteenth century. While the popularising of this issue was very much a legacy of these antislavery campaigns, the Congo Reform Association adopted strategies of organisation and single-issue lobbying tactics that authors such as Adam Hochschild and the Peruvian Nobel laureate Mario Vargas Llosa have identified as foundational to the work of international non-governmental organisations today, such as Human Rights Watch or Amnesty International.

Furthermore, in any inclusive study of the roots of modern British socialism and internationalism, Casement's collaboration with ED Morel should be cited as a critical conjuncture in a tradition of English radicalism and the struggle for the fairer distribution of land. The Congo campaign, that placed the issue of the ownership of the land by the people for the people, might be traced back to the seventeenth century Diggers and forward to Brazil's *Movimento Sem Terra*, the Landless Workers' Movement that over the last two decades has protested for the fairer distribution of land for Brazilian peasant-farmers and small-holders. Similarly, their thinking on questions to do with liberty, cultural rights, social justice and both individual and corporate responsibility might be legitimately associated with the republicanism of Tom Paine, the United Irishmen of 1798 and the late nineteenth-century Land War in Ireland. Other aspects derived from the secular and religious activism of humanitarian endeavour as embodied in missionary enterprise, antislavery protest and aborigine protection. The relevance, too, of fundamental Marxist critiques on the division of labour, the abuse of the work force and the alienation of workers from the market place are also discernible in their broader analysis.

The Congo Reform Association may have started out by borrowing from Gladstonian Liberal principles and supported by proselytising Evangelical missionaries; however, in a relatively short time Morel, Stopford Green and Casement had reoriented the CRA towards a position that identified with socialist and internationalist aims. After the British general election of 1906, when the Labour Representation Committee won twenty-nine seats and the Labour Party became an entity in British party politics, leading advocates supported the Congo campaign. The first Labour Prime Minister, Ramsay MacDonald, the trade unionist and politician John Burns, the historian and political activist Robert Bontine Cunninghame Graham, and the social activists Leonard Woolf and Beatrice and Sidney Webb (all members of the social reform group, the Fabian Society) supported the movement. Congo reform in Britain led the way for the formation of associated Congo reform groups in France, Belgium and the US and a broad front of activists determined to confront the abusive practices resulting from unregulated, free market capitalism and to promote a more secularly-driven, rights-based internationalism.

Following the annexation of the Congo in 1908 and the death of King Leopold, Casement sought to extend the campaign beyond the Congo and take on slavery in its various incarnations around the world. In 1911, the Congo Reform Association mooted its intentions to expand its horizons. A testimonial luncheon in the heart of Whitehall to raise money for Morel and his family was organised by Casement, Stopford Green, and Arthur Conan Doyle. With this event the CRA made a clear statement of how it had shifted away from dependence on Evangelical missionary support towards a new internationalism. Casement expressed his aspiration to turn the CRA into a global operation and confided to Morel shortly before the event:

> Tackling Leopold in Africa has set in motion a big movement – it must be a movement of human liberation all the world over. You must not limit your vision to the African. You concentrate on him because that's your special task for which you are fitted more than any other man – but you must remember that the cause of human freedom is as wide

as the world — that if the slaver wins in Mexico or Peru, he stands, too, to win elsewhere.[18]

The next chapter will show how Casement's investigation of labour practices in South America was part of this bigger 'movement of human liberation', as were his hopes for Irish independence. The main speeches at the testimonial luncheon were delivered by representatives from different European support groups. These included Emil Vandervelde, René Claparède, founder in 1908 of the International Office for the Defence of Indigenous People, and the prominent French anticolonial intellectual, Félicien Challaye. Socialists from across Europe were now aware of the Congo Reform Association and its work, and the need to build transnational responses and solidarities able to confront the abuse of human rights and the crimes against humanity resulting from a widening of the industrialised global horizon. But the outbreak of world war would see diplomatic discussion on the Congo disappear out of sight. In November 1914, James Larkin's newspaper, *The Irish Worker*, published a front page article by James Connolly that quoted extensively from Casement's report and asked the question:

Why was the exposure of these outrages suddenly stopped; why did the British and French Governments suddenly exert themselves to choke off all further revelations, and to re-establish cordial relations with the Belgian Court?[19]

The economy of extractive rubber – or 'red rubber' as it was termed after the publication of Morel's book with that title in 1905 – had unleashed the next generation of slavery across the tropical regions of sub-Saharan Africa and South America. What Morel, Casement and Stopford Green had pioneered was a movement determined to challenge the excesses born of untrammeled transnational capitalism and turn a political and economic system in a more compassionate direction. In achieving this end, the work of the Congo Reform Association shifted the conversation on both human rights, international responsibilities and individual and collective freedoms in creative directions. Ultimately, this discussion would impact on questions to do with national sovereignty, anticolonialism and the rights and status of peoples dispossessed by imperial expansion and dehumanised by the impact of modernisation.

But any long-term intentions planned by Morel, Stopford Green and Casement were overtaken by events into which they were rapidly swept as the world prepared for war. In June 1913, the Congo Reform Association wound up its operations, as Casement and Green channeled their energy into the crisis in Ireland. On the outbreak of the First World War, Morel found a new role in helping to organise the Union of Democratic Control, an anti-war pressure group that denounced the expanding role of secrecy in diplomatic relations and opposed the manipulative influence of what we now call the industrial-military complex in questions of foreign policy. In one of his last surviving letters to 'Bulldog' Morel, 'Tiger' Casement made a prediction:

> I am convinced that when the whole story of the Congo has passed into history, the Belgian people will feel that the work of the Congo Reform Association was a work of friendship and enlightenment on their behalf, no less than a struggle in the interest of those distant Africans whose welfare has been committed to their trust.[20]

Chapter Six

· · · · · ·

1906-1913

South America

After more than a year and a half of absence from active
official duty, Casement was recalled to the consular service on the request of the new Foreign Secretary, Sir Edward
Grey. He departed from England for South America in September 1906, destined for the port of Santos in southern
Brazil, where he would be responsible for a consular jurisdiction stretching across the expansive states of São Paulo
and Paraná.

His appointment coincided with a greater determination
on his part to bring about the political and cultural separation of England and Ireland. During his long leave of absence,
Casement had involved himself with the cause of advanced
nationalism (or revolutionary nationalism) and the Sinn Féin
movement in Ireland. In his own mind, he now sought to
bring about the symbolic and practical severance of Ireland

from its constitutional union with Britain. Both his private and official correspondence made a deliberate national distinction. 'Remember my address is: Consulate of <u>Great Britain and Ireland</u>, Santos – not British Consulate!' he wrote to Alice Stopford Green as he arrived by steamship into Brazil.

Until recently, Casement's Brazilian years were overshadowed by his two decades in Africa and the tragic complications entangling the end of his life. However, in terms of his own intellectual formation, which led to his wholesale rejection of imperial hegemony and the formulation of a distinctly pluralist and tolerant Irish nationalism, this would prove to be a most influential transfer. His rejection of what he considered to be objectionable features of Brazilian nationality helped shape his own model for Ireland. His analysis of the political economy in Brazil, and his investigation of the rubber industry in the northwest Amazon, coupled with his wider knowledge of the geopolitics of the Atlantic sphere, further consolidated his determination to overthrow an unjust system which fostered division and suffering.

From the private and official communications to his colleagues, friends and family during his first three years in Brazil, the most unsettling aspect of Casement's commentary was his overt and often quite offensive criticism of Brazilian people and national life. 'Brazilian life is the most perverted, comfortless and dreary of any in the world. The country is beautiful beyond words & the people uninteresting, pretentious shams beyond conception. Everyone is overdressed – dress is their religion and vanity their High Priest.'[1] Critics have been quick to employ such comments *ad hominem* to imply a racism towards Brazilians ingrained in Casement's outlook. Certainly Casement's racial views are difficult to measure against the standards of today, but they contain quite an elaborate understanding of ethnicity that is worth considering briefly.

Casement recognised that national identity was principally about cultural survival. Much of his racial commentary on Brazil and the Amazon extended from his evaluation of the encounter between pre-colonial indigenous people and the forces of imperial power. He understood colonial society in Brazil as constructed upon waves of conquest and exploitation: centuries of Portuguese government, transatlantic slavery, the on-going frontier war against indigenous communities, and the endless cycles of natural resource extraction. This was the legacy he read into the faces of the acculturated Brazilians and prompted his often quite intemperate outbursts: 'Give me the real black – not this mongrel half-black, half white, half Portuguese, half Jew mongrel Indian mestiço.'[2] The mores of Brazilian society collided with his inherent sympathy for the indigenous 'native' still under siege from the internal colonialism of the South American republics, whether Brazilian, Peruvian, Colombian or Bolivian. Initially he censured those same republics and their ruling elites for their collective failure to extend the Enlightenment hopes of liberty, equality and fraternity to indigenous populations, whose suffering was not in any way eased by the advent of the republics after the wars of independence in the early nineteenth century.

After his experience in 1910 investigating atrocities along the Putumayo river basin of the northwest Amazon, Casement rejected the possibility of top-down reform and believed that organised resistance, of both a violent and non-violent nature, amongst oppressed people was the only way of delivering a fairer and more egalitarian world. His representation of the South American Indian (if at times romanticised) recognised their vulnerability. He recorded his thoughts during a conversation with a slave-driver:

> I said I had "great sympathy for the Indians" – and he could only smile. I have more than sympathy – I would dearly love to arm them, to train them, and drill them to defend them-selves against these ruffians ... I never carried a revolver against African natives, and I certainly shall not begin to do so against these very human South American Indians who are so much gentler and less able to defend themselves. The innate gentleness of their dispositions is revealed in a score of ways. But it is strikingly visible in their countenances.[3]

In 1913, he came to compare the struggle of the South American Indian with the struggle of the increasingly alien-ated and dispossessed Irish language communities of the west of Ireland. The comparison was in some respects question-able: could the brutal hardships endured over four centuries by the Native American communities really be measured against the war of cultural attrition suffered by the communities of the Gaeltacht? Or was his comparison intended to foment solidarities of resistance and to encourage Irish citizens to think transnationally about their own history?

His initial expectations about Brazil were quickly dashed by the mundane monotony of his work and the high cost of living. Within a few weeks of arriving in Santos he wrote to his cousin Gertrude Bannister describing how dejected he was by the drab and demeaning pace of life there. His correspondence described a mounting sense of frustration: he felt his time was wasted by menial duties facilitating drunken sailors and processing marriage licences. In spite of his dissatisfaction, he still managed to keep a steady stream of missives flowing back to his colleagues in the Foreign Office.

The most sustained piece of writing he produced during this first term of duty was his report on the trade of Santos for the years 1905-06.[4] He confirmed with candour how British economic dominance was beginning to face fierce opposition from the Germans. 'In paper and cement Germany has practically superseded British and all other exporters to this part of Brazil, and she is steadily entering into competition in a variety of other articles once largely supplied from the United Kingdom.' His report made further perceptive comments about the 'invisible exports' economy, (the sizeable amounts of money that left the country through seasonal migrant workers from Europe and Argentina).

In an effort to draw attention to a distinctly Irish manufacturing industry, he made deliberate reference to the increased import of Guinness stout into the country 'owing partly to the recommendation of the medical faculty.' He mentioned too the popularity of some key goods manufactured in Belfast, notably linen and steamships; of the latter, the Brazilian steamship company, the Lloyd Brazileiro, had two under construction in Belfast. Nevertheless, he noted that all goods coming from Great Britain were generally described as 'Ingleze' and Brazilians were unable to distinguish between what was manufactured in Britain and what was made in Ireland.

In February 1908, after several months back in Europe, he was assigned a new consular post at Belem do Pará, the prosperous city at the mouth of the Amazon, with responsibility for a vast consular jurisdiction stretching across the states of Grand Pará, Amazonas and Maranhão, an area much large than western Europe. Initially, his private correspondence described his preference for the life in Belem do Pará compared to the south of Brazil.

His priority on arriving was the urgent need to put the British consular house in order and to deal with years of neglect by previous consuls, as well as to reorganise an archive in utter disarray. He found life in Belem do Pará impossibly expensive and his letters home were filled with details about the unaffordable cost of living. Due to the lucrative rubber trade, Belem was enjoying the zenith of its boom years. The gracious, mango-lined avenues shaded an extensive public transport system and, under the state governorship of Dr Augusto Montenegro, generous works of civic improvement had turned the city into the most modern tropical metropolis in the world.

Despite his complaints, Casement produced a highly informative sixty-two page report for the British Foreign Office and the Board of Trade, which demonstrated why he was such a valued and respected official.[5] When compared to the previous eight years of consular and diplomatic reports, this was a substantive piece of work, which went much further than mere dry analysis of trade figures and the talking-up of British interests in the region. Illustrated with a fold-out map of the Amazon, the contents included a rich mix of historical and geographical descriptions, economic information, and candid observations about sociolinguistics, population, tariffs, river traffic, tourism, education and public health. Attention was drawn to the disproportionate levels of profit made by the federal state in Brazil from the country's economic interests in the Amazon, and how little was invested back into the region in order to improve social well-being, health and education.

In the light of subsequent shifts in the geopolitical economy of rubber, his prescient comments about the Amazon trade contained a discreet warning about the impending collapse of the extractive industry once rubber production from the emerging plantation economy of southeast Asia was able to meet the market demand. The overdependence of the Amazon on extractive rubber would inexorably lead to collapse once the economy shifted.

> Tropical America contributes 63 per cent. of the world's total – all of it wild rubber gathered in swamp and forest from virgin soil; Africa comes next with 34 per cent., collected by even more primitive methods in still wilder regions; leaving to Asia the modest contribution of 3 per cent., but all of it the product of careful cultivation, supported by capital and scientific application of labour. That this agricultural outlay in Ceylon, Malaya and elsewhere, where rubber plantations are being systematically extended, must in future years largely influence the supply of rubber cannot, I think, be disputed.[6]

His forecast was consolidated with thoughtful criticism of an economic model which was over-dependent upon the extraction of resources. He cited the demise of the turtle oil industry, which had resulted in a lesser but noteworthy boom in the region in the decades before the dominance of rubber extraction. The annual slaughter of turtles and the exportation of their oil to burn in the street lamps of western Europe had left rivers bereft of turtle life and had pushed some species of river turtle to the brink of extinction. Further criticism was aimed at the widespread shooting and trapping of tens of thousands of ibises and the use of their brightly-coloured feathers by European fashion designers and milliners.

The main event of his posting to Pará was a trip to report on the progress of works on the Madeira-Mamoré railway, the infamous railway project in the depths of the forest. The journey gave Casement insight into the extravagant and often hallucinatory life on the frontier of rubber extraction, where a minority were richer than Croesus and the majority lived in appalling poverty. He reported back to London how in Porto Velho, the main settlement at one end of the railway line, most of the Canadian and American managers were down with malaria and the labourers imported from Cuba were not up to finishing the task. Referring back to his own experiences organising railway construction in the Congo during the early 1890s, he suggested that the company should 'look to Africa or the Africans, for the completion of their task.'[7] The line was finally opened in 1912, just as the bottom fell out of the Amazon rubber market.

In mapping Casement's own intellectual formation with respect to the history and natural history of the Amazon, it is apparent from surviving fragments of notes held in the

National Library of Ireland that Casement's reading on the Amazon, and Brazil in general, was wide-ranging and comprehensive.[8] Hours, days, weeks and even months spent aboard riverboats and transatlantic steamships afforded him plenty of time (when not writing) to read around his subject. His correspondence, reports and notes were referential to works by the botanists and natural scientists of the Amazon waterways, including the Victorian naturalists Henry Walter Bates and Alfred Russel Wallace, and the botanist Richard Spruce. Other archival fragments reveal his deference to the wider European tradition originating with the Enlightenment journeys of the Portuguese naturalist Alexander Rodrigues Ferreira, the Prussian geographer Alexander von Humboldt, the Bavarian botanist Carl Friedrich von Martius, the Austrian palaeontologist Louis Agassiz and the French voyager, the Baron de Santa-Anna Nery. He also read lesser-known accounts by Henry Lister Maw, an officer of the Royal Navy, who made a reconnaissance trip across the Amazon basin in 1827, and the exploration of the Amazon valley undertaken by William Lewis Herndon under the instruction of the US Navy. Both voyages helped explain, at an official level, the strategic value of the Amazon for both British and US interests in the greater Atlantic region.

Moreover, he studied with sympathy and understanding the history of missionary influence in South America and was aware of the life and work of both the historian and

Dominican friar Bartolomé de las Casas, the first Bishop of Chiapas, who chronicled the atrocities committed by Spanish colonist against the pre-Colombian communities, and the Jesuit missionary Antonio Vieira. Several references in his correspondence defend the 'lingua geral' (a language developed by Jesuit missionaries to facilitate communication between different language groups on the Amazon) and the Quechan-speaking people of the Andes. The language politics which increasingly informed his construction of Irish national identity was projected into the South American context.

The unifying intention of all his reading on the Amazon was to decipher and evaluate the treatment of the indigenous people of the region and to ascertain how different cycles of economic and political interference in the area had affected the culture and lifeways of the people who had lived in the Americas before the arrival of the Europeans in the late fifteenth century.

Casement's interest in the natural wonders of the region he experienced and his ethnographic eye can be understood in the objects he collected and sent back to Ireland. These included a ceremonial bark costume and a large signalling drum from the Putumayo.[9] More controversial in terms of contemporary standards was his purchase and supply of birds and animals to the Dublin Zoological Gardens in the Phoenix Park. During his trip to inspect progress on the

Madeira-Mamoré railway, he sent back an animal he described by its Indian name *iguati*, which was possibly a tamandua, related to the great ant-eater. A 1911 letter from LC Arbuthnot, the superintendent of the Zoological Society's Gardens, thanked Casement for the delivery of a number of different Amazon animals.[10] The list included a small rainforest cat or ocelot (*Leopardus pardalis*), a coati or Brazilian aardvark (*Nasua nasua*), a Capuchin monkey, a colourful Arara (a type of large parrot) and a pheasant-like curassow. However, the most precious of his surviving artefacts from his Amazon travels is his collection of iridescent blue Morpho butterflies, a curiosity doubtless stimulated by his reading of the renowned Victorian entomologist, Henry Walter Bates.[11]

Over the years Casement developed a substantial knowledge of botanical affairs. By the time he arrived in Brazil he had nurtured a close friendship with the most distinguished Irish botanist of the age, Augustine Henry, who had identified hundreds of new plants during two decades as a medic and customs officer in central China.[12] A significant part of Casement's consular brief in both Africa and South America was to report on the economic value of natural products. He was aware of how the botanical potential of the region was a resource which had sustainable value and was of greater long-term worth than the boom-bust cycles of the extraction economy, or 'vegetable filibustering' as he termed it.

He recognised, too, that the botanical richness of the region was unlimited and potentially an almost infinite source for scientific investigation. Coupled to this was his concern about levels of deforestation, a subject which he regularly referred to in his official writing. In two undated notes he compared the felling of timber from the Amazon rainforest with the history of the deforestation of Ireland and argued how control of habitat was intrinsic to colonial domination.[13]

The cross-fertilisation of Casement's thinking on Ireland with his experience of Brazil is most evident in his writings on the mythical island of Hy-Brasil. Here he endeavoured to argue (not altogether convincingly, it must be said) for Irish origins of the name 'Brazil'.[14] In the Irish poetic imagination, Hy-Brasil or 'Hy-Brazil' (as Casement wrote it) was an expression of utopia, an island paradise lying off the western seaboard of Ireland. At the turn of the century, as the Irish nationalist project began to connect its own past to a more ancient Atlantic tradition, the myth of Hy-Brazil became prominent among cultural revivalists. Some of Casement's friends involved in the northern revival in Belfast, among them Dora Sigerson Shorter and Ethna Carbery, had engaged directly with the myth of Hy-Brazil, which had become part of the cultural re-imagining of Ireland.[15]

Casement, however, examined the myth of Hy-Brazil as a way to critique historical orthodoxy. He argued that the influence of ancient Irish belief systems, myths and stories in the writing of Atlantic history had been silenced by a dominant Anglo-Saxon version. Building on the work of the Irish folklorist TJ Westropp and other antiquarians, Casement demonstrated how the official Portuguese name for the country, 'Terra de Santa Cruz' (Land of the Holy Cross), had been usurped by the name Brazil, a vernacular term used by seafarers to describe this fabled land in the western Atlantic. But such an origin had been lost because historians overlooked and largely dismissed vital Irish language sources that illuminated the contribution made by Irish trade and monastic culture to the spheres of Atlantic and European culture.

The argument is well-informed with critical reference to the dominant popular accounts of South American history by Washington Irving, William Robertson, WH Prescott and Robert Southey and the criticism derives from the influence of a new national historiography under construction by Casement's intellectual mentor, Alice Stopford Green. With the publication in 1908 of her history on medieval Ireland, *The Making of Ireland and its Undoing*, Green had provocatively expressed how aspects of Irish influences had been persistently suppressed by more dominant structures of historical narrative.

At the start of 1909 Casement was promoted to be British consul general in Brazil, based in the capital, Rio de Janeiro, and arrived in March of that year to take up his position. For several months he commuted by train each day from Rio to the diplomatic colony at Petrópolis. There he bore witness to the declining years of the administration of Brazil's legendary minister for foreign affairs, José Paranhos, the Baron of Rio Branco, who had facilitated Brazil's transition from empire to republic in 1888. Casement, however, expressed frustration in private to his colleagues at the Foreign Office about the slow and challenging nature of Brazilian bureaucracy.

These frustrations with Brazilian life were partly alleviated with his interest in the rapidly developing situation in Ireland. His letters home are filled with angry asides at the continued prevarication of the Liberal government to deliver Home Rule for Ireland. He rebuked leading statesmen of the time for their duplicitous dealings with both Ireland and the Congo. Arthur Balfour, Lord Rosebery, Herbert Asquith, and the head of his own ministry, Sir Edward Grey, were persistently targeted.

Elsewhere, he censured British power for its pursuit of self-interest at the cost of the wider common good. In one particularly far-sighted letter, he predicted the advent of war between Britain and Germany unless British animosity was stopped. Writing to ED Morel on 15 September 1909, he predicted how 'things have reached so evil a pass that peace between the two great powers of Europe can hardly be kept. Both are preparing for war and faster than the world at large suspects – but the fault lies far more with England than with Germany.'[16] Some years later, once his treason had been identified and the British authorities picked through the details of his life in an effort to understand his treacherous turn, they were no doubt shocked to discover how, from behind the cover of his consular post in Brazil, he was discreetly redistributing significant amounts of money from his civil service salary to sustain emerging national revolutionary initiatives in Ireland.

Casement arrived back in England on leave in the late spring of 1910 just as news of another scandal about the extractive rubber industry was breaking in London. A young American railroad engineer, Walt Hardenburg, had stumbled across a brutal regime of slavery inflicted on the native Putumayo Indians in the northwest Amazon in the disputed frontier region between Peru, Colombia and Brazil. The offending rubber company, the Peruvian Amazon Company, was owned by a local Peruvian entrepreneur, Julio César Arana, and his family. In 1907, however, Arana had floated the company on the London stock exchange and raised over a million pounds of investment capital to underwrite its operations. A board of British directors was nominated to oversee the company's activities.

The Anti-Slavery and Aborigines Protection Society took up the cause at a political level and a weekly London-based journal, *Truth*, specialising in financial affairs, began to investigate and report on the escalating developments. The story was branded by the press as 'a British-owned Congo' and comparisons were quickly drawn with King Leopold II's discredited activities.

Casement put pressure on the foreign secretary, Sir Edward Grey, to send him on a special mission as the British government's representative. In July of 1910, he embarked with a five-man commission selected by the Peruvian Amazon Company to investigate the allegations internally and on the spot. His main brief was to report on the condition of nearly two hundred Barbadians, all of them British subjects, recruited by Julio Arana in 1903. The commission travelled directly by ship from England to the Amazon, with brief stops in Belem and Manaus, arriving in the remote, forest-girt town of Iquitos, headquarters of the Peruvian Amazon Company, in early September.

Over the next three months Casement dutifully recorded his daily observations, thoughts, concerns and actions in an extensive journal, edited by Angus Mitchell in 1997 as *The Amazon Journal of Roger Casement*.[17] During a period of ten weeks Casement moved with the commissioners through the Putumayo district, known as the 'devil's paradise', where the main rubber-gathering operations were located. Through conducting extensive interviews with the Barbadians and the murderous white managers of the rubber stations, Casement detailed and cross checked an extensive body of testimonies describing this widespread crime against humanity. His jour-

Above: Roger David Casement (1864-1916).

Right: Roger Casement (father) (1819-1877). After a spell of military duty in India, where he was influenced by Sikh mysticism, he acted as a messenger for the Hungarian freedom fighter Louis Kossuth. He supported the Paris Commune and showed early sympathy for the civic ideals of Irish republicanism.

Left: Roger Casement's elder sister Agnes Jane (1856–1927), known as 'Nina' by her younger brothers.

Below: Roger Casement standing at back on right in white suit with Mary Kingsley (centre, front), Claude Macdonald (seated) and others at the British consular residency in Old Calabar.

Above: Roger Casement photographed with the American explorer May French-Sheldon in December 1904 as he returned to Europe after his investigation of the upper Congo.

Below left: King Leopold II, a first cousin of Queen Victoria, whose administration in the Congo Free State was condemned by Casement's 1904 report for the British government.

Below right: Joseph Conrad, author of *Heart of Darkness*, a novel quite probably inspired by Conrad's conversations with Casement. The two men shared a mud hut in Matadi in 1890 and remained on friendly terms for many years.

Left: The Irish historian Alice Stopford Green (1848-1929) collaborated closely with Roger Casement and ED Morel (below) in the foundation and organisation of the Congo Reform Association. Her friendship with Casement proved to be one of the most progressive intellectual alliances of the age.

Right: Journalist and activist ED Morel (1873-1924) served as acting secretary of the Congo Reform Association 1904-1913 and on the outbreak of war in August 1914 established the Union of Democratic Control.

Above: Roger Casement standing beside Juan Tizon, the managing director of the Peruvian Amazon Company, at the main rubber station of La Chorrera on the Putumayo in 1910.

Right: Roger Casement's camera was skilfully used to capture visual evidence to support the written revelations of his report. The following two pages reproduce photos taken by Casement.

Right: A Barbadian
overseer of the Peruvian
Amazon Company's
operation in the Putumayo
region stands behind two
armed *muchachos de confianza*
and a child.

Below: A group of
Putumayo Indian women,
with painted bodies and
adorned with feathers,
assemble before a dance
organised to entertain the
commission of inquiry.

Right: 'An Indian father
& tiny son just in with
their loads of rubber. I saw
many children carrying
loads … The whole family
had to take part in getting
[the rubber] down to the
station—a trip of 100 kms.'
Below: 'Indian youths
with rubber at Entre Rios.
Some of the loads weighed
74 or 75 kilos often carried
60 miles & no food given.'

COMMISSION EXPOSES RUBBER HORRORS.

Inside a prison, showing whipping post (x) and natives who were flogged.   Wooden drums used by natives.

A native custom: women's legs bound with fibres.

Types of Boras women employed by the company.

Rubber at Iquitos, the port of exportation.

Juan Tizon.   E. S. Bell.   H. L. Gielgud.   W. Fox.   L. H. Barnes.   Sir R. Casement.

Terrible stories of the unspeakable cruelty inflicted on Indians and British subjects during the collection of rubber in Peru are told by Sir Roger Casement, who is seen above with members of a commission of inquiry. The photographs were taken at the time the commission were collecting information. The drums are used by natives as signals of warning.

Above: *The Daily Mirror*, 15 July 1912.

nal maps a litany of abuses: mass killings, gratuitous violence and murder, torture, sexual violation, interminable flogging and acts of public humiliation. Of the extensive body of text produced from the profits of rubber and about the rubber industry, this journal survives as the most emotive and instructive window into the last years of the Amazon rubber industry as the market boom for extractive rubber went bust.

The Amazon Journal is a work of candid and harrowing description. Casement uses various approaches – official representative, private investigator, empathetic Irishman, lawmaker and ethnographer – to penetrate through the web of deception, violence and terror which formed the basis of the company's operations in the area. His compassion towards the Indian victims of the crime is discernible at every level of the inquiry. As he listened to the stories and observed the daily activities of the company, he gradually unpicked the layers of secrecy and deception masking the regime and contextualised the atrocity as part of an historical continuum of exploitation unleashed when Columbus first set foot in the 'New World' in 1492.

> The crimes of the Putumayo, or, as they should be called, the crimes of the Amazon basin, although today less in sum total than the recent crimes of the Congo basin, represent a far older, more enduring and more fatal wrong to humanity than that mystery of evil called the Congo Free State. The Congo crime was an effort on the part of a European

ruler to put back the clock; the Putumayo crime shows that on one of the Continents occupied for four hundred years by two European races, the clock was stopped four centuries ago.[17]

As a supplement to what he witnessed, heard and transcribed, Casement also turned his camera to effective use. As photographs had proved such an effective instrument in provoking people to take action in the Congo campaign, he now focused his lens on the abused body of the Putumayo Indian. From references he made later on in official correspondence, he compiled various albums of pictures which captured both the tragic exploitation of the people as well as their extraordinary strength and fortitude.[19]

Returning down-river at the end of 1910, Casement was a changed man. His beliefs in the 'civilising' potential of the British Empire had evaporated and his concerns with modernity and civilisation's promise of progress had disintegrated. To describe that shift by adopting a fictional analogy, it is possible to contend that if he had travelled up-river to investigate the 'devil's paradise' in the guise of Marlow, the protagonist of Conrad's *Heart of Darkness*, he now returned to Europe with the cynicism of Kurtz: utterly disillusioned by the hollow promises of 'civilisation' and more determined to overthrow the system.

On his return to London in early 1911, Casement wrote two substantive reports and transcribed, with the help of a secretary, the testimonies by the Barbadians, which formed the bulk of his evidence. The main report, delivered on St Patrick's Day, 17 March 1911, was quite different from his initial brief, which had restricted his investigation to the condition of the Barbadians. Instead Casement concentrated his report on the mistreatment of the indigenous communities of the Putumayo.

In August 1911, Casement returned to the upper Amazon. Part of this brief was to follow up on his investigation, but there were other, more secretive, aspects to his journey. On his way upstream he stopped off in Belem and Manaus to meet with local traders and British officials and discuss the way ahead once the full impact of the collapse of the Amazon rubber boom was felt. In the eyes of those allied with the Peruvian Amazon Company, his highly damning revelations were already well known and his presence was considered to be extremely unwelcome. Operating once more in the shadowy intersection between diplomacy, intelligence-gathering and discreet advocacy, he attempted to take the investigation onto another level, testing the efficacy of Peruvian law by seeking to have the perpetrators of the atrocities arrested and prosecuted. But his efforts were largely futile. The Peruvian judiciary proved corrupt and incompetent. Known criminals walked freely through the streets of Iquitos, while others had disappeared undetected into the far ends of the Amazon wilderness to seek employment elsewhere. Casement spent several uncomfortable weeks in Iquitos trying to activate the local judiciary and preparing for the arrival of a new British consul, GB Michell, a colleague from his Congo days.

His time was not wasted, though, and he made important alliances with an anti-Arana group conspiring to overthrow the local dominance of the Peruvian Amazon Company. Among them was Rómulo Paredes, who had recently returned from the Putumayo after making an official investigation on behalf of the Peruvian government. Paredes supplied Casement with confidential excerpts from his report, which Casement studiously translated from Spanish into English. His findings confirmed Casement's own conclusions and went much further in recording testimony gathered directly from indigenous witnesses. While this added substantially to the case describing the greater crime against humanity, it did little to improve the condition of the victims. There was still no competent authority in the Putumayo region protecting the rights of the Indians.

At the end of the year Casement returned to Europe via Washington. With the support of the British ambassador, James Bryce, a noted historian and lawyer, he presented his case to the US President, William Howard Taft. The American State Department was persuaded to apply pressure on the Peruvian government under the emerging special relationship between the British and US governments, and a mutually agreeable way forward was arranged. In July 1912, the British government published the Blue Book containing Casement's reports and his transcription of the Barbadian testimonies.[20] Early the following year, the US published an equally comprehensive compendium of official documentation and reports, also containing much of Casement's correspondence.[21]

Despite the publication of the Blue Book in mid-July, when public interest was at low ebb because of the holiday season, the investigation attracted widespread coverage from around the world. Based partly on Casement's findings, Pope Pius X issued an encyclical advocating the protection of the South American Indians.[22] Pervasive negative publicity contributed towards the retreat of international investment from the extractive industry of the Amazon towards the increasingly productive plantations of Anglo-Dutch colonies in southeast Asia. The great years of prosperity built upon the profits of Amazon rubber came to an abrupt end.

Still concerned with what might happen to the Putumayo Indians, Casement set about raising funds to support an Irish Franciscan mission, and a group of five missionaries arrived in the region in early 1913. They remained in the district until 1917, working to stabilise the rapidly disintegrating situation and to serve as intermediaries between the company representatives and those terrorised by the regime. But by then the Peruvian Amazon Company had downsized their operation in the area, as extractive rubber was no longer as profitable. One of Casement's strategies to raise awareness for the mission was to write an article for the popular weekly publication *The Contemporary Review*.[23] This amounted to a coherent defence of indigenous life and revealed Casement's empathy for Amerindian culture as well as his support for missionary work. Although the tone had to conform to some of the expectations of potential donors, and adopted a language which was accessible and comprehensible to a British public, it revealed a progressive reading of the historical tragedy underpinning the colonial encounter on the American frontier. His comparison of cultural differences between central Africans and Amazon Indians added to the authority of his approach. At another point he commented how the Indian 'was, and is, a Socialist by temperament, habit, and, possibly, age long memory.'

Over the summer of 1912, the sense of public anger in Britain obliged Prime Minister Asquith to take the decision to set up a Parliamentary Select Committee inquiry. This initiated the last chapter of Casement's involvement in the Putumayo atrocities. Towards the end of 1912 and beginning of 1913, a cross-examination of those involved in the scandal was conducted in central London. Casement appeared twice before the select committee and, on one occasion while giving evidence, brandished a Winchester rifle above his head in court in a gesture intended to draw attention to the destructive potential of the modern armaments industry.

Behind the scenes he worked tirelessly to keep the chairman of the select committee, Charles Roberts, up-to-date with developments in the Putumayo as news reached him from his network of informants based in the Amazon.

At the end of the year, with his health broken by the long campaign, he left England and headed for the Canary Islands in search of winter sun and relaxation. He took with him a trunk of papers to do with his Putumayo investigation, so he could continue to work on the case. While staying at Quiney's hotel in Las Palmas, he sent Roberts his substantive Amazon journal, written in long-hand during his Putumayo journey of 1910, and agreed for the manuscript to be typed up and used in evidence.[24] He then continued on to South Africa and made a brief visit to his brother Tom in the Drakensburg Mountains. He spent a few weeks collecting his thoughts, digging in Tom's vegetable garden, and riding out to visit some caves containing ancient Bushman petroglyphs. It was appropriate that Casement ended his involvement with the Putumayo atrocities whilst travelling by ship to Africa for the last time. It neatly integrated his two official enquiries into one coherent whole.

But Casement's feelings of frustration with his position as a British official, combined with the escalation of tensions in Ireland led to his decision to resign from the consular service, something he had been threatening to do privately for quite some time. In the Coronation honours list of 1911, he had been bestowed with a knighthood for his services to the Crown and in recognition of his selfless years of duty. Though Casement had no time for such entitlements, he realised that the prefix of 'Sir' to his name empowered him and some of his causes. In the summer of 1913, when Sir Roger Casement tendered his resignation to the Foreign Office, he had secured his reputation as an exceptional official and was widely recognised for his personal courage and compassionate integrity. But that image was about to change utterly.

Even though the Putumayo Indians held Casement's memory sacred to their own struggle for survival for many years after the collapse of the rubber economy, it has taken Europe more time to acknowledge this painful story. In October 2012, exactly a hundred years after the publication of the Blue Book and to coincide with Spain's Día de la Raza (Columbus Day), a delegation of government officials from Peru, Colombia and Brazil, including the British ambassador in Bogotá, gathered at the old rubber station at La Chorrera, district capital of the Colombian Putumayo, to recognise the ethnocide committed against the Putumayo communities during the rubber boom. Official government statements were forthcoming from Peru and Colombia and 'ethnocide' was the officially-recognised term to designate the crime.[25] Local chiefs (caciques) officiated at a ceremony to exorcise the evil memories of the rubber era and banish them to what is called in their belief system the Basket of Forgetful-ness.[26] Pope Benedict XVI issued a statement reconfirming the papal encyclical circulated by Pope Pius X in 1912 in defence of the South American Indian.[27] In Madrid, the historic administrative centre of the Spanish-speaking world, Casement's legacy was honoured with an exhibition, 'Roger Casement in Ibero-America', at the Casa de América. This was co-curated by Professor Laura Izarra at the University of São Paulo and organised by the Irish ambassador, Justin Harman, and Ireland's Department of Foreign Affairs.[28] The contemporary relevance of Casement's South American history, which had not previously received the attention it deserved, was at last recognised.

Chapter Seven
• • • • • • •

1905-1913

Building an Irish Network

A lingering fallacy in the interpretation of Casement's life suggests that his enthusiasm for Ireland did not surface until relatively late. This view emerged at the time of his trial and advanced the notion that it was a sudden and somewhat erratic malice that turned his apparent loyalty into treason: 'blinded by a hatred to this country, as malignant in quality as it was sudden in origin', was how FE Smith, his prosecutor at the treason trial, phrased it in his opening remarks.[1] Such a line of thinking excludes the possibility of an evolutionary continuity within Casement's intellectual formation and downplays the possibility that it was his prolonged exposure to the frontiers of empire that altered his view of Ireland's political and cultural relationship with England. Did Casement's specific conceptualisation of Irish independence evolve in response to his disillusionment with systems of imperial power? He remained a Home Ruler for as long as he could. But as the prospect of the implementation of Home Rule diminished, his antagonisms were accelerated by the failure in Westminster to deliver workable political solutions. His identification with the Irish cause was no sudden awakening, but is evident from a very early point in his life and never went away. His cousin, Gertrude Bannister, wrote:

> Roger Casement from his earliest days was before everything else a lover of Ireland. In his school days he begged from the aunt, with whom he spent his holidays, for possession of an attic room which he turned into a little study, and the writer remembers the walls papered with cartoons cut out from the *Weekly Freeman*, showing the various Irish Nationalists who had suffered imprisonment at English hands for the sake of their belief in Ireland a Nation. Many years later, when he himself was a prisoner in an English gaol he wrote: "I have felt this destiny on me since I was a little boy: it was inevitable: everything in my life has led up to it."[2]

Casement's sense of preordained destiny and the pursuit of a pre-determined course are not apparent beneath the surface of the work he carried out for the Foreign Office. It was a humanitarian ideal that first drove him to Africa and he upheld a deeply moral sense of justice and humanity. This was at least partly informed by a sense of Irish difference and 'otherness'. Casement engaged with much of the progressive thinking of his day on such matters as prison reform, labour rights and health care, and applied it to his analysis of colonial conditions on the frontier. Therefore, it is important to recognise that Casement's aspirations for Ireland and his own disaffection with European empires are interrelated. Though he identified with the grand-narrative of Irish nationalist history striving for a united and independent Ireland, he would connect that aspiration to a much wider understanding of human liberation based on internationalism and anti-colonial struggle. If his writings made few direct references to an emerging socialist voice and the rise of a Labour Party in both Britain and Ireland, his actions belonged to the social reform movements of his time. The struggle for national self-determination was a necessary first step towards internationalism.

It was not until his return from Africa in 1904 that his anxieties about colonial administration fused with his reconnection to the intellectually progressive energy that defined Ireland in the years building up to 1916. This energy electrified a spectrum of activities beyond the well-known literary revival and language movement. Its voltage spread into the arts and crafts industry, the co-operative movement, and a wide engagement with social reform and community building. As the constitutional crisis in Ireland deepened over the next decade, Casement aspired to more than merely a constitutional break with the British parliament. He yearned to define Ireland as a flag-bearer of international humanity, committed to the battle for justice, equality and decency rooted in a language of inclusion, empathy and rights. His beliefs were clearly influenced by the Sinn Féin movement and a broader strategy to promote the local cultural and economic strengths of the country. He practised a type of responsible citizenry, dressed in clothes woven on an Irish loom, and from 1905 scribbled much of his personal correspondence on letters bearing the Irish Trade Mark letterhead. He encouraged his friends to buy Irish and to work above everything for the preservation of the Irish language.

At the core of Casement's local activism was a re-visioning of education in Ireland. In this he supported the new pedagogical approaches advocated by a core of progressive national educationalists, notably Patrick Pearse, Arthur Griffith, Alice Milligan, Alice Stopford Green and others.[3] At the heart of this endeavour for Irish education was the central role of the Irish language. In the last twelve years of his life, Casement emerged as an extremely generous supporter of Irish language educational initiatives in the four provinces. These included the building of new Irish schools, most notably at Tawin island (Connaught) and in the typhus-stricken region of south-west Connemara. He helped to sponsor (and visited whenever he could) Irish language colleges in Ballingeary (Munster) and Cloghaneely (Ulster). Patrick Pearse's Dublin-based school, St Enda's, also benefitted from Casement's generous support, and he provided regular funding for Bulmer Hobson's work organising youth groups such as Fianna Éireann and the Dungannon Clubs. In London, he communicated closely with the essayist Robert Lynd in nurturing interest in language support groups and arranging Gaelic League events for sympathisers in England.

The event that is rightly identified as the moment when Casement's engagement with Ireland entered a new phase was the first *Feis na Gleann*, held in Glenariff in the Glens of Antrim in the last days of June 1904. This was a celebration of all things Irish. There were competitions for vocal and instrumental music, plenty of Irish dancing, and prizes awarded for essays on local history and for short stories and poetry written in Irish. A local industries' section encouraged arts and crafts and domestic skills, notably knitting, lace-making and home baking. There were over one hundred competitive sections. Casement judged the contests for the best hand-knitted pair of gloves and the best specimen of wood-carving. A specially-commissioned copper shield – The Shield of the Heroes – was presented to the winners of the hurling final. Beyond its intention as an exercise in community building, the day allowed for the catalysing of a cultural network of nationalists.[4] Casement linked up with many individuals who would emerge as his closest allies for the rest of his life. Writing soon after the event, Padraic Colum noted:

> The Feis of the Nine Glens showed in a startling way the distance we had advanced towards a united Ireland, and

how many Protestants in the Black North have accepted the Irish nation. Many of the promoters were Protestant. Catholic, Protestant, and Presbyterian clergymen worked together. Orangemen subscribed.'[5]

The 1904 *feis* was a manifestation of that brief political and cultural cross-community synergy that would be quickly extinguished by the deepening political divisions that emerged in the next decade. Several of the principal organisers belonged to those families who had known Casement since his boyhood, including the Irish language devotees Ada MacNeill, Margaret Dobbs, and Rose and Ella Young. The event was supported by a new generation of cultural nationalists, scholars and grassroots activists who would collaborate intimately before surfacing as key figures in Ireland's revolutionary movement. The secretary of the *feis* was a local Irish language scholar and historian, Eoin MacNeill, destined to become the Chief-of-Staff of the Irish Volunteers in 1913. Another organiser was the young republican and Quaker, Bulmer Hobson, who founded Fianna Éireann with the Countess Markievicz.[6]

The main patron of the *feis* was the Belfast solicitor and antiquarian Francis Joseph Bigger, who had devoted his life to amassing an extraordinary archive of material on every aspect of Irish culture, history and natural history, with the emphasis on the heritage of Ulster. His large, comfortable home, Ard Righ on Belfast's Antrim Road, served as a popular location for frequent informal gatherings, *feiseanna* and pageants performed by the Fianna. Through Bigger, Casement communicated with a wider circle of Belfast-based national activists, including Cathal O'Byrne, Denis McCullough and the poet Joseph Campbell. Over the next decade, during his regular trips to Belfast, Casement stayed with Bigger and spent many hours discussing the future of Ireland and learning of the progress of Bigger's various local history projects (such as the restoration of Jordan's Castle at Ardglass). Ard Righ became a space for participative gatherings where traditional music and song, harp recitals and storytelling were enjoyed around the glow of the warm, turf-stoked fireplace of Bigger's impressive library.

Perhaps the most important outcome of the 1904 *feis* was how it consolidated Casement's belief that the Irish language was the integral component of national consciousness. Over the next decade, he wrote and lectured at length on what persists to the present day as a very vexed issue: the role of the Irish language in Ireland. He carried on correspondence with many of the leading figures involved in the language movement, including the German philologist Kuno Meyer and the future professor of Irish at UCD, Agnes O'Farrelly. When his leave from the Foreign Office allowed, he attended Irish language summer schools and engaged personally in the public debate on the place of Irish in the university curriculum. His correspondence, surviving lecture notes and published statements demonstrate a coherent and pragmatic understanding of the cultural capital invested in a language.

The death of Irish as a spoken daily tongue was, to his mind, a deliberate act of cultural sabotage. 'The language of a people is the fortress which the enemy first assails; and once that fortress is captured and its stones levelled with the ground, every other stronghold of nationality must inevitably fall.'[7] During Penal times, the imposition of the English language under law was a manifestation of British economic and cultural hegemony. But despite his bold support for the language movement, Casement had little hope for its long-term survival. 'When the Irish language is quite dead, our patriots and publicists, our economists and politicians will realise, in that silencing of worldly cares and strivings which the awful moment of death brings, that a race has passed away from the family of men, and that an ancient nation has ceased to exist.'[8]

This engagement with the Irish language movement was both encouraged and reciprocated by his close friendship with the socialist and republican, Alice Milligan. A founding editor of the feminist-nationalist newspaper *Shan Van Vocht*, Milligan was one of a coterie of Belfast activists, including the poet Anna Johnston, working for progressive reform in terms of women's rights, republicanism and social justice.[9] She wrote in 1916 of her collaboration with Casement in 1905:

In the winter following my first meeting with him, he organised a series of five lecture entertainments for me along the Antrim coasts, and I vividly recall how we drove past the foot of Glenariff, the scene of that delightful summer *Feis*, in a snowy blast which swept down from the mountain heights. Just as we passed under the sandstone arch at Red Bay, the Irish travelling teacher of the district rode by us on his bicycle, and we could scarcely hear the greeting he shouted to us, for the roaring of the wind and sea. The house of a kinswoman and friend of his was our headquarters, and there we had talk till late in the nights, about how the cause of Ireland might best be served and the old tongue revived.[10]

This is one of several such examples attesting to how Casement worked tirelessly to both preserve and extend the frontiers of Irish. On various occasions he undertook journeys into the Gaeltacht districts and remote islands such as Rathlin and Tory. Several surviving photographs of Casement seated among groups of Irish language students, teachers and Gaeltacht communities provide evidence of this high level of commitment to the cause. As well as encouraging friends and family to attend, he was also able to critically and comparatively apply the erosion of language on the fringes of Ireland to his analysis of the colonial frontier in South America. In an essay outlining the historical background to the Putumayo atrocities, he argued how schooling was exclusive to the language of the conquering power. He lamented the destruction of Quechua-speaking peoples as a symptom of Spanish rule:

> Whilst the civilisation of the Incas was ruthlessly trampled under foot their language survived, but no steps were at any time taken to instruct the Indian people of the Andes through the medium of their own tongue ... The only school at which he could learn the ruling tongue was in the service of those who were bent upon exploiting him.[11]

In August 1953, as a mark of respect, Éamon de Valera, Seán MacBride and Frank Aiken (all of them former IRA Chiefs-of-Staff) made a spontaneous cross-border visit to Murlough Bay in County Antrim, to the very spot in the Glens where Casement expressed a wish to be buried, to speak at a Casement commemorative gathering. In his oration, de Valera spoke at length about Casement's work for the language movement and how his life was valid to every new generation of Irish citizen:

> The essential thing is that in each generation those who see the importance of what Casement stood for will do all in their power fully to realise his ideals.[12]

If those ideals referred to by de Valera were synonymous with Casement's belief in the sanctity of the language, they were also ideals associated with his desire for a new form of society based on the ethics of civic republicanism and empathy for the oppressed. In pursuit of those ideals, Casement developed the most profound of all his intellectual friendships with Alice Stopford Green, the now-forgotten High Priestess of the Irish revolution. In his foreword to *Labour in Irish History* (1910), James Connolly paid homage to Stopford Green's work *The Making of Ireland and its Undoing* (1908), claiming it was 'the only contribution to Irish history we know of which conforms to the methods of modern historical science.'[13] In the decade before the 1916 Rising, Stopford Green built up an extensive network of support for the independence struggle. Her web of contacts linked Boston to Berlin and Lagos to London and successfully tied the question of Irish sovereignty into much larger questions on empire, nationality and colonial reform. When Casement's collaboration with Stopford Green was initiated in the spring of 1904, their networks of influence were fused in pursuit of a common objective: the achievement of Irish independence and the disestablishment of the British Empire.

Alice Stopford was born in Kells on 30 May 1848 at the height of the Irish famine. From her privileged upbringing as the daughter of the Rector of Kells and Archdeacon of Meath, Alice developed a compassionate love for Ireland. In 1877, she married the Oxford academic John Richard Green, and over the next six years served an extraordinary apprenticeship to the historian often credited as the founder of British social history. The Greens inhabited the intellectual demesne of Gladstonian England and Stopford Green formed alliances with several of the most influential statesmen of the late Victorian world, and some eminent historians, notably WH Lecky, John Morley, James Bryce and Lord Acton. After her husband's premature death in 1883, she continued his work and was provided with a degree of financial independence as a result of the regular royalties accruing from his best-selling book, *A Short History of the English People* (1877). She developed as a historian in her own right, building her reputation on a short biography of *Henry II* (1888) and an ambitious, wide-ranging social history on *Town Life in the 15th Century* (1894).

Contingent with her view of history was a social activism and a resolve to participate in national and international affairs. Her stated position on the need for women to reclaim influence within the domain of imperial and political power encouraged her to forge friendships with other leading women of the age. As well as Mary Kingsley, these included two leading social reformers, Florence Nightingale and Beatrice Webb. From 1880 to 1921, her London home was transformed into a crucible for the unfettered discussion of new ideas about women's rights, social reform, positivism, the demise of the Liberal Party and the rise of the British Labour Party, Irish Home Rule and the direction and destiny of the British Empire.

In the 1890s, her romantic relationship with the Dublin barrister John Francis Taylor brought her into close association with Eoin MacNeill and Kuno Meyer. Under their influence, her historical interests now turned more directly towards Ireland and the popularising of a narrative of early medieval Ireland rooted in the new scholarship deriving from Irish language sources. This retrieved the significant economic and cultural links joining Ireland to Europe before English interference brought about the demise of the Gaelic world, and the political, commercial and cultural changes resulting from the plantation system.

Like Casement, Stopford Green's disenchantment with the British Empire helped to shape her own aspirations for Ireland. She was part of a vital minority voice in Britain opposed to the Second South African War, which she believed was motivated by commercial interests. In 1900, following her independent inspection of the condition of Boer prisoners-of-war held in British concentration camps on the island of St Helena, Stopford Green founded the African Society in honour of her recently deceased friend, Mary Kingsley. Through this work she established herself at the centre of an information hub on African affairs, and a vital imperial network for commercial, cultural, scientific and academic interests in Africa. In 1904, when Stopford Green and Casement initiated their correspondence, her influence on African affairs and the British Empire was already extensive.

In his opening letter, Casement wrote how 'the claim of the Congo people must appeal to every sincere and genuine Irish national: the more we love our land and wish to help her people the more keenly we feel we cannot turn a deaf ear to suffering and injustice in any part of the world.'[14] Casement's direct knowledge of the colonial history of Ireland had provided him with the insight to see the horrors of the Congo, 'when I made up my mind to tell, at all costs, it was the image of my poor old country stood first before my eyes. The whole thing had been done once to her – down to every detail – she, too, had been "flung <u>reward</u> to human hounds" – and I felt that, as an Irishman, come what might to myself, I should tell the whole truth.'[15] In a letter written to Stopford Green from Santos he further reflected on his Congo experience:

> I realised then that I was looking at this tragedy with the eyes of another race – of a people once hunted themselves, whose hearts were based on affection as the root principle of contact with their fellow men and whose estimate of life was not of something eternally to be appraised at its market "price".[16]

What Casement and Stopford Green would develop together over the next decade was a very specific and alternative place for Ireland in international affairs. Stopford Green's identification with Irish separatism extended from her deep reading and wide-ranging writing on British social history. As she engaged with the crisis of Home Rule, she believed Ireland had been not merely politically oppressed, but was demoralised by a history imposed by the conquerors. In response to this, she pioneered the writing of a history that was socially engaged, deliberately uplifting and unequivocally identified with the cause of Irish national resistance to the oppressive formations of English rule.

Through his friendship with Stopford Green, Casement sharpened his perspectives on the Irish past and harnessed a distinct sense of history to his activism. He read through Green's manuscript of *The Making of Ireland and its Undoing* and intervened in the controversy surrounding the refusal of the Royal Dublin Society to purchase the book for their library, because they considered her perspective offensive. In 1915 he would collaborate on a German translation of the book with Kuno Meyer's sister. In 1911 he helped to plan the publicity campaign to advertise her book *Irish Nationality*, a small pocket history which was circulated widely in the years before the Rising. Ultimately their shared historical sensibility allowed them to assert a moral claim to Irish sovereignty based upon a revised view of the past, thereby shaping the ethical foundations for political independence.

Stopford Green also encouraged Casement to write. He submitted regular contributions to the advanced nationalist press during his eighteen months out from the Foreign

Office between January 1905 and the summer of 1906. *The United Irishman, Uladh* and *Sinn Féin* published poems and short essays that unequivocally indicated where his sympathies lay.[17] Under different guises he wrote about his father's involvement in Hungarian independence, the Act of Union, the Irish College at Lisbon, anti-enlistment and even aspects of Irish sports. His style ranged easily between the historical, satirical and a scurrilous anti-monarchist position, which became even more pronounced in his writings from Germany (which will be considered in a later chapter).

Beyond contributing to the nationalist press, Casement discreetly funded several newspapers from his Foreign Office salary. These included Bulmer Hobson's newspaper *The Republic*, and the voice of nationalist women *Bean na hÉireann*, edited by Helena Molony. WP Ryan, the editor of two newspapers supported by Casement, *The Irish Peasant* and *The Irish Nation & Peasant*, remembered how 'when he came to our rescue in a financial crisis he said he looked for nothing but the continuance of the policy, and no diminution of the Gaelic features.'[18] In the years immediately preceding the Rising, Casement supported with both copy and cash other organs of insurgency and independence, notably *Saoirse, The Irish Review* and *The Irish Volunteer*.

Increasingly, the control and influence of newspapers was the critical instrument in validating political action. The sophisticated propaganda strategies developed in Britain during the First World War had their antecedents in the battle for hearts and minds fought in Ireland during the previous decade. Casement's campaign in the Congo and the attempts by King Leopold II to discredit his report had prepared him for how the press and other avenues of representation could be used to manipulate and obscure the truth. Both text and image had been wielded in that contest to garner support, spread lies and influence public opinion. But from 1904 until he was marched to the gallows in 1916, Casement never ceased using or influencing the press for his own ends.

Casement's belief in Irish freedom verged often on the side of proselytising; he tried to convert doubters to the cause wherever he went. His endeavours building an Irish network, once largely hidden from view and conducted under the cloak of anonymity, is quite visible a century on. His work for the Irish language movement, his contribution to nationalist print culture and his extensive archive of correspondence with socialist and republican activists indicate his long and deep engagement with the separatist cause. This is what rendered his trajectory into treason even more abhorrent to the authorities. The fact that he was a paid-up government official who was filtering considerable amounts of his salary into emerging Irish revolutionary causes and using his privileged access into realms of power to further his own agenda was unpardonable, whatever good he might have done in the name of humanity.

What is harder to map accurately in terms of determining Casement's Irish network is the scale and scope of his trans-national support. As later chapters will show, both his correspondence and anonymous writings make regular reference to Britain's imperial relations with India and a comparative analysis of colonial Ireland and colonial India informs much of his political writing. Connecting the cause of Irish independence to other struggles around the world and building up support within the Irish diaspora were integral to the plan. Fragments of information would suggest that from his arrival in South America in 1906 he was using his Foreign Office work as a convenient mask to push the Irish independence agenda to the limits of the Atlantic world. But much of this story is either lost to history or remains to be unravelled.

In March 1910, on his return to Europe from Brazil, he made a month-long diversion to Argentina where he linked up with part of the extensive Irish diaspora that settled there after the Famine. He talked with the businessman and land-owner Thomas Duggan, a pillar of the Irish community in Buenos Aires. He was present for the launch of the nationalist broadsheet *Fianna* in Mar del Plata on St Patrick's Day 1910, a short-lived newspaper published by the Irish-Argentine republican Patrick McManus. It was indicative of the muscular republican links between Ireland and Argentina, most symbolically embodied in the figure of Eamon Bulfin, son of the Irish–Argentine newspaper editor William Bulfin, who was schooled at St Enda's, fought bravely in the GPO in 1916 and was imprisoned in Frongoch in Wales. In 1919, Bulfin was sent as the Sinn Féin envoy to Buenos Aires to help raise funds and increase the Irish support base in South America.

This seditious connection with Irish republicans in Argentina testifies to Casement's recognition that if the independence struggle had any chance of defeating the most powerful empire in the world, then it had to deploy every potential national and international ally to achieve that end. His vast correspondence, now catalogued in libraries and archival collections across Europe and North America, substantiates this tireless determination. When Casement resigned from the Foreign Office in the summer of 1913, his network of support for Irish independence reached from the open pampas of Argentina to the docklands of New York and the farthest pavilions of empire in India and then back to the exclusive drawing rooms of Hampstead and Westminster; wherever the Irish diaspora was located. Operating underneath the radar of his Foreign Office peers, he had rewired parts of the communications circuitry of the British Empire to the cause of Irish freedom.

Chapter Eight

• • • • • • •

1913-1914

Raising and Arming the Irish Volunteers

As soon as Casement returned from his last trip to Africa in the spring of 1913, he was swept into a public controversy over British administration in Ireland. Outbreaks of typhus fever in southwest Connemara had reawakened the spectre of the Famine. Casement wrote about the incidents in a letter to the *Irish Independent* on 20 May 1913. Under the title of 'Irish Putumayo', he made the controversial connection between his Putumayo investigation and the administrative failures in the west of Ireland.[1] He travelled to Connemara in early June to inspect the situation and establish an appeal to raise money, staying overnight at the Hotel of the Isles and signing his name in Irish in the hotel register, giving his address as 'Hy-Brazil'. With his tireless efficiency, he sent out a series of letters seeking contributions and quickly built up a network of support. A food distribution scheme was set up. Casement's close friend, William Cadbury, pledged to supply free cocoa to the local school, and within weeks children from the outlying district were lining up to receive bread and hot chocolate. The one condition requested by Casement was that all prayers be recited in Irish and that Irish be the prevailing language in the classroom.

Similar schemes feeding under-nourished children were already well established in Dublin. Casement used the appeal to raise money and sympathy for the suffering, and to draw attention to the failings of British administration on the margins of Ireland. Publicity was vital and he kept the matter alive in the press for over a year. The *Financial Times* devoted an entire magazine page to the issue and even printed an Irish language version of their letter of support.[2] Casement organised for the journalist Oscar Schweriner of the *Vossiche Zeitung* to travel through the district and report on the story for the German press. Over the following months some £211 was collected from the Irish community in Argentina and another appeal was launched in New Zealand. Royal Irish Constabulary agents watched Casement closely during his journeys to Connemara and detailed police reports of his movements remain on the record.[3] Both Alice Stopford Green and Douglas Hyde also undertook separate journeys to the region.

Casement saw the neglected margins of the country as

symptomatic of the deepening political crisis. At the start of the year the Home Rule Bill, which had passed through the House of Commons the previous November, was defeated in the House of Lords. The Lords' opposition demonstrated the power of a deep-rooted and intractable element in British politics that was ruthlessly determined to block any form of devolution. Casement came to target this as a principal obstacle to all progressive constitutional change. In August 1913, the Dublin Lock-out exposed to the rest of the world the appalling slum conditions of the working classes of the city and opened the space for the organisation of a citizens' militia. Casement's own energies now shifted exclusively towards Ireland.

In the summer of 1913, the CRA was wound up after almost a decade of operations and Casement finally resigned from the Foreign Office on a small pension. If Ireland had not become his priority, his plan had been to go out 'to the Cape for a period of repose and quiet, within which to place on record my African and Amazon experiences in the field of tropical research'.[4] Instead, he was now propelled into the whirlwind of a political and cultural crisis in Ireland as the battle lines were drawn between a Protestant majority in Ulster, under the leadership of Dublin-born barrister Sir Edward Carson, and a nationalist and mainly Catholic south. Casement vehemently opposed the division:'In Ulster, where I was most at home, I tried to keep together the small band of "scattered Protestants" there who desired friendship with our Catholic fellow countrymen, based on an equal recognition of their common Irish identity, against which the forces of intolerance and enmity were openly arrayed.'[5] Over the next year he would devote himself to trying to prevent the descent into sectarian division augmented by the deafening blast of 'Carsonism'.

Newspapers became the main outlet for his views. He railed against the intensifying level of discrimination entering political discussion and over the next year he explained, as transparently as possible, his clear critical analysis of the situation. One of his principal issues was the failure to think through the underlying assumptions in the representation of the crisis in the press. He wrote a letter to the editor of *The Ulster Guardian* on 14 May attacking the concept of the 'Ulster Scot' and the language of intolerance now permeating the public conversation. The letter ended angrily: 'when Irish history ceases to be written by buffoons and English music-hall artistes we shall begin to see that the simple title "an Irishman" is the common and glorious heritage of every son of this soil.'[6]

He knew that the intellectual battle over Ulster was where the war would be either won or lost. 'Ulster is, in many respects, the most typically Irish province of Ireland,' he claimed in a letter tracing the historical solidarities binding Protestant Ulsterman and Catholic Irishman.[7] Instead of division and difference between communities, Casement looked for common ground, stating, for example, that the 'melodies of the Orange bands that annually parade the streets of Ulster towns in warlike defiance of Ireland are mainly of pure Irish origin.' He realised how the tried and tested imperial strategy of divide and rule was being ruthlessly deployed to sustain political leverage in Westminster: 'It has been at once the curse and justification of English rule in Ireland that it can only exist by dividing Irishmen against themselves, and then must continue to exist because of this division.'[8] Over the following weeks he expanded his support-base in Ulster to mount a campaign to try and dissuade the Protestant and Presbyterian communities from dancing to Carson's divisive tune.

It was a question of taking the issue to the people. On 24 October he was one of several speakers who took part in 'A Protestant Protest' in Ballymoney, a parish in the heartland of Protestant Ulster. Casement shared the platform with a number of like-minded allies, including the Liberal Home Ruler, the Reverend JB Armour, the MP Alec Wilson, and his trusted ally Alice Stopford Green. The principal organiser of the event was Captain JR White, a free-spirited individual from a well-known local family with land and property in Broughshane, County Antrim. For several years Jack White had lived in the Whiteway Colony, an experimental community influenced by the Utopian writings of Tolstoy. The mystic and Hegelian philosopher, Francis Sedlak, was one of the more prominent members of the community, and Mahatma Gandhi visited there in 1909. White, like Casement, had a progressive and humanist view of the world based upon his direct experience of British colonial rule, and an insider's understanding of the prejudice and discrimination built into the structure of class privilege and vested interest underwriting British hegemony.

On the night of the meeting, a strong police presence patrolled around the five hundred locals who attended. The persistent beating of a drum in a nearby Orange hall exacerbated tensions. White initiated proceedings by making an impassioned statement about the deception and bigotry underlying those who opposed Home Rule. Significantly, he evoked the term 'human rights' to defend the Home Rule position, in what appears to be the first use of the term in the context of Irish politics:

> When will Ulstermen see that this question of Home Rule is not, and never has been, a religious question, but a question of human rights in which the Catholic hierarchy has intervened to hinder rather than to help.[9]

White was followed by Stopford Green, who tried to draw from history the many examples of when Ulster Protestants had supported the Catholic community. Casement spoke next and used the moment to try and pacify the deepening rift in the community resulting from recent inflammatory incitements by Carson and the Unionist leadership. Some form of self-government was inevitable and the Unionist Ulstermen, he argued, would be much better placed to play a constructive role in the building up of a devolved and united Ireland. The difference in faith should be no bar to a common nationality.

> While the Empire has been expanding and consolidating, Ireland has been contracting and falling apart. A hundred years ago there was only one Ireland. The Wexford Catholic and the Antrim Presbyterian were then equal rebels in the cause of that one Ireland … Where do they stand today? Disunited and severed … while the Ireland they died to make one, has lost millions of her people to build up greatness abroad, she has been growing poorer in men, poorer in heart, more abject in spirit, until today it is actually hailed as a triumph of Unionism that here at the very heart of Empire … there are not one Irish people, but two.[10]

This association between the construction of Britain's empire with the decline and disintegration of Ireland would become a key argument in Casement's political writings. He made the argument for the first time in public that it was the very concept of imperialism that must be defeated, as well as the insidious idea that one people had the right to exclusively determine the destiny of another.[11] With the benefit of hindsight, after decades of sectarian struggle and insecure peace-making efforts, the views expressed that night at Ballymoney would only become politically acceptable in the efforts in recent times to build cross-community understanding after the signing of the Good Friday Agreement in 1998. The contemporary rhetoric that endeavours to build partnerships and 'shared histories' between the divided Catholic and Protestant, Unionist and Nationalist communities in the North can be constructively compared to the inclusion espoused that night.

Coverage of the event in the press was mixed. The London *Times* dismissed the event as representative of a 'small and isolated pocket of dissident Protestants', and Casement as one who 'combines citizenship of the world with an enthusiastic attachment to romantic Nationalism'.[12] The comments infuriated Casement, who wrote an incensed reply, claiming that his personal knowledge of the people of Ulster gave him a more profound and authoritative insight into the region than that possessed by someone like Edward Carson. Casement felt affronted by the widespread accusation that his nationalism was 'romantic' or over-idealised. He believed adamantly that it was not.

> Your correspondent is good enough to refer to me as one who "combines citizenship of the world with an enthusiastic attachment to romantic Nationalism," and he adds that, with the exception of Mr Wilson of Belvoir park, we were

somewhat out of contact with everyday life and feeling in Ulster, and might incur the reproach of being "cranks and faddists" to the Philistines who make up so much of Ulster's muscular Christianity.

It was doubtless an enthusiastic attachment to romantic humanitarianism that led my footsteps from Ulster up the Congo and Amazon rivers, and probably without that quality I should have failed in the very practical investigations I was privileged to conduct alone, in both regions, and to bring to a not unsuccessful issue.

That humanity has lost from my being an Ulster crank or faddist of this kind I must leave to a wider public to decide.[13]

The brief collaboration between Casement and White at Ballymoney would continue over the following months as both men played anchor roles in the founding of the Irish Citizen Army and the Irish Volunteers. Beside their Antrim Protestant backgrounds, White and Casement together concealed a millenarianism with regard to the part revolutionary Ireland might play in the much greater shifts in world events. When White was selected to train the Irish Citizen Army, Casement sent a telegram in support: 'Strongly approve proposed drill and discipline Dublin workers, and will aid that healthy national movement, as I am also prepared to aid wider national movement to drill and discipline Irish National Volunteers throughout Ireland.'[14] Their ideological differences, however, would emerge over the coming months and were first evident in White's desire to frame the protest at Bally-money in terms of Carson's 'lovelessness', attacking the spirit of hatred he felt underpinned Carson's rhetoric. In contrast, Casement felt the argument would be more usefully served by upholding the sense of lawlessness implicit in Carson's divisive populism and the language of anarchy underscoring his public discourse.

After Ballymoney, Casement stepped up his interventions in the press. His anti–sectarian argument was made more forcefully in a longer article that appeared in *The Fortnightly Review* in November 1913. There he assailed the 'belliger-ent creed' of Protestantism and exposed the constitutional shortcomings that kept Ireland in abeyance. He roundly condemned the anti–Home Rule agitation as an unnatural development from a historical perspective, although it was itself a form of Home Rule for Unionists. The 1800 Union had failed to unite Ireland and Great Britain into one people and yet 'a separation of one people into two hostile bodies, artificially achieved in the face of nature, is to be regarded as a natural law, and enforced in defiance of reason, judgment and religion.'[15]

His article appeared on the same day as the publication of Eoin MacNeill's article 'The North Began' in *An Claid-heamh Soluis*. MacNeill's piece is generally cited as catalys-ing advanced nationalist thinking and bringing the Irish

Volunteers into existence. The tenet of MacNeill's argument evidently harmonised with the Stopford Green-White-Casement position articulated at Ballymoney and he picked up on several points raised in Casement's *Nation* letter of 11 October and referenced above. Most significantly, Mac-Neill noted how 'the British army cannot now be used to prevent the enrolment, drilling and reviewing of Volunteers in Ireland. There is nothing to prevent … from calling into existence citizen forces to hold Ireland "for the Empire."'[16] Given the long intellectual friendship between Green, Casement and MacNeill, based on their shared love of Ulster and their common historical interests, it is not unreasonable to assume that there was a close level of collaboration and discreet coordination in their actions during the weeks leading up to the founding of the Irish Volunteers.

MacNeill was born in 1867, the year of the Fenian Rising, in Glenarm, a village in the Glens of Antrim. By the time he completed his formal education at Queen's College in Belfast he had an exceptional knowledge of Irish history. In 1893 he had co-founded the Gaelic League with Douglas Hyde and was involved actively in the politics of the language movement. In 1908 he was appointed professor of early Irish History at University College Dublin. His scholarship, infused with his engagement with medieval Irish texts, had been popularised through Stopford Green in her histories on medieval Ireland. Stopford Green and MacNeill had started a correspondence as far back as 1894 and had worked closely on stimulating national and international interest in the language movement. MacNeill was also close to Francis Joseph Bigger and the coterie of Ulster nationalists involved in the organisation of the *feis* back in 1904. What is clear is that Casement and MacNeill had been personally acquainted for almost a decade by the autumn of 1913. They would co-operate closely in the months before and after the founding of the Volunteers, although Casement preferred to operate behind the scenes, preferring others to take the limelight.

Within days of the publication of the article, Bulmer Hobson, a member of the Irish Republican Brotherhood, approached MacNeill and the two began to talk about the founding of a Volunteer movement. Hobson later wrote: 'MacNeill's value to us lay in the fact that he was an important intellectual figure, able, clear-headed, sincere and well liked, that he quarrelled with nobody.'[17] On 11 November a meeting was organised by Hobson at Wynn's Hotel in Dublin. Present were Eoin MacNeill (Chair), Bulmer Hobson, PH Pearse, Seán MacDiarmada, WJ Ryan, Eamonn Ceannt, Sean Fitzgibbon, James A Deakin, Piaras Beaslaí, Joseph Campbell, The O'Rahilly, Robert Page, Seamus O'Connor, Eamonn Martin, Colm O'Loughlin, Michael J Judge and Colonel Maurice Moore. The committee agreed to despatch a letter to various national organisations, placing the basic aims of the Volunteers before their members, and giving details of another meeting to be held in Dublin towards the end of the month.

On 20 November, *The Daily Chronicle* published a front-page story about the founding of the Irish Volunteers (Óglaigh na hÉireann). The article spoke openly of a 'citizen force' and identified the two leaders of the movement as Sir Roger Casement and Captain JR White. The same edition of the newspaper carried an interview with Casement. When asked about the exclusion of Ulster from the Home Rule Bill, Casement commented: 'I certainly do not think any policy of excluding Ulster is either possible or workable, and I have met no Ulsterman who put it forward as a solution. This proposal, you may remember, did not come from any Ulster or Irish representative; it was first made, I think, at Dungannon by Mr FE Smith, who is not an Ulster member.' The irony of this comment would become shockingly apparent in 1916, when Smith would lead the Crown prosecution against Casement at his trial for treason. Public antagonism between Casement and Smith can be traced back to this statement.

At the founding of the Irish Volunteers at the Rotunda on 25 November 1913, Pearse, MacNeill and Laurence J Kettle were the principal speakers. Hobson was considered too extreme to put on the platform. Casement chose not to be present, but within hours of the meeting MacNeill wrote to him, outlining the enormity of the task and asking for Casement's assistance: 'In the constructive work we need the help of men like you who can stand out detached.'[18] Casement took MacNeill at his word and acted immediately. Within days he had drafted the *Manifesto of the Irish Volunteers*, setting out the aims and objectives of the movement:

> The object proposed for the Irish Volunteers is to secure and maintain the rights and liberties common to all the people of Ireland. Their duties will be defensive and protective, and they will not contemplate either aggression or domination. Their ranks are open to all able-bodied Irishmen without distinction of creed, politics or social grade. Means will be found whereby Irishmen unable to serve as ordinary volunteers will be enabled to aid the Volunteer forces in various capacities. There will also be work for women to do, and there are signs that the women of Ireland, true to their record, are especially enthusiastic for the success of the Irish Volunteers.[19]

Over the following months, Casement continued to play a vital organising role and worked with Hobson, Pearse and others in determining the direction of the Irish Volunteers. Casement realised that a principal requirement was to find officers able to train the Volunteers and he corresponded with Colonel Maurice Moore, the brother of the writer George Moore, to find a suitable candidate. In 1918, Bulmer Hobson's *A Short History of the Irish Volunteers*, including a

preface by Eoin MacNeill, was dedicated to the memory
of Roger Casement and partly explained his role. Volunteer
recruitment rallies were held across the thirty-two counties
of Ireland. Thousands of men signed up each week.

After the success of the Rotunda meeting, Casement, Pearse
and MacNeill travelled to Galway in December. An initial
discussion held at the University was followed by a torch-lit
procession and a well-attended rally at the Town Hall. Casement and MacNeill then moved on to Cork, but matters
did not go as smoothly. At a large gathering of sympathisers, trouble broke out when MacNeill asked for three cheers
for Edward Carson. His gesture was intended as a display of
solidarity for Carson's vindication of the right of Irishmen to
arm for the assertion of their political beliefs. But some elements in the crowd misinterpreted the act as direct support
for Carson's cause. Disorder and confusion ensued. The idea
was ill-judged by both Casement and MacNeill.

Casement had other business in Cork. For several months
he had discreetly organised an initiative to re-orientate
German ships through Queenstown (Cobh) harbour and
thereby establish an Irish stopover for transatlantic German
liners. Such a move had been prompted by a decision by
the British-owned Cunard Line to cease its calls to Queenstown on its way to and from the US. The excuse given by
the company was the decline in Irish emigrants to the US,
but Casement and other nationalists saw this as a deliberate

act to isolate Ireland. In an effort to improve the situation, Casement opened up communication with the Hamburg-Amerika line, Germany's principal transatlantic shipping company. His intention was to persuade steamships to stop in Queenstown on their transatlantic voyages and thereby maintain Ireland's shipping link with both Europe and the US. A welcoming party was organised by Casement of local Cork dignitaries to meet the first ship, the *Rhaetia*, when she docked on 20 January 1914. However, as the appointed day approached, problems emerged and, at the last moment, the plan was cancelled. Casement was convinced that this was the result of direct interference from Whitehall and a culture of anti-Irish feeling in the Foreign Office. In a letter to a Cork solicitor, John J Horgan, who had collaborated with Casement on the scheme, he wrote how England 'holds Ireland in a grip of economic servitude. Most Irishmen are slaves in their outlook on life – England has made them so – by hideous cruelty and oppression in the past, carried on today by rigorous seclusion from contact with others and by the control of every means of advancement.'[20]

For Casement the incident demonstrated the servitude of Ireland and the need to reorientate Ireland's political economy towards Europe and away from its oppressive dependency upon the British Empire and what he termed 'the Anglo-Saxon alliance'. His bitter disappointment at the blocking of his Queenstown plan became a frequent bugbear in his political writings and private correspondence over the coming months. His historical condemnation of the act was expressed in three consecutive monthly editions of *The Irish Review* published under the title, "From 'Coffin Ship' to 'Atlantic Greyhound'", written under the pseudonym 'An Irish American'.[21] This placed the Queenstown incident into the broader context of the Irish Famine, as Irish poverty and emigration in the latter half of the nineteenth century had resulted in large profits for British shipping companies. The argument was orientated towards attracting both the attention and sympathy of the Irish-American lobby. In apportioning blame to an institutionalised, anti-Irish attitude in British administration, Casement pointed a finger of blame at the First Lord of the Admiralty, Winston Churchill. He criticised Churchill directly for his interference and his plans to refocus Queenstown towards its value as a naval base protecting the interest of the British Empire.

The Queenstown incident was just one of several new fronts now opened up by Casement as the battle lines over the Home Rule crisis hardened. The New Year of 1914 was ushered in at the house of FJ Bigger in Belfast with a procession of the Fianna through the streets of the city. Over the following months, apart from brief visits to London and Belfast, Casement based himself in rooms in Malahide, just north of Dublin. From there he could reach Belfast, Dublin and London by rail with relatively short journeys. He now started to widen the revolutionary conspiracy.

Early in 1914 he despatched Bulmer Hobson to the US with a secret memorandum outlining the position of Irish-German relations in the event of war. Since 1908 he had predicted the inevitability of conflict between European powers, which he believed would be motivated by British determination to maintain her trade monopoly. As the crisis in Ireland and the wider world deepened, he understood the need to expand the network of support for Irish independence onto a diplomatic level. To that end he opened a more direct line of communication with the centres of power in both the US and Berlin. He devoted all day and most of the night to writing either letters or articles, walking along the sea front to collect his thoughts, and conversing with the few who knew his whereabouts. A Royal Irish Constabulary intelligence file demonstrates that Casement's movements were being closely monitored and he tried to keep his actions as secret as possible. The advanced nationalist press published a good deal of Casement copy over the coming months; some was written under his own name, some pseudonymously, and some is still to be identified. Occasionally he would take a break to take the platform at an Irish Volunteers recruitment rally.

On 25 January he visited Limerick in the company of Pearse. They spent much of the time in talks with James Daly, a prominent local republican, at his fine Georgian house at

15 Barrington Street, and met with other noted Limerick republicans, including the mayor, Michael O'Callaghan.[22] A recruitment meeting was convened and assurances were given at the outset that the gathering to enlist Volunteers was not intended to derail the passage of the Home Rule Bill. Pearse delivered an impassioned speech, while Casement placed the Irish Home Rule struggle into the context of the British Empire. In his opening he referred to an army of Boer volunteers: 'they now had self-government and were living in peace and happiness and in the utmost loyalty to the Empire.'[23] In public he was still maintaining the moderate line of advocating a constitutional settlement, but in private his comments suggest a more seditious line that had abandoned all hope of a peaceful solution.

On his way back to Malahide from the mid-West, Casement met with Tom Clarke in Dublin, who wrote to John Daly: 'Sir Roger Casement called this evening & told me of the meeting yesterday and how delighted he was with his stay with you. Both he and Pearse say your Limerick meeting was the best in many respects of any they have been at yet.'[24]

He returned to Limerick on St Patrick's Day, this time without Pearse, staying once again in the Daly household. Over three days and nights, various inspections of local Volunteers and meetings were arranged. During the parade, he marched through the city at the head of a corps of Volunteers and inspected them on the outskirts of the city. That evening he was invited to a meeting of a branch of Fianna Éireann in Little Barrington Street and, after speaking of his time in Africa and South America, he encouraged the assembled to respect the virtues of the Fianna of old by being 'truthful, honest, straightforward, kind, self-reliant, and ready to act if called upon in defence of the rights and liberties of their native land.'[25]

Beyond Casement's busy schedule in the first six months attending recruiting rallies, building Volunteer capacity and writing for the advanced nationalist press, he involved himself in various conspiracies against British administration in Ireland. From his years fighting bitter campaigns over crimes against humanity in the Congo and Amazon, Casement understood how the dynamic of propaganda and the battle for hearts and minds was critical to the success of every political campaign. Over the previous decade, Sinn Féin had developed a highly efficient and effective public relations machine that would soon be met by various legislative measures from Westminster intended to curtail free speech, most notably the Defence of the Realm Act. Casement recognised the requirement to nurture stories that would reflect badly on British administration in Ireland. The Connemara campaign had served as a means of damaging the reputation of various arms of British administration, notably the Congested Districts Board. But as divisions deepened, other ways of indicting British authority in Ireland were now deployed.

In many respects this is the most controversial aspect of his revolutionary turn and it would eventually leave him vulnerable to counter-conspiracies. Fostering such nefarious intrigue merely antagonised his diminishing support in the British government and has alienated Casement from straightforward historical treatment, because conspiracy is mainly unacceptable within the parameters of academic study and the history sanctioned at an official government level. Governments do not admit to conspiracies, however strong the evidence is either for or against them.

In early 1914, Stopford Green, MacNeill and Casement collaborated in the purchase of two important archives of papers that they felt, once publicised or circulated within sympathetic circles, would seriously compromise the image of British administration. The first collection of papers was offered to Casement and MacNeill by a disaffected public servant in Ireland, William Henry Joyce (not to be confused with his namesake William Joyce, or Lord Haw-Haw, the Nazi propagandist executed by the British for treason in 1946). Joyce was a sub-inspector and resident magistrate who had retired from the public service with an intimate knowledge of the working of British executive power in Ireland. Angered by his treatment, Joyce compiled a secret history of his career, largely levelled against AJ Balfour's years as chief secretary in Ireland and the Tory administration. In early 1914, Joyce opened secret communications with Casement about selling these papers. Casement believed that the papers would be enough to bring the government down. In a letter to Stopford Green he wrote: 'It is a statement that, if published, would do more to wreck the Anglo-Saxon alliance than anything I have seen – if properly edited and written up. The evidence is there, the corruption is there, the shamelessness is there, the debauchery of the 'public service' by the higher servants of the State is there; all for political ends against Ireland.'[26]

The other collection of papers disclosed murky aspects of the 'Crossmaglen Conspiracy', a particularly unpleasant incident in the Land War that led to the wrongful conviction of thirteen men in 1883 on charges of treason-felony and conspiracy to murder. This scandal suggested the presence of a culture of corruption and collusion linking politicians, the judiciary and landowners in oppressing tenant farmers. At the time, it had rocked the Liberal government and forced the resignation of two high-ranking civil servants. Of equal concern was how the legal process itself had involved false testimony and the use of concocted evidence, including a forged book, referred to as the 'Crossmaglen Book', detailing the activities of a fictitious revolutionary organisation called the Patriotic Brotherhood.[27]

This archive of material was transported to America and deposited with Joe McGarrity in Philadelphia, but the full story was not published until the 1960s, by which time the wind had largely gone from the sails of the intrigue. In hindsight, Casement's view, expressed in his letter to Stopford Green, appears somewhat exaggerated, but it does demonstrate how the stakes in this seditious entanglement were escalating.

News of a different kind of conspiracy reached Casement's attention as he left Limerick after the St Patrick's Day celebrations. On 20 March sixty British cavalry officers, led by Brigadier-General Hubert Gough, threatened to resign their positions rather than go to Ulster to coerce (as they wrongly believed) the unionists into accepting Home Rule. On 28 March Casement and MacNeill jointly signed a letter to the *Irish Independent* where they defined the military build-up in the North and the Curragh mutiny as evidence of a coup d'état.[28] Casement once more pointed an accusing finger at two of the most powerful Anglo-Irish voices, Lord Lansdowne and Lord Wolseley. When serving as British Foreign Secretary, Lansdowne supported Casement unequivocally during his Congo campaign, while Wolseley had enjoyed for many years the close confidence of King Leopold II in the Congo.

Fears of a coup deepened at the end of April with the successful landing of a large shipment of guns for the Ulster Volunteers. An estimated load of 25,000 rifles and three million rounds of ammunition arrived into the port of Larne and were quickly dispersed to Loyalist arms dumps across Ulster. On hearing the news, Casement made a visit to Larne with Alice Milligan and was reported to have said to her, 'We'll have to do something like this.'[29]

He was a man of his word, and within days a plan to run guns into Ireland for the Irish Volunteers was in the making. On evaluation of the surviving evidence, it would seem that the planning of the Howth gun-running was largely master-minded by Casement. His experience in Africa gathering intelligence on the movement of arms to the Boer Volunteers in the Orange Free State and his secret intelligence reports on the shipping of weapons up both the Congo and Amazon had provided plenty of insight into the clandestine world of arms smuggling. His speech-making and correspondence of early 1914 made persistent reference to the fundamental necessity of arming the Volunteers, which he considered was critical to the success of the movement. He saw the arming of the Volunteers as a defensive act, undertaken on one level in response to the Ulster Volunteers and on another level to give real agency to the Irish Volunteer force. But this deci-sion would force Casement to confront John Redmond and the leaders of the Irish Party at Westminster in a series of strained encounters.

According to his own account, on 7 May Casement and MacNeill had a meeting with John Redmond at the Houses of Parliament. During the course of this meeting it became clear that Redmond intended to take control of the Volunteers and to 'use them as a sham army for political purposes on English party platforms.'[30] Both Casement and MacNeill wished the Volunteers to remain free from political control. During the course of the meeting, the question of guns was discussed, but Redmond was highly opposed to any such idea and said to Casement: 'Rifles were the last things to give [the Volunteers].'

Redmond's attitude only spurred Casement and MacNeill on. The following day, a meeting was arranged in the drawing room of Alice Stopford Green, at her house on Grosvenor Road overlooking the Thames. Erskine Childers and Darrell Figgis joined MacNeill, Casement and Stopford Green to discuss the financing and logistics of a gunrunning operation. A moving description was later set down in words by Figgis. His tone pays literary homage to the opening paragraphs of Joseph Conrad's *Heart of Darkness* and the descriptive intonations of *The Riddle of the Sands*, the first spy thriller written by Erskine Childers, who would steer the guns into Howth Harbour, just north of Dublin, a few months later.

> It was a grey afternoon. The windows gave on to the Thames, and against the grey sky the warehouses on the southern bank were, through the gathering mist, lined in an outline of darker grey and black, the tall chimneys uplifted above them. The tide was out, and beside the distant quayside some coal-barges lay tilted on the sleek mud of the

river-bottom, with their sides washed by the silver waters that raced seaward.

Against this picture, looking outward before the window-curtains, stood Roger Casement, a figure of perplexity, and the apparent dejection which he always wore so proudly, as though he had assumed the sorrows of the world. His face was in profile to me, his handsome head and noble outline cut out against the lattice-work of the curtain and the grey sky. His height seemed more than usually commanding, his black hair and beard longer than usual. His left leg was thrown forward, and the boot was torn in a great hole – for he gave his substance away always, and left himself thus in need, he who could so little afford to take these risks with his health. But as I spoke he left his place by the window and came forward towards me, his face alight with battle. "That's talking," he said, throwing his hand on the table between us; and I remember the whimsical thought crossing my mind that language had wandered far from its meaning when one man could say to another that he was talking, when his appreciation and brevity betokened an end to talking.[31]

Piecing together the precise history of the Howth gun-running is not easy as much of the planning was undertaken in secrecy. Stopford Green chaired the committee, oversaw the financing of the operation and contributed a significant sum herself to the overall cost. The generous royalties paid to her over the years by her publisher, Macmillan & Co, for the editions of her late husband's popular *A Short History of the English People* were used to purchase guns. Other subscribers included Mrs Erskine Childers, Lord Ashbourne, George Berkeley and a group of Anglo-Irish landowners from County Limerick, including Mary Spring Rice and the accomplished yachtsman Conor O'Brien. When Casement's plan finally came to fruition towards the end of July, he would be on the other side of the Atlantic drumming up support among the Irish-American community in the United States.

After their plans had been made, Casement left London and returned to Ireland to undertake an intense itinerary of recruitment drives across Ulster with both MacNeill and White. They spoke at Greencastle (23 May); Carrickmore and Sixmilecross (24 May) Omagh (25 May) Derry (26-7 May) Strabane (28 May) Dungannon and Belfast (5 June); Fintona and Dundalk (7 June). 'We preached nationalism versus imperialism yesterday to the hillside men of Tyrone,'[32] Casement scribbled to a comrade.

Negotiations continued between the Irish Parliamentary Party and the leadership of the Irish Volunteers over the summer. In early June, however, control of the Volunteer movement hit a crisis when Redmond declared the need for the governing body to be fully representative and demanded the addition of twenty-five committee representatives allied to the Irish Parliamentary Party. Casement hurried to Dublin to consult with Hobson and MacNeill, and to negotiate with Redmond. His prevailing determination was to avoid a split. At a meeting on 16 June, Casement, Hobson and MacNeill acceded to Redmond's demands. A split was avoided, but at enormous cost. A rift now opened within the IRB ranks between Tom Clarke and Bulmer Hobson. Casement resigned his seat on the committee and was replaced by Clarke. Frustrated by Redmond's stance, Casement wrote to Green:

> The country is being sold – for place & posts & profit – into the hands of the English. I feel it & see it proceeding. These men do not want Irish freedom – they want merely majority rule, i.e. Catholic rule in Ireland – & under it England will more & more strangle Ireland & emasculate the minds of the people.[33]

His letter finished with reference to his immediate intention to spend a few days of undisturbed peace before disappearing. Casement's attentions were now shifting towards America and to his ambitious plan to turn the question of Irish independence into an international issue. He returned to Ulster for a few last days of relative peace amongst family and close friends before, as he hoped, to slip away unnoticed to the US and to build up Irish-American support in preparation for the landing of arms. His last public appearance in

Ireland occurred on 28 June 1914, the same day as the Arch-
duke Ferdinand was assassinated in Sarajevo.

As wire services around the world spread the news of the
assassination in the Balkans, Casement stood on the cairn dedicated to Shane O'Neill above Cushendun and 'harangued
in a cracked voice' to the assembled, including a gathering of
newly recruited Antrim Volunteers. The stone platform from
where he spoke marked the spot where O'Neill had been
slain by the MacDonnells in 1567 as he sought to unite local
power interests against English authority in Ireland. Since
1904, the annual procession and oration from this cairn had
become a centrepiece of the *feis*. Among the speakers who
had stood on the spot before Casement were Eoin MacNeill,
Francis Joseph Bigger and Winston Churchill's first cousin,
Shane Leslie. According to one of the few written accounts
of the occasion, Casement's address dwelt upon O'Neill's life,
his skills as a diplomat, his bravery as a warrior and his deep
desire for peace.

A few days later Casement took the ferry to Glasgow
where he met with other activists and nationalists before
embarking on the SS *Cassandra* bound for Montreal on that
auspicious day in the minds of the American people, the
fourth of July.

Casement's threat to imperial security might be measured
by the intelligence that his actions now generated. From
late 1913 British secret service agencies were keeping a

very close eye on the renegade consul. Throughout 1914 his movements were under close surveillance by the RIC and his frequent public appearances at recruitment rallies were carefully reported. In the nine months to elapse since the founding of the Volunteers, Casement had emerged as one of the main coordinators of the movement, operating at the nerve centre of the Volunteer network. Drawing together disparate nationalist, internationalist and socialist elements in Britain and Ireland, he realised that if Ireland was to break away from the largest empire on earth then it needed maximum support from its allies both at home and abroad. In America, the two main Irish revolutionary organisations, the IRB and Clan na Gael, had to know what was happening on the ground.

When he departed Ireland he had done as much as he could for the time being. The first 100,000 recruits, perhaps as many as 140,000 men and women, had now signed up. He had a trusted structure of leadership, notably MacNeill and Hobson, organising from the top of the command centre. The bridge between advanced nationalists and the Irish Citizen Army had also been built with the co-operation of White, Connolly, Milligan and other socialist republicans. In the next few weeks the last stages of his gunrunning strategy would fall into place. In London, Stopford Green continued to work her influence at the highest level of state power, speaking informally to Liberal Party cabinet members. Even though Redmond's intervention had been disastrous, the show must go on. If arms could be obtained then the power dynamic would change once more.

On a personal level, Casement was finding it increasingly difficult to hold his own life together. The question of his paper trail was of increasing concern. He wrote to Gertrude how his papers 'are scattered all over the "Empire"'.[34] His nomadic existence was proving increasingly difficult to contain. Trunks of papers were held with friends in London, Belfast, Dublin, Antrim and several other haunts where his head had lain over the years. From his complex understanding of the structure and process of history, Casement realised the value of the primary source. He had read and re-read Wolfe Tone's *Diary*, John Mitchel's *Jail Journal*, and other key texts of the Irish republican movement. He knew that every revolutionary leader must be aware of the need to protect his narrative and be vigilant against the determination of the authorities to construct and disseminate an official version of events that sustained their sense of moral order and the rule of law. His account of his investigations in the Congo and the Putumayo had left on the official record the most measured indictment of colonial power relations, but his Irish narrative was not quite so straightforward to manage.

For a decade, Casement had worked tirelessly in the shadows for Irish independence, protected within the cocoon of anonymity and his privileged position as a respected British official. By the summer of 1914, Sir Roger Casement had broken free from that cocoon to emerge as an exotic addition to the Irish Volunteer movement. But this was no sudden coming out, as some would have it. Few could understand the extraordinary levels of energy, personal sacrifice and financial contributions that Casement had channelled towards different national independence initiatives over a sustained period of time. In emerging into the open, Casement knew that the stakes and risks were now far higher.

Chapter Nine

• • • • • •

1914

America

The steamship that conveyed Casement to America was called the *SS Cassandra* – a curiously appropriate name. In Greek mythology, Apollo gave Cassandra the gift of prophecy in an attempt to seduce her. But when his advances were rejected, Apollo placed a curse on her, so that none of her predictions would be believed. She warned the Trojans about the Trojan Horse and later foretold her own demise and descent into madness. In the Greek imagination, Cassandra was a representation of both the tragedy and dilemma of one who is constrained by the conflicting combination of powerful insight and powerlessness. This was the bind in which Casement now found himself. Exposed, as he had been, to the inside knowledge of imperial power, Casement had developed a unique acuity into the secret machinations of transnational relations. Since 1911, he had committed his

thoughts to paper in an effort to try and divert the impending conflict. In Ireland he had worked tirelessly to prevent
the division of the country into two warring factions as he
could clearly foresee the endless spiral of troubles that would
result. When that failed, he set about arming the Irish Volunteers in order to deliver some level of agency to an insurgent
people long denied real power and marooned in a world
spinning towards Armageddon.

In July 1914, he made his departure to the US as discreet
as possible, travelling 'emigrant' class under the name 'R. D.
Casement' and bound for Montreal, rather than New York –
fearful that he would be caught by the 'British spy bureau'.[1]
His intention now was to cultivate support for revolution
within the US. A rough sketch of his journey to the US and
his movements over the forthcoming weeks is included in
the diary he started after arriving in Berlin in early November of 1914. In that document he refers to an earlier diary
he kept during his three months in America, but which he
threw overboard when he left the US in October, fearful that
it would fall into the wrong hands and be used in evidence
against him and his revolutionary co-conspirators. In this
diary, Casement recalls his last glimpse of Ireland, of Mount
Errigal in County Donegal and Tory Island, which he had
visited in the summer of 1912. He then described the large
number of icebergs off Newfoundland as the boat headed
for the St Lawrence Seaway and its final destination of

Montreal. From there he took the train south to New York.

Casement was not a stranger to the US. For several years he had been cultivating clandestine alliances with leaders of the Irish-American diaspora working for independence. In the first days of 1912, on his return to Europe after his second journey to the upper Amazon, he had stopped off in New York on his way to Washington to speak with President William Taft about the Putumayo atrocities. He had used that opportunity to meet with various Irish-Americans sympathetic to the cause, although he kept his movements secret because he was officially on Foreign Office business. At this point he also met with both the legendary Fenian leader John Devoy, editor of the *Gaelic American*, and Joe McGarrity, the chief of Clan na Gael. Michael Keogh, in his memoir of Casement's Irish Brigade, remembered meeting Casement at this time in New York.[2]

Moreover, Casement was in contact with other networks of resistance as he moved into the revolutionary underworld. In July 1911, he had met briefly with the African American intellectual, WEB Du Bois. During their brief conversation at a house in Brixton in London, they found many points of contact and in the months following their meeting, Casement used his power to speak out against the appalling racial prejudice in the US and the outrageous culture of lynching. His Congo investigation had won him sympathy with the Black prophetic tradition in America. Du Bois would later write a moving obituary on Casement.

On arrival by train into Grand Central Station, Casement checked into the Belmont Hotel and within hours of arriving had, according to his diary, met up with a Norwegian comrade, Eivind Adler Christensen. Over the following days the two struck up a friendship and Casement, conscious of his own vulnerability, employed Christensen to work as a minder and personal assistant. Christensen was destined to play a complicated and controversial role in Casement's life over the following months, implicating himself in the clandestine efforts by the British Foreign Office to capture Casement as he passed through Norway on his way to Berlin at the end of October. Casement's decision to trust Christensen ultimately proved to be poor judgment. Whether you believe the two men became lovers depends on the version of events you favour. Even when Christensen's behaviour in the months ahead became erratic, Casement remained loyal, and there is nothing to suggest their relationship was more intimate than friendship. The British intelligence archive, in contrast, provides a narrative attesting to an indiscreet love affair that helps to buttress their attempt to smear Casement in 1916.

The first important matter that Casement had to attend to was to make a convincing case to the Irish revolutionary directorate, explaining Hobson's capitulation to Redmond and his own reasons for resigning from the committee of the

Irish Volunteers. He appeased both Devoy and McGarrity by letting them in on the gunrunning plan. After staying a few nights at a hotel, the Irish American attorney John Quinn invited Casement to stay at his penthouse overlooking Central Park. Quinn is another intriguing figure involved in the Irish Cultural Revival; a regular visitor to Lady Gregory's circle at Coole Park, he is often credited with introducing modern art into America and patronising some of the leading modernist writers of the age, among them the poets WB Yeats, Ezra Pound and Joseph Conrad.

On 24 July, Casement drove with Quinn down to Norfolk, Virginia, to speak in the sweltering heat to a large fund-raising gathering of members of the Ancient Order of Hibernians. His thoughts, however, were focused elsewhere. The gunrunning plans were entering their final stages. The landing of the rifles at Howth was imminent. Casement stayed for the next few days at the house of McGarrity, waiting anxiously for news. He remembered:

> During the period of waiting for Sunday 26 July (the day I had arranged with Hobson and E. Childers that the two yachts should arrive at Howth and the Dublin Volunteers should march out to meet them and get the rifles) I got a letter from Mrs. Green telling me all was well and that "our friends were on the sea." ... That Sunday I spent at McGarrity's in great anxiety and on tenterhooks. It was a very hot day. At 7 p.m. Joe and I walked down the fields in front

of his house until full twilight fell and darkness came. We lay on the grass and talked of Ireland and often, watch in hand, said, "now it is midnight in Dublin now 1 a.m. soon something must come over the cables." About 9 p.m. one of the sub-editors of a Philadelphia paper I need not name rang up Joe over the 'phone and told him a news message had just come in that instant saying that a landing of rifles for the Irish Volunteers had been effected near Dublin that day, that the British troops had been called out to disarm the Volunteers and had fired on them killing several persons and securing the rifles. Joe flew down to the Hibernia Club. Later on a message came from him to his wife to tell me that the guns had not been captured by the troops but retained by the Volunteers.[3]

News of the success of the Howth gunrunning, followed later in the day by the shooting of Irish civilians by British troops on Bachelor's Walk in the centre of Dublin, echoed around the world. As the mastermind of the operation, Casement's credibility soared in the eyes of the Irish-American republican leadership. Plans were now put into motion to maximise the propaganda of the deed. On 2 August, at a demonstration of solidarity for the victims of the Bachelor's Walk shooting, a mock funeral was held in Philadelphia. More than 1,000 men, many of them dressed in the uniform of the Irish Volunteers, assembled at the graveside of the revolutionaries who had died for American Independence in

1777-8. Casement and Devoy followed the column in an open carriage. The photograph of the two men captured an air of confidence mixed with a certain sense of detachment and trepidation. Devoy later revealed how Casement was anxious not to be photographed and was increasingly concerned about having his image circulated in the newspapers.

When Casement stood to speak, his message was one of peace and reconciliation, not war and division: 'I look to the day … when all Irishmen will march under one banner and show the world at length, that Thomas Davis's words have been fulfilled and that Orange and Green have carried the day.'[4] But such a day was still far off. The following afternoon, on 3 August 1914, the British Foreign Secretary, Sir Edward Grey, made his epoch-making speech in the House of Commons announcing that 'the peace of Europe cannot be preserved,' thereby committing Britain to war.

Casement knew Grey well. The two had worked closely together over the Putumayo campaign, but as Casement's frustrations with the direction of the Liberal government had intensified, he singled out Grey as the embodiment of much that was wrong with the politics of the day and, in particular, the conduct of British foreign policy. Casement's career coincided with a huge shift in the political ideology of the Liberal Party. Since the 1880s, when the star of Gladstone and his supporters was in the ascendant and Irish Home Rule was first debated, the Liberal Party had moved towards a position less to do with constitutional devolution and more to do with defence of imperial interests. To Casement's reckoning, the failure to deliver constitutional reform in Ireland had brought about the crisis now facing not just Ireland and Great Britain, but the wider world. Conservative fears about the implications of Home Rule had driven much of the open discussion on foreign policy into a space of secrecy and the controlling interests of a reactionary elite. The deteriorating political situation in Ireland was part of a spectrum of domestic and international reasons as to why Britain committed to war. Casement would never forgive Grey for his speech of 3 August 1914.

Over the next two years, until he was finally hanged on the gibbet in Pentonville, Casement directed an extraordinarily ferocious attack on Grey, perhaps only matched by his assault on one of the intellectual anchormen of Liberal England, the statesman and historian James Bryce. In various essays he argued how an ascendant faction of 'military and naval experts' (referring to Winston Churchill among others) had usurped British foreign policy with hawkish intentions for the Empire. Since the 1890s and the premiership of Lord Salisbury, foreign policy had been removed from democratic parliamentary process and had become the game of a few political and financial insiders. He deemed Grey to be both willing stooge and compliant puppet of this staunchly Unionist and imperialist faction. After a decade of secret treaty making, the world had now stumbled into a crisis that would produce four years of unmitigated slaughter in Europe.

Even if the tone was brusque and accusatory, the argument made by Casement was not unique to him, but reflected the position of a group of informed intellectuals. Within days of the outbreak of war, ED Morel took up the challenge to serve as acting-secretary of the Union of Democratic Control (UDC). This pressure group was established through the co-operation of several prominent politicians including Charles Trevelyan, a Liberal MP (and a direct descendent of his namesake who played such an infamous part in Ireland during the famine) who resigned his seat in the House of Commons in objection to Britain's declaration of war. Other founding members included the future Prime Minister Ramsay MacDonald and Norman Angell, winner of the Nobel Peace Prize in 1933. The UDC would become the first organised body of dissent in the First World War and it campaigned vigorously throughout for a more transparent system of diplomacy. Several of its members were imprisoned for their anti-war beliefs, including the philosopher Bertrand Russell.

Casement had predicted for several years the inevitability of war if Britain continued on its anti-German course, but the hope always remained alive that it could somehow be avoided. In response to the enormous level of betrayal he felt at the outbreak of war, he immediately set about assembling and editing a collection of essays for publication, entitled *The Crime against Europe*, in order to make his views clear as to why he believed the war was unjust and why Irish men and women should not fight.

In 1921 the British government produced an official report entitled *Documents Relative to the Sinn Féin Movement* detailing the collusion between Germany and Ireland during the War of Independence. The report opened by describing the publication of these essays by Casement and the widespread influence they had on their time. In the British official imagination these articles wielded a threatening influence in building up international support for Sinn Féin and contesting the legitimacy of Britain's justification for going to war in defence of small nations. 'Large quantities of the pamphlet were printed in Germany as well as in America. Excerpts were also issued in leaflet form and large numbers were smuggled into Ireland and circulated by Sinn Féin.'[5] Diarmuid Lynch, a member of the pre-1916 Supreme Council of the IRB, related how, in September 1915, he picked up hundreds of copies from the print room of the *Enniscorthy Echo* in potato sacks and distributed them around the country in envelopes advertising seed catalogues.[6] This prominent reference to *The Crime against Europe* would indicate that Casement's views on world affairs held great sway in Ireland, Germany and the US and these essays became a key component in the battle for hearts and minds.

Between 1914 and 1916, the essays were published in a number of different editions in both the US and Germany. Individual chapters appeared in editions of *Saoirse*, the *Irish Review* and the *Gaelic American*. The initial collection was gathered under the title *Ireland, Germany and the Freedom of the Seas: A possible outcome of the war of 1914*. A second edition appeared as *The Crime against Ireland and How the war may right it* (1914). After that, various editions were available under the main title *The Crime against Europe*. In 1915 the essays were translated and distributed widely in Germany along with other essays published in Berlin's leading English-language newspaper, *The Continental Times*.

In these essays Casement came close to communicating the logic of his evolution from faithful servant of the British Empire into its sworn enemy. It was a trajectory he believed all Irishmen and women should take. During his trial he hoped the essays would one day speak for themselves and contribute towards his ultimate vindication and a more measured understanding of his 'treason'. In one of his final letters (only released on 21 December 2012) he asked Gertrude Bannister if the essays, along with his other political writings, could be collected and published, claiming in a somewhat self-important comment that *The Crime against Europe* 'was the foundation and inspiration of the Rising.'[7] An indication of the confusion that has surrounded Casement's place in Irish history might be appreciated by the failure to as yet properly respect the dead patriot's wishes. Although small reprints of *The Crime against Europe* appeared in 1958, and more recently through the efforts of a Belfast imprint, Athol Books, in 2003, Casement's political writings are waiting to be properly collected, edited and included into the intellectual history of the First World War.

A century on, and lost in the crush of an immense body of historiography on the causes of the 1914-18 war, his essays endure as a perceptive critique of the political crisis of the age by a knowledgeable and informed opponent of imperial systems. Casement's pro-German sentiment and his support for German culture and intellect, however, became unpopular as the war progressed and subsequently lost all their appeal in the light of later Nazi war crimes. While they can in places appear overly partisan toward Germany, it should be remembered that when most of these comments were written, many countries were still undecided as to who to support in the war, America included. On another level, the essays reveal dimensions of the workings of imperial power that were immensely threatening to British security. With his astringent attacks on secret diplomacy, the immorality of the arms race and the armaments industry, and his intentions to expose the undeclared causes of the war, Casement could be viewed as a whistleblower as much as a revolutionary.

If there is an overarching theme to the essays, it is that

Ireland must liberate itself from English rule as a first step to dismantling the British Empire and hastening the unavoidable reconfiguration of power in Europe caused by the emergence of a united Germany. The articles were written with an international audience in mind. Their principal purpose was to rethink and recalibrate Ireland's relationship with the British Empire and explain how Irish independence could be used to improve international relations. 'The Irish question was in truth a European question,' he stated on several occasions.

The essays ranged widely between historic, economic, political, legal and military determinants to argue that from Tudor times Ireland held the key to imperial strategy. 'The British Empire is founded not upon the British bible or the British dreadnought but upon Ireland.'[8] For centuries Irishmen had supplied the manpower to enable expansion: 'Ireland is the English peon, the great peon of the British Empire', and had 'given cheap labour to England ... built up her great industries, manned her shipping, dug her mines, and built her ports and railways.' The maintenance of that relationship was vital to the security and continuance of the Empire.

While Britain had understood the integral importance of Ireland to its own safety and control of the Atlantic, Europe, in contrast, had missed this geo-strategic importance. Philip II of Spain, Louis XIV and Napoleon had all failed to militarily defeat England because they underestimated Ireland's significance. According to Casement, restoring an independent Ireland to her rightful place within European power relations would stabilise international relations in Europe and allow Ireland to play a valid role in world affairs, based upon compassion for and empathy with the marginalised. The withdrawal of Ireland from English control would be 'a very necessary step in international welfare and one very needful to the progress of German and European expansion.'[9]

These positive aspirations for a reconfiguration of power relations between Ireland and Britain required him to take an aggressive stance towards the British Empire – 'nations are born, empires rise from hell,' he confided in a letter to Gertrude Bannister. Tropical imagery was invoked in order to illustrate the ruthless, suffocating relationship between the two islands. He compared the British Empire to the 'Sipo Matador' (or murdering creeper of the Amazon rainforest) that fastened onto the limbs of other trees and grew 'great from a sap not its own.'[10] He likened the indomitable power of Irish resistance to the *Diodon*, a small fish occasionally swallowed whole by a shark. Once inside the belly, the *Diodon* gradually gnawed through the flesh of the stomach, eventually eating its way out of the body and killing the shark in the process. This, he felt, perfectly illustrated Ireland's contest with the Empire. Within his writings, jingoism was unmasked along with the vast strategy of deceit required to keep the 'great illusion'[11] of Empire afloat and to maintain 'a supreme and absolute England to which Ireland, India and Scotland are subject'.[12]

In his predictions about the future of international relations and world power, Casement feared the reconfiguration of the Empire through a strengthening of the Anglo-American alliance, a concern that he discussed with the former US President, Theodore Roosevelt, in a private audience on 4 August 1914, the day of Britain's open declaration of war. 'You will become imperialists & join her in the plunder of the earth,' he warned the president, adding that only a German victory could deliver a true balance of power in Europe.'[13] 'Were the "Anglo-Saxon Alliance" between Britain and the US ever consummated it would be the biggest crime in history'.[14]

Another dimension of these essays was what they revealed about the origins of the conflict between Britain and Germany. For well over a decade, Britain had fought a covert war against German economic expansion. Casement was alerted to this during his time as a consul, and his reports detail the shift. Britain, he argued, was not prepared to tolerate German economic development if it in any way threatened Britain's dominance of the seaways and her advantageous hold on global trade. European diplomacy had been deliberately directed towards protecting British trading interests and in isolating Germany. He was particularly critical of the *Entente*

Cordiale and the Triple Entente whereby German militarism was challenged by, as he saw it, an unnatural alliance between Britain, France and Russia. Britain used this alliance to start the war and France, he predicted, would be the real victim of the conflict. Britain required a disunited Europe for its continued existence as master of the seas, upon which its trading advantage rested. It would do everything in its power to avoid losing that advantage.

While objecting to the war on a number of levels, Casement realised that the conflict presented an opportunity for Ireland to strike for freedom and to end centuries of oppressive interference. Simultaneously, if Britain was defeated, the war could bring about an end to the Empire or, at least, a reconstitution of colonial relations into a commonwealth of nations. But he realised that the human cost would be immense.

As he prepared these essays for publication, he embarked on an extraordinary fund-raising tour, visiting Baltimore (6 August) and Buffalo (9 August) to build up the profile of the Irish Volunteers among the extensive networks of Irish-Americans. He believed it was also critical to start building bridges between Ireland and Germany, for the key to Irish sovereign independence was one that Germany must now be persuaded to uphold.

In the aftermath of the Bachelor's Walk incident, Casement contacted senior officials at the German Embassy, including the military attaché Franz von Papen, a future German Chancellor, and the propagandist Georg von Skal. Von Papen informed the German Foreign Office that Roger Casement, 'the leader of all Irish associations in America', had contacted him. Within three weeks of the outbreak of the war Casement had drafted a substantial memorandum *How Ireland might help Germany and how Germany might help Ireland*.[15] In this he set down a series of proposals concerning the procurement of more arms and the preparation of German officers for a military invasion. Other objectives included the formation of an Irish brigade from among captured POWs and the publication of a statement articulating Germany's positive intentions towards Ireland. Casement also drafted a letter to Kaiser Wilhelm II expressing support and respect for Germany, while emphasising the importance of Ireland to the ultimate freedom of the seas.

Conveying his views through diplomatic channels to Berlin was relatively easy, as British Naval Intelligence had not yet started intercepting these communiqués, but transmitting his message to the people of Ireland was much harder. One of the few available spaces for expressing his views was in the letters page of Irish newspapers. On 17 September he wrote to the *Irish Independent* saying that Irishmen should not fight the war, as their responsibility lay with Ireland, and that the Irish had no quarrel with the German people. 'If Irish blood is to be "the seal that will bring all Ireland together in one nation and in liberties equal and common to all", then let that blood be shed in Ireland, where alone it can be right-eously shed to secure those liberties … If this be a war for the "small nationalities", as its planners term it, then let it begin, with one small nationality, at home.'

The following day, Home Rule was finally placed on the statute books on the condition that it would not be granted until the war was over. On 19 September, Redmond made his Woodenbridge speech committing Ireland to the impe-rial battlefield 'wherever the firing line extends'. Casement wrote to John Quinn: 'I am so distressed at Redmond's treachery, and the deplorable state of things in Ireland … that I am raging, like a caged animal at the impotence enforced upon me here.'[16] Redmond's pledge certainly represented an extraordinary about-turn in the thinking of the Irish Party at Westminster. Home Rule debates back in the 1880s had been closely connected to the interrogation of imperial affairs, and the empathy felt by Irish nationalists for other nationalist and anti-imperial causes. And yet now the Irish Party was prepared to bargain the loyalty of the people of Ireland in defence of an Empire that was the instrument of its own subjugation.

Redmond's speech effectively broke the Volunteer move-ment. The majority remained with Redmond and became the National Volunteers. A much smaller core, the Irish Vol-unteers founded by Casement, Hobson, MacNeill, Pearse and others, broke away and would form the nucleus of the 1916 rebels.

Casement's letter in the *Irish Independent* on 5 October 1914 argued for Irish neutrality and for Irish sympathies to reside with Germany, not Britain: 'Let Irishmen and boys stay in Ireland. Their duty is clear – before God and before man. We, as a people, have no quarrel with the German people. Germany has never wronged Ireland, and we owe her more than one debt of gratitude.' But his argument now found little official support. A leader in the same edition of the newspaper expressed both surprise and sorrow that Casement no longer cared for the Empire 'in a struggle for justice and righteousness.'

Casement's negotiations with the German embassy continued. On 10 October another meeting was held and the decision taken formally that Casement would travel to Berlin to try and implement some of the proposals he had previously discussed with the embassy officials. In the aftermath, Johann Heinrich von Bernstorff wrote a letter of introduction for Casement to present to the Imperial Chancellor, Theobald von Bethmann Hollweg. In a letter written to his friend Dick Morten hours before his departure, Casement scribbled:

> The war has upset and changed everything – including my heart. It is a crime. Grey and Asquith are *greatly* to blame. England could have prevented this war altogether had she

wanted to – but she wanted to get Germany down and could not resist the chance that came – as the direct result of her own planning and contriving with France and Russia … It is a monstrous crime and calamity and will ruin half the world.[17]

Casement and Christensen left New York on board the *Oskar II* on 17 October. Casement travelled under the false name JE Landy, a cover arranged for him by another senior Irish-American supporter, Judge Daniel Cohalan, a close ally of Devoy. He tried to disguise himself by shaving his beard and lightening his complexion with buttermilk. Before leaving, the Irish-American leadership gave him $2,500 (£500) in American gold. He entrusted the money and all his papers to Christensen just in case his identity was discovered before leaving. Every precaution had to be taken. He wrote to Alice Stopford Green how he 'was spied upon on all sides wherever he went.'

On 24 October, as the ship was passing near to the Faroe Islands, a British battleship, *Hibernia*, ordered the *Oskar II* to steer a course to Stornaway on the island of Lewes, so the passengers and cargo could be inspected. One of the passengers, the Austro-Hungarian ambassador, protested and six members of the crew were taken on shore because they were German. 'Mr Landy' kept a low profile and, to his relief, his identity was unchallenged. After a hold-up of two days the ship was allowed to continue to Christiania in Norway, where it arrived late at night on 28 October. But the British secret services had by then figured out that Mr Landy was their renegade official. From the moment he arrived into the Norwegian capital he was conscious of being followed 'by the usual type of British spy'.

Chapter Ten

• • • • • •

October 1914–April 1916

Imperial Germany

ritish intelligence activated plans to have Casement reined in when he arrived in Christiania (Oslo). During the two day stopover, as he waited for entry papers to Germany, officials at the British Legation opened a line of direct communication with Christensen and unlocked yet another conspiratorial dimension. Once again the official narrative describing the events during these days (held in the British secret service archive) is seriously at odds with Casement's, as is evident from the trail of references in his diary, correspondence and journalism.

The Christiania incident, or Findlay affair, would become the major point of confrontation between Casement and the Foreign Office. Casement wrote about the matter obsessively and used it as a way of exposing in public the nefarious activities of his former employers. As the plot developed over the coming months, Casement faked both letters and entries in his diary in a purposeful strategy to misinform and deceive his past colleagues.

What the historian has to grapple with at this juncture is two incompatible versions of the same story. In many ways this bifurcation in the narrative mirrors the confusion created later on by the presence of the Black Diaries. According to the version in official British records, Christensen, on his own initiative, went to the British Legation in Christiania and told an official that he had information on a well-known 'Englishman'. The following day he returned to continue the conversation, this time with the British ambassador, Mansfeldt de Cardonnel Findlay. He then revealed further information about Casement and his work.

According to the official version, Christensen confessed that he was having 'unnatural relations' with Casement.[1] To supplement this sudden admission, there is a series of sworn statements by various Norwegian witnesses attesting to the openly sexual nature of Casement's relationship with Christensen.[2] This narrative maintains that on three occasions in his two-day stopover, Casement was caught *en flagrante* by members of the hotel staff. All these affidavits are dated July 1916 and were collected by Basil Thomson, the head of the British Special Branch, but they were not released into the public domain until the 1990s. The idea, for instance, that Casement would have left the door of his hotel room open for a bell-boy to barge in and discover the two men in bed together shifts the story from the absurd to the ridiculous. This narrative of Casement's indiscretion, according to the secret services, is harder to sustain when it is considered that Casement was also under close surveillance from Germany and there is not an iota of evidence from that quarter to support the official British intelligence account.

Casement's version of events seems more probable, given the security threat he now posed. According to his explanation, Christensen was approached by a stranger in the lobby of the hotel and taken to the British Legation, where he was questioned about his activities and his relationship with the renegade Irishman. On returning to the hotel, he told Casement what had happened and the two then hatched a plan to deceive the officials. Christensen returned to the Legation the following day and, during the course of his conversation with Findlay, Christensen was told that if he 'knocked Casement on the head' he would be well rewarded. In Casement's mind this amounted to an assassination plot.

Over the next months, Casement entered into a high stakes conspiracy against the British Foreign Office and its associated agencies. He would send Christensen back to Norway, continuing the surreptitious negotiations with Findlay to deceive the embassy officials. Eventually, Christensen managed to convince Findlay of his good faith, and on the authority of the British Foreign Secretary, Sir Edward Grey, a promissory note was drawn up offering Christensen £5,000 in gold for supplying information leading to Casement's capture. Over the next eighteen months, this promissory note, written on headed British Legation notepaper, provided the hard evidence of the conspiracy. Casement had it copied and reproduced repeatedly as he broadcast the details of the plot in an effort to discredit his former employer.

Though the story reflects badly on both sides, whom do we believe? Several aspects of the official version of events do not add up. Firstly, there is no corroborating evidence in the German archive supporting Casement's sexual relationship with Christensen. The sense from the British archive is that Casement was living more or less an open relationship with Christensen, but was he really risking everything for the forbidden love of this Norwegian comrade? Secondly, if the homophobic German authorities had had the slightest indication of any such impropriety they would have dropped Casement's cause without hesitation. Even before Casement arrived into Berlin he was under intense surveillance by the German authorities as well as from the British side. Richard Meyer, the assessor who would work with Casement throughout his stay in Germany, linked up with Casement and Christensen in Christiania and helped both men across the border. In all the time Casement and Christensen were together in Germany, there is no evidence corroborating the narrative in the British intelligence files.

In 1915, Casement felt so strongly about his mistreatment that he attempted to take the matter to the Norwegian courts but, unsurprisingly, both the British and Norwegian governments declined to cooperate. The clash of these contradictory versions throws up awkward questions. Is the narrative contained within British official sources a creative invention intended to counter the accusations levelled by Casement against the government-sanctioned conspiracy? Is the body of evidence produced by Basil Thomson's Special Branch part of a targeted campaign of defamation, requiring the deliberate concoction of evidence to vilify Casement's character? Although the material was not used during Casement's lifetime, it came into circulation in the 1950s as the campaign to subvert Casement's historical reputation entered a more aggressive phase. This practice of circulating compromising sexual material in order to discredit an adversary remains a standard way by which intelligence agencies control and subvert rebellious agents and enemies of the state. The tactic is generally associated with the communist Stasi and KGB, but such strategies are also part of the modus operandi of Western intelligence agencies then and now. A recent history of MI5 revealed how in advance of the US entering the First World War, a photograph of German ambassador Count von Bernstorff, with his arms around two women in bathing suits, was circulated by a British agent in New York in order to ridicule the German ambassador.[3]

In 1915, after Christensen had returned on a mission to

America, he decided to exploit his collaboration by trying to extort money from John Devoy for the maintenance of his wife and child. The fact that Casement trusted Christensen was a serious misjudgement, as was his decision to enter into such a dangerous and self-destructive game with the Foreign Office. It would appear that Christensen was untrustworthy, unscrupulous and ultimately harboured no enduring loyalty to Casement's cause, but was motivated principally by money. When Casement met up with Christensen on arriving in New York in July 1914, he needed a minder and personal assistant to help him with his increasingly dangerous activities; his mistake was taking Christensen into his confidence and involving him in a vortex of conspiracies.

What further complicates this conspiracy is Findlay's own history, and his involvement in an atrocity against a community of Egyptians, in a celebrated case known as the Dinshawai incident. In June 1906, a group of British soldiers needlessly provoked local hostility when shooting pigeons near the village of Dinshawai in the Nile Delta. Local opposition to the soldiers' presence led to shots being fired. Four locals were wounded by gunfire, and in the ensuing skirmish some of the British soldiers were harshly clubbed and received broken bones. In retaliation, and on the authorisation of Findlay, fifty-two villagers were rounded up, and following a brief sitting of a kangaroo court, four men were sentenced to be hanged, nine to imprisonment and five to public flogging. The punishments were seized upon by critics of empire as an act of ruthless imperial oppression and significantly diminished the legitimacy of British authority in Egypt. George Bernard Shaw referred to the episode in his preface to *John Bull's Other Island* as a reason why the British Empire could no longer be tolerated. Although Findlay was reprimanded for his heavy-handed actions, it was Lord Cromer, the legendary Pro-Consul in Egypt, who had presided over Egypt since the British occupation in 1883, whose reputation suffered the most. Cromer, it should be added, was a prominent supporter of Casement; his name and authority had endorsed the 1904 Congo report and had backed the work of the Congo Reform Association. In the many accounts of the Findlay affair circulated by Casement over the next twelve months, he made various references to Findlay's involvement in the Dinshawai affair as a way of entangling the story into his wider campaign against the British Empire.

The Findlay Affair has become and will doubtless remain an unpleasant dimension in the Casement story and reflects badly on all parties. It propels history into a dimension of conspiracy where facts mutate and historical 'truths' are impossible to determine. Some of the official documentation to do with the case is contained in a file titled 'Irish Conspiracy' that readers to the National Archives (UK) are still required to consult in a designated secure reading room, where unusually sensitive material must be viewed.[4]

On 1 November, Casement arrived into Berlin and was given yet another new identity, Mr Hammond, by the German Foreign Office. The journey had been extremely arduous, but the outcome successful. Back in 1884, Berlin had been the city chosen by Chancellor Bismarck to convene European and US diplomats to discuss the future of sub-Saharan Africa. That same year, Casement found himself on a boat destined for the Congo to take up a position in King Leopold's colonial administration. Now, almost thirty years on, he found himself in Berlin as the chosen emissary of the Irish independence movement.

Despite the casualties returning from both the Eastern and Western Fronts, morale remained generally high in the German capital. By the late autumn of 1914, the Schlieffen Plan, which had intended to deliver the defeat of France within forty days, had failed, but Belgium was vanquished and occupied. Celebration of the victory of the German army against the Russians at the Battle of Tannenberg on their Eastern Front had kept confidence high. However, the conflict had now entered into a stalemate and trench warfare locked all sides into a long war of attrition. Casement quickly linked up with his network of German friends, arranging meetings and familiarising himself with the city.

General narratives of the First World War tend to overlook how Ireland's relationship with Germany on the eve of war was quite different from the deepening antagonism felt in

England towards its Saxon cousins. Casement made frequent reference to this in his public statements. Over the previous decade a vibrant, cultural bridge had been built by a group of like-minded European scholars working in the field of Celtic philology and the study of Old Irish. The most eminent of these was Kuno Meyer, a close friend of Stopford Green, MacNeill and Casement. In the early twentieth century, Meyer founded the School of Irish Learning in Dublin with the stated intention of bringing about 'a second golden age of Irish learning.' The vehicle for this aspiration was the academic journal *Ériu*, which published the work of leading Irish language scholars, including Eoin MacNeill; the future director of the National Library of Ireland, RI Best; and the Norwegian linguist, Carl Marstrander. In 1911, Meyer returned to Berlin to take up the Chair of Celtic Philology at the Friedrich Wilhelm University in Berlin. Meyer's brother, Eduard was also a Professor of History at Berlin University, and through his influence other senior German academics interested themselves with the Irish question. The most notable of these was Theodor Schiemann, a close friend of Kaiser Wilhelm II, who would translate some of Casement's writings from *The Crime against Europe*. Another was the medieval historian, Dietrich Schäfer.

Over many years Casement had built up a network of German friends. While serving in Portuguese East Africa, he had formed a lasting friendship with Gebhard Blücher, the great-great grandson of Marshal Blücher, the saviour of the Duke of Wellington at the Battle of Waterloo. During Casement's eighteen months in Germany, Blücher became a steadfast supporter of his propaganda offensive against the British Foreign Office, offering advice and contacts whenever needed. Other friends included Ferdinand and Adelheid Nordenflycht, part of the German diplomatic mission in Brazil.

Casement also linked up with a community of Germans and expatriates sympathetic to the cause of Irish independence. Among them was the US consul in Munich, Thomas St John Gaffney; the philosopher and sociologist, George Chatterton-Hill, now editor of *The Continental Times*; and the adventurer, Edwin Emerson, a graduate of Harvard University who had served as a personal clerk to Theodore Roosevelt during the Spanish-American War. For the first months Casement based himself in Berlin and lived in a series of simple hotel rooms in the centre of the city. But as his initial enthusiasm for the German war effort waned, he grew tired of the oppressive presence of Prussian militarism and, in the summer of 1915, relocated to Bavaria.

Though he spoke no German, Casement had developed quite a deep knowledge of the country and the culture. In May 1912, he had toured through Germany with his friend, Richard Morten, in a motor car. Their route took them to Strasbourg, Lake Constance, Nuremberg, Coblenz, Rottenburg, Wiesbaden, Heidelberg and Frankfurt. Through a combination of established contacts and with his letters of introduction from von Bernstorff, Casement gained rapid and privileged access to both the Prussian Court and the German Foreign Office. Within days of his arrival he met the Undersecretary of State for Foreign Affairs, Arthur Zimmermann, and the head of the English section at the German Foreign Office, Count Georg von Wedel, who would remain his most trusted government ally over the next eighteen months. From the outset, the main subject of discussion with all senior officials concerned the formation of an Irish Brigade. The negotiations were complicated as the idea needed to be accepted by a number of different arms of the German military command.

On 16 November, Casement received orders to leave immediately for the headquarters of the German General Staff at Charleville-Meziérès, just inside the French border with Belgium, where he was to meet with senior German officers to discuss his plans for the brigade.[5] The next day he travelled on the overnight train to Cologne where a German staff car met him. He was then driven the 270 kilometres through the wintery frozen hillsides of the Eifel region of Westfalia and northern Luxembourg to his destination. On arriving at Charleville, he met with two senior officials: a high-ranking diplomat, Kurt von Lersner, whom he had met in New York in the autumn, and the Director of the Political Department of the German Foreign Office, Wilhelm von

Stumm. In a brief conversation he convinced them both of the sincerity of his mission.

On the return to Cologne, the car followed the course of the river Meuse and drove Casement through much of the terrain ravaged by the advance of the German army into France a few months earlier. Casement was able to judge for himself the level of damage, the morale of the people living under German occupation, and to discern the extent of German atrocities. Since the outbreak of hostilities, British propaganda had been making disturbing claims about the extent of German brutality and the mistreatment of the civilian population in Belgium. Allegations of atrocities were deployed to swing world opinion against Germany, and the argument over the level of German brutality in Belgium in 1914 persists as one of the essential controversies of the First World War. Casement wrote about the issue at some length and, as the official who had investigated more atrocities at first hand than any man alive, he was in an informed position to assess the situation and knew how atrocity claims could be cynically deployed for propaganda requirements. As he stood before a wall in Namur, site of a notorious atrocity perpetrated by German soldiers against Belgian civilians, he reflected:

> Sometimes, I must confess, when the present 'agony of Belgium' confronts me – and it cannot well be minimised it is in truth a national agony – I feel that there may be in this awful lesson to the Belgian people a repayment. All that

they now suffer and far more, they, or their king, his government and his officers wreaked on the well nigh defenceless people of the Congo basin.

In assessing the German army's treatment of Belgium,
Casement was questioning whether, during the autumn
of 1914, Britain's justification for going to war in the first
place was viable. Was gallant little Belgium really so gallant
if its colonial record in the Congo was taken into account?
Had prolonged mistreatment of the people of central Africa
brought on this national agony?

On Casement's return to Berlin, German newspapers officially announced the appearance of Sir Roger Casement in
Germany. The story was picked up by news services around
the world. To mark his arrival, a Declaration of Goodwill,
drafted by Casement, was simultaneously circulated to the
press. The document underlined Germany's peaceful intentions towards the Irish people: 'The Imperial Government
formally declares that it entertains no hostile designs against
the Irish people, their institutions, their lands or their country.'[6] Besides reinforcing German-Irish amity, another intention of this declaration was to defy the propaganda now circulating through British agencies in Ireland, which suggested
that German plans for Ireland were no different to their 'rape'
of Belgium. After this significant achievement, Casement's
energies now focused on the formation of an Irish Brigade.

There is a long history of Irish soldiers prepared to take

up arms against British power, both at home and abroad. An Irish brigade raised in France had battled through much of the eighteenth century, most notably in the war of the Austrian Succession (1740-48). During the Second Boer War, Arthur Lynch and John McBride established an Irish brigade to fight against the British. What was different about Casement's brigade was that while previous Irish brigades had fought on behalf of France, Spain, Austria or the Boers, Casement was adamant that his would fight exclusively for Ireland, or in the wider conflict to bring down British rule in the Middle East.

Plans to set up the Irish Brigade had been discussed at length and approved by Devoy, McGarrity and Judge Cohalan while Casement was in America. However, despite strenuous efforts over the forthcoming months to make the scheme work, it proved a spectacular failure. In early negotiations with the German Foreign Office and German General Staff, ambitious forecasts were made of several hundred men enlisting, but recruits never rose above fifty-five, too few to make the force viable at any stage. Part of the problem was that responsibility for the organisation of the Irish Brigade was shared between different sections of the German military complex, and conflicts soon erupted. The German spymaster, Rudolf Nadolny (director of the military secret service, Abteilung IIIb), developed a particular aversion to Casement and a climate of distrust grew between the two.

From the outset there were considerable logistical difficulties in segregating potential recruits from those soldiers who were steadfastly hostile to the scheme. Beyond merely determining who was Irish and Catholic, it was necessary to work out who might be sympathetic to such a venture. By early December, a process of separation had started. A prison camp at Limburg in the Lahn valley, north of Frankfurt and east of Coblenz, was designated for the project. But it was a day's train journey from Berlin, which only added to the logistical problems.

Most prisoners at this early stage of the war were from the ranks of the regular army's Irish regiments: the Irish Guards, Munster Fusiliers, the Connaught Rangers, Royal Irish Rifles, Royal Dublin Fusiliers and Royal Iniskilling Fusiliers. What would be their motivation for throwing in their lot with Casement? Casement's own political views were largely lost on soldiers whose main reason for joining the British army in the first place was principally financial and often to escape a life of poverty. His plan to reconfigure Ireland's place within the balance of power in Europe, combined with his anti-imperial views, were as likely to offend as they were to impress. Soldiers can often be oblivious to the real political circumstances of the wars in which they fight – theirs not to reason why, theirs but to do and die. Casement felt that the anti-German views of the English press had so infected their views that no amount of persuasion would work.

Casement first entered Limburg camp on 4 December, where he spoke to around twenty non-commissioned officers. He returned on various occasions over the forthcoming weeks. Copies of the *Gaelic American* and the anti-British broadsheet, *The Continental Times*, were left for the prisoners to read at their leisure. But the uptake was very slow. Few men displayed much sympathy for the Irish struggle and no one supported Germany. 'We may hate England, but that doesn't make us love Germany,' was a prevailing attitude among the men. In a note sent by some NCOs to the camp commandant, the message was unequivocal: 'in addition to being Irish Catholics we have the honour of being British soldiers'.

Casement persisted despite indications from very early on that this would prove a hopeless and humiliating task. He recognised that it was important for the spiritual needs of the prisoners to be attended to and three priests were engaged: Father John Crotty, a Dominican, Father John Nicolson from Philadelphia, and Father Canice O'Gorman, sent via Clan na Gael. The priests played a role in administering to the men and keeping Casement discreetly supplied with information.

Over Christmas week of 1914, Casement drew up an agreement setting out the terms of engagement for the Irish Brigade. After several days of quite strenuous negotiation, the Undersecretary of State, Arthur Zimmermann, signed the document. Although it was never formally authorised by the IRB, Casement would claim the 'Treaty,' as he called it, was a moment of great historic significance in advancing Irish sovereignty at a diplomatic level in Europe. In signing this document the German government was officially committed to securing Irish national independence, based upon its recognition of the Irish Brigade's objectives. The first two of the ten articles read:

> Article 1: With a view to securing the national freedom of Ireland, with the moral and material assistance of the Imperial German Government, an Irish Brigade shall be formed from among the Irish soldiers, or other natives of Ireland, now prisoners of war in Germany.
>
> Article 2: The object of the Irish Brigade shall be to fight solely in the cause of Ireland, and under no circumstances shall it be employed or directed to any German end.

But even with the German government's imprimatur, the recruiting drive did not improve. Privileges offered to the Irish prisoners prepared to join the brigade were open to abuse; some prisoners expressed interest for no better reason than to improve their prison conditions. Efforts by three recruiting sergeants to build capacity were unsuccessful. On various occasions Casement addressed large groups of prisoners when an individual approach might have proved more effective. Momentum was rapidly diminishing. On 5 January, Casement received a hostile reception when he addressed a group of men, although the claims made at his trial that he was physically assaulted proved to be invention. Another problem was the ineptitude of the German military representatives selected to look after the prisoners, who often had limited knowledge of the men.

By April 1915, the senior German officers were losing patience with the scheme. Nadolny, in particular, believed the renegade Irishman could be a double agent and he wished to divest his responsibilities to the brigade altogether. The arrival of Joseph Mary Plunkett, on a mission from the IRB in May, gave a brief boost to the initiative and Casement delivered a moving address on 15 May to the soldiers in Limburg, setting out the objectives of the war for Irish freedom. In June, fifty-five recruits were transferred to another camp at Zossen, south of Berlin, where they were supposed to receive supervised training in machine-gun practice. In October, Robert Monteith, a highly capable organiser with good military experience from his time in the British army, arrived to take over the training. He quickly built up an *esprit de corps* in the men by encouraging sports, drilling and marching.

The failure, however, to make the Irish Brigade into an able fighting unit would be assiduously used against Casement during his trial and for many years afterwards. Several of his closest friends felt this to be a step too far. The critic Pauric Colum could see his declaration of sympathy for Germany as wise and patriotic, but felt that his determination to form an Irish Brigade was useless and unworthy. For many, the

First World War was a conflict that demanded unconditional loyalty. Casement upset deeply-held notions of patriotism. His own turn against the British Empire and his determination to separate the cause of Irish freedom from British war aims unnerved the politics of national allegiance. For this, his role in the First World War remains hard to include because it intrudes upon those dominant myths of loyalty, sacrifice and valour that helped to justify the slaughter and are annually rehearsed in Remembrance Sunday commemorations.

Casement was only too aware of the implications of his actions. The diary he maintained for his first four months in Germany made regular reference to his treason, but his confessional comments, by early 1915, had started to unsettle even him as his own confidence in his venture started to lapse. In a letter to the Countess Blücher he wrote:

> You know the charm of a diary is its simplicity. Its reality and the sense of daily life it conveys to the reader depends not on style, but on truth and sincerity. It should tell of things ... I kept one for the first three months or so of my stay in this country, & then I gave it up because I became too personal! I found myself writing things best left unwritten – even unthought.[7]

But his fury at the British government still found an outlet. On 1 February Casement addressed a long letter to Sir Edward Grey and divested himself of all his honours and his state pension while defending the logic of his actions: 'To save Ireland from some of the calamities of war was worth the loss to myself of pension and honors and was even worth the commission of an act of technical "treason".' He argued that his own treason was lesser to the treachery of Grey, Asquith and the British ruling elite, whose decision to commit Britain to war and unleash carnage upon the people was a far worse crime.

From the spring of 1915 onwards, as his interest in the Irish Brigade diminished, Casement spent longer periods of time in Bavaria, at a small resort town named Riderau on the banks of Lake Ammersee, north of Munich. Here he was able to reconnect in peaceful surroundings with his daily routine of writing and walking. A memoir, *Casement in Deutschland*, published the year after his execution, described the deep and lasting impression Casement left locally. The author, Dr Franz Rothenfelder, referred to Casement in almost reverential terms and described his walks to the Benedictine Abbey at Andechs and the extraordinary effect his acts of kindness and generosity had on local people.

Faced by the failure of the Irish Brigade, Casement now channeled his energies into the propaganda war. Every biography on Casement to date has chosen to either entirely ignore or make the most hesitant reference to Casement's propaganda writings of 1915. Compared to his essays in *The Crime against Europe* they are far more revealing and seditious. A century on, they still make disturbing reading in their candid commentary of the war on truth and how the hidden hand of British intelligence manufactured global hatred against Germany. The articles speak frankly of a culture of deception, lying and skullduggery underpinning British war policy. When reading these essays, it is necessary to factor in Casement's own political grievances and place them in the environment of deep animosity that is inevitably conjured by war. Nevertheless, in the light of what we now know about the sophisticated methods of disinformation which governments deploy to deceive their own people and to justify atrocities during the time of war, much of what Casement says is plausible. Revelation of secrecy had been a continuous theme of his life and was bound to his belief that secrets were anti-democratic, anti-republican and anti-social.

The National Library of Ireland holds what is perhaps the most critical and overlooked file in helping to unlock the mystery over Roger Casement's complicated place in British history. It is a folder of manuscript writings containing a series of pseudonymous letters, drafted essays and satirical fables by Casement.[8] Many of these were published pseudonymously or anonymously in *The Continental Times*, an English-language newspaper published out of Berlin three times a week and distributed within Germany and central Europe. Unfortunately, a complete set of *The Continental Times* has not apparently survived, but some writing was eventually published elsewhere. Casement used a series of different pseudonyms, including 'Will E Wagtail', 'By One Who Knows', 'An American Scholar', 'Henry Bower', and 'Diplomaticus'. Doubtless there were other names.

The most controversial accusations are made in four long letters signed 'John Quincy Emerson LLD, an American citizen'. They deal loosely with some of the aspects of the Findlay affair, but also weave into this account other serious issues of the clandestine operations of the British secret state as well as the corruption of the mainstream press, or 'reptile press' as Casement called it, and the 'hired pens' and embedded journalists of Fleet Street. Ireland, in particular, had been carefully controlled by a policy of strict news censorship. Reuters was named as one particularly untrustworthy source.

Beyond the scathing comments about the British press, these letters also accused the more secretive agencies of the British Foreign Office of engaging in plots and intrigues. His brandishing of Findlay's promissory note was one example of which he had both direct knowledge and hard evidence. He made further allegations against another British ambassador in Bulgaria, Henry Bax Ironside, claiming that he plotted against the life of King Ferdinand of Bulgaria. Another claim, and not unreasonable when considered in the light of what is known and officially admitted to today about secret services operations during war, was the charge that the espionage system had infiltrated post, telegram and telephone services as well as railways and hotels. The intelligence gathered from intercepted signals (SIGINT) was then and is now the bedrock of every secret service agency in the world. The knowledge revealed about the activities of British Naval Intelligence and other agencies during the First World War largely vindicates Casement's accusations, proving they were not the feverish paranoia of a mad, fugitive consul.

A further dominant theme of these essays and an issue that had informed Casement's writing from as early as 1907 was his concern for how truth was manipulated and an official version of history constructed for public consumption. The essays make bold and unequivocal accusations about the management and censoring of history for political motives. Over the years, Casement had described many examples of this in his analysis of the relations between England and Ireland. Such an outlook was informed by the historiography of Alice Stopford Green, and the argument that history was inescapably subjective and driven by agendas. It is a view that was disputed vigorously at the time, but is now recognised as a legitimate concern. In undertaking this attack on the relationship between 'truth' and history, Casement assailed two of the most venerated historian-statesmen of the age: Winston Churchill and James Bryce.

Both Churchill and Bryce had been habitués of Alice Stopford Green's London circle. In 1904, when Churchill crossed the floor of the House of Commons and became a

Liberal Member of Parliament, he showed his new colours by openly backing the inaugural issue of the *West African Mail* with a letter of support for ED Morel. But as political tensions over Ireland deepened, coupled with the crisis of the Liberal Party, Churchill's own sympathies rested more and more with the hawkish voice of the Unionist Party. As mentioned earlier, Casement blamed Churchill for being the main antagonist in scotching his efforts to have German ships stop at Queenstown. Added to this was Churchill's support for the leadership of the Ulster Volunteer Force and his intimate political ties with Casement's future prosecutor, FE Smith. In *The Crime Against Europe*, Churchill was forthrightly attacked for his belligerency towards Germany. By 1915, Casement's hostility had extended to attacks on Churchill's honesty and his embroidered approach to writing history.

An essay that is critical to comprehending why both the British ruling elite turned on Casement so ruthlessly, and historians find it difficult to accommodate him into the intellectual history of the age, is 'The Far-Extended Baleful Power of the Lie'. [See Appendix] This essay amounts to an attack on the writing of official history and the use of what Churchill described euphemistically as 'terminological inexactitude' (lying) as one of the principal weapons of the British Empire. While Churchill came in for scathing treatment, Casement's most trenchant attacks were leveled at James Bryce, part of the Liberal imperialist intelligentsia and, arguably, the most able legal mind of his generation. He had collaborated closely with Casement over the Putumayo campaign when serving as British Ambassador in Washington and had a particular legal interest in the issue of atrocities. This extended back to his intervention in the Bulgarian atrocities of the 1880s and later on to his outspoken condemnation of the Ottoman treatment of the Armenians.

At the end of 1914, Asquith chose Bryce to head a commission to investigate the allegations of German atrocities in Belgium. This was a matter Casement had watched closely from the outset of the war, and he believed that he was well able to ascertain the power of propaganda in the reporting of how stories of German barbarism were deliberately spun for the benefit of the recruiting sergeants and to justify Britain's intervention in the war. Be that as it may, Casement's flight to Germany makes him susceptible to counter-accusations of bias, although he was not the only voice making such allegations. On his return from the Western Front in November 1914, Casement had made a forthright statement:

> Of all the lies England has distributed in recent years throughout the world, by her admirable system called 'free trade', I guess this lie of German barbarism and 'German atrocities' is the most willful, the most perverse and the most evil intentioned.[9]

Written three months after the start of the war, this comment was already unequivocal in its condemnation of officially spun lies, and while the Germans had undoubtedly committed appalling acts in their advance through Belgium, Casement felt that the construction of German barbarism was intended to do little more than accentuate the climate of fear and hatred of Germany.

The publication in the spring of 1915 of the 'Report on the Committee on Alleged German Outrages', by the committee overseen by Bryce, inspired an even more ferocious attack. Casement accused Bryce of essentially selling his good name as a historian and defiling the professional standards of his discipline in order to produce a view of the war that suited British propaganda requirements. What infuses Casement's accusation with particular gravity is the fact that he was able to compare and contrast his own investigations in sub-Saharan Africa and South America with Bryce'e methodology. In constructing his case, Casement made a direct reference to the deliberate falsification of documents and records, which he maintained was part of the operating procedure of the British Foreign Office:

> It was Napoleon I think said that the falsification of official documents was more common with the English than with any other nation. Sir Edward Grey is claimed by his friends to be thoroughly English, and no one who has read his famous White Paper giving his version of the origin of war, or his speeches in Parliament explaining what the white

paper omitted to make clear, can doubt for a moment his nationality. The White Paper has already been revised twice I think – certain lacunae having been discovered, even after a triple editing, that gave the mockers occasion to revive Napoleon's calumny. There were dates that had gone astray and curious discrepancies that showed a later hand at work than that ostensibly penning the despatch. At the second revise it was hoped that the present edition (the 3rd edition let us call it, second million, cheap or popular issue at 1d.) was above detection even by an expert. The most careful revising eye in the Foreign Office could find no opening for attack. Alas, for the reputation of the experts …'[10]

In making this argument, Casement contested the official version of events and insinuated how elaborate lies could be constructed and propagated as truths. His propaganda writings of this time are filled with similar accusations. *The Continental Times* ran several such pieces. In an article entitled 'England's Care for the Truth', Casement sarcastically referred to the Bryce report:

'England has always taken care of the truth. Her solicitude for it has ever been great and never so remarkable as in the present war.

That Truth was a woman and could be taken care of was first perceived by England many centuries ago, and John Bull chivalrously took steps to house and secure the unprotected female long before less adventurous and far-seeing minds were aware of the necessities of the case. And now England has her reward.

Truth, no longer at the bottom of a well, to be drawn up painfully and with much spilling in inadequate buckets-full by a rotting cord or rope, is distributed by a magnificent system of high pressure pumps in vast and fructiferous floods over the surface of the whole earth.[11]

It is hard to ascertain how the British government or, indeed, the British press was reacting to Casement's indiscretions and accusations. But it is almost certain that both his treason and his writings were being discussed in the corridors of power. Even if *The Continental Times* had a limited distribution in Europe, there is good reason to believe that the Foreign Office was well aware, through their network of spies, of the embarrassing revelations made in these articles. As war censorship deepened, Casement's treason was constructed along specific lines by news services across the British Empire. Some sources questioned Casement's sanity and suggested that years in tropical climates had somehow unhinged his thinking; others claimed he was in receipt of German gold. But this did little to dissuade Casement, and his acts of defiance only increased.

By mid-1915 Berlin was a hotbed of different seditious and revolutionary movements and crosscurrents. The German General Staff was giving credence and clandestine support to various revolutionary causes to further its national war aims. But some struggles were deeply opposed to both the Kaiser and the war. Rosa Luxemberg, the Marxist revolutionary, referenced the Putumayo investigation in her indictment of the relationship between capitalism and militarism in *The Junius Pamphlet: the War and the Workers*. She wrote of the 'forty thousand men on the Putumayo river … tortured to death within ten years by a band of European captains of industry.' Whether Casement was fraternising with this part of the revolutionary underground is unclear, although he had conceptualised Irish revolutionary activity as part of a much wider commitment to anticolonial action. Article 7 of his Treaty had controversially stated that 'it might be possible to employ the Irish Brigade to assist the Egyptian People to recover their freedom by driving the British out of Egypt … a blow struck at the British invaders of Egypt, to aid Egyptian national freedom, is a blow struck for a kindred cause to that of Ireland.'[12] In December 1915, he entertained plans to visit Constantinople in order to discuss the deployment of the Irish Brigade 'in the Eastern warfield' and he drew up a detailed memorandum with his plan.[13]

Another kindred cause was India. A British Foreign Office cipher written after Casement had arrived in Berlin commented: 'Casement has been seeing Indians at Berlin & is trying to organise rebellion in India.'[14] The Hindu–German conspiracy is the umbrella term for a series of insurrections against the British Raj during the First World War, fostered with both German and Irish support. Irish and Indian revolutionaries had been conspiring over many years for the common goal of independence. One of the more active individuals involved was Margaret Noble, or Sister Nivedita as she was known in India. Born in Dungannon in 1867, Noble dedicated her life to social work, and after her harrowing experience of British rule in India preached the gospel of national independence and the use of physical force to achieve those ends. India was the largest jewel in the imperial crown and its potential nemesis. Casement confided to his diary: 'Once India falls the whole house collapses – for it is chiefly on India and her plunder the colonial scheme of robbery depends.'[15] In 1917, Casement's friend in Berlin, Agatha Grabisch, published a pamphlet – *Roger Casement and India* – drawing together much of his writing on this theme and showing how he developed a coherent comparative understanding of colonial Ireland and colonial India.

There is a more direct reference to Casement's widening conspiracy with India. During his weeks in Germany, Joseph Plunkett made reference in his diary to Casement's friendship with Virendranath Chattopadhyaya (Chatto), a prominent Hindu revolutionary and seasoned anti-British conspirator.[16] By 1915, Chatto had a following among the diaspora of Indian intellectuals in Europe and was in touch with various national revolutionary networks. Since his participation in the Stuttgart conference of the Second International in 1907, Chatto had been in communication with other socialist delegates, including Rosa Luxemberg, Karl Liebknecht, Ramsay MacDonald and Jean Jaurés. He had served on the board of the *Indian Sociologist* and was part of the India House Circle, a hot house for Hindu agitation in London.

In 1914 Chatto went to Berlin to organise exiled Indians through the 'German Friends of India', an association endorsed by Kaiser Wilhelm II. The result was that many revolutionaries from the rest of Europe migrated towards Berlin. Over the next few years and with the support of the German Foreign Office, Indian revolutionaries were well supported from the US, most generously by Joe McGarrity. Casement's friendship with Chatto suggests that Casement was deepening the link between the Irish struggle and other configurations of anti-imperial resistance. It was a high stakes game and one that had started to play havoc with his health and nerves.

From his years in the tropics, Casement had developed a susceptibility to periodic fevers, probably malaria. These bouts often came on when his immune levels were low and would leave him with no alternative but to take to bed, often for several days at a time. Both Plunkett and Monteith confided in their diaries that Casement's health was increasingly fragile. With the approach of winter in 1915 his health deteriorated, his anxieties exacerbated and his depression deepened. There is an identifiable difference between the confident and buoyant Casement who visited the German Foreign Office on the Western Front in November 1914 and the Casement of early 1916. After fourteen months in Germany he had become dejected by Prussian militarism, outraged by the daily slaughter of the world war, and frustrated by his own gradual isolation from the main Irish revolutionary decision-making centres in the US and Ireland. He was physically and mentally exhausted, and in early 1916 he spent significant amounts of time bed-bound in a sanatorium. In February 1916 he wrote to Blücher:

> The only thing I really want is peace − peace all round. I am sick to death of all the rest − the hopeless folly of the whole thing − the organised madness − the scientific insanity − called "war", "victory", "glory" − how vain and hopeless it is.[17]

Despite the setbacks and his disillusionment, Casement's natural authority and his clarity of vision were reinvigorated when confirmation of the plans for the Rising reached him in February. He now revived his diary-writing routine in order to document his lengthy negotiations with officials from the German General Staff, the Foreign Office and the German Admiralty. In *A Last Page* − as this diary was titled − Casement's dogged determination to continue to shape events, even though he had lost direct authority, is evident on every page. He was also deeply troubled by doubt.[18]

His description of his final weeks in Germany is extraordinarily candid and provides honest insight into what he justifiably considered to be an impossible situation. He described himself at the mercy of a regime of military power that had largely lost sympathy with his cause (quite possibly influenced by the Kaiser's tacit objection to the idea for a rebellion in Ireland). His sense of isolation and misgiving was deepened by his inability to communicate secretly and efficiently with the Irish revolutionary network. His web of informers, sympathisers and comrades – that once stretched from Mar del Plata in Argentina to the Gaeltacht of Connemara – had been seriously disrupted and reduced.

In February 1916, he tried to get word through to Devoy, in advance of the Irish Convention held in New York, and sent messengers in different directions to influence the revolutionary command centre. John McGoey was dispatched to Ireland to contact Eoin MacNeill, the Chief of Staff of the Irish Volunteers, and convince him that without the right military support from Germany, the Rising would be little more than a sacrificial slaughter. But the fate of these various messengers is obscure. British intelligence was by now keeping abreast of the revolutionary build-up in Ireland through the interception and deciphering of secret communiqués.

In his diary, Casement set down exactly why he objected to the Rising on military, political and moral grounds. Without a direct commitment of German officers and soldiers, the plan was nothing more than a gunrunning venture and unlikely to succeed. From a political perspective the Rising was likely to be bitterly resented in Ireland by the bulk of the population who are 'law abiding and peace loving'.[19] This would only deepen the anger and contempt felt towards Germany. Much of this argument proved highly prescient. But in adopting this oppositional line he knew that he was himself open to accusations of 'treason' against the very independence struggle that he had worked so hard to initiate and organise. The failure of the Irish Brigade had left Casement in an extremely compromised position. He was convinced that both the German General Staff and Foreign Office were only supportive of the Rising in order to rid themselves of the Irish question and the Brigade. In his reckoning, their commitment to supplying a shipment of arms was little more than an empty gesture; without the right military support, the rifles were worthless and the rebellion inevitably doomed.

Even though Casement helped to negotiate the arms shipment, he had little belief in the potential success of the plan, which he felt was ill-prepared and unlikely to succeed. The energies of the rebels, he believed, would be more effectively deployed in properly organising the rendezvous with the arms shipment and getting the guns into the right hands so that a sustained guerrilla war could be mounted in the west of Ireland.

The level of Casement's tactical influence might be measured by the fact that both the German General Staff and Foreign Office commissioned an internal report on Casement in the weeks before his departure to determine whether it was more strategically valuable to keep him in Germany, or to send him back to Ireland to meet his fate. Both advantages and disadvantages were advanced, but Casement was unwavering in his desire to return to Ireland. In his last days in Germany, deep frictions began to open up in his negotiation with the different departments of war. His succession of meetings with the German spymaster, Rudolf Nadolny, were particularly hostile and the diary entries in the spring of 1916 identify the breakdown in trust as the primary reason for his deteriorating relationship with German military officials.

Casement's principal concern was to maintain the guarantees obtained in the treaty signed at the end of 1914 and to ensure some level of security for the Irish Brigade after his departure. But the German government was trying to back away from the treaty; the low number of recruits to the Irish Brigade had, in its eyes, rendered it invalid. Casement had to argue hard to stop the German General Staff from sending the Brigade back aboard the arms ship, the *Aud*. Eventually he won his point by predicting that if the men returned to Ireland without the 'efficient military support' promised in the treaty, it might result in a humiliating public relations disaster for Germany.

The most dramatic aspect of his negotiation was his determination to persuade the German General Staff to provide a submarine, or U-boat, for his return to Ireland. Nadolny and other senior officials were hesitant. They believed there was little chance of the vessel arriving in time or breaking the naval blockade. Casement argued that he could supply valuable intelligence on the landing of the arms, an excuse concealing his real intention: to be put ashore on reaching Ireland and do his best to stop the Rising. At the last moment the hard-fought request to make a U-boat available was granted through pressure from the Admiralty and various German officials who had Casement's interests at heart. It was a significant victory at the end of some very awkward negotiating.

But there was another reason for returning to Ireland by submarine because, as Casement later wrote, 'the submarine was invented by an Irish rebel'.[20] The inventor, John Philip Holland, a native of County Clare, had died in New Jersey within days of the outbreak of war in August 1914, and could never have predicted the part his invention would play in naval warfare. Much of Holland's early research into submarine design was financed with Fenian support in the US. Always conscious of the need to promote Irish innovation, Casement was further motivated by his determination to foster embedded fears of invasion, latent in the British military imagination, by deploying the most advanced mechanism of war for his revolutionary ends. Nothing symbolised the modernity of the First World War quite as brazenly as the submarine. In this sense, Casement's return to Ireland is the stuff of not just history but science fiction. The symbolism of the moment would fuse the futuristic imagination of Jules Verne with the paranoid invasion fears informing Erskine Childers' espionage classic *The Riddle of the Sands*. Ironically, the design of the submarine required a huge number of rubberised components.

In the last weeks, Casement made various trips to Zossen in the company of Father Crotty and Monteith to prepare the members of the Irish Brigade as best he could for the impact that his departure would have, although he was vigilant not to disclose what he was about to do. In his communication with von Wedel, the only senior official Casement now trusted, he sought guarantees of safety for the men, even though he knew that their individual destinies would be condemned in the light of his own actions.

He was also concerned about his large archive of papers gathered since arriving in Berlin. He left complicated instructions with Charles Curry to bury the more important documents, including his copy of the treaty, and to publish his diary after the war.[21] Casement believed that by explaining why he went to Germany and detailing his entanglement with the British secret service, the logic of his 'treason' would be vindicated. To achieve this end, it was vital that his papers were distributed in such a way as to guarantee their survival.

The circumstances of Casement's return to Ireland with Monteith and Daniel Julian Bailey (aka Sergeant Beverly) are complicated and controversial. Under a mantle of secrecy, the three men made their way to Wilhelmshaven, Germany's main naval port. Casement met with Lieutenant Karl Spindler, captain of the *Aud*, and the finer details of the plans were agreed. Both men considered the chances of the *Aud* beating the British naval blockade were slim. In theory, the arrangement was straightforward. Casement would travel via submarine while the *Aud*, carrying the arms – 20,000 rifles and three million rounds of ammunition – would follow a separate route. They would rendezvous in Tralee Bay and Casement would help in any way he could to distribute the arms.

On 12 April, Casement, Monteith and Bailey boarded the U-20, but two days out from port the submarine developed engine trouble and was forced to turn back. After arriving at the naval base at Helgoland, a replacement U-boat, the U-19 under Captain Reimund Weisbach, was placed at their disposal. Once the necessary transfer of provisions was complete and the officers briefed, the U-19 departed Helgoland at 1.26pm on 15 April. But the delay had thrown the plan off-kilter.

The journey to Ireland took five days. Much of it was

made on the surface but every day there were two practice dives, each lasting a couple of hours. Monteith described the routine as follows:

> As we submerged, I noticed the expression on the faces of Casement and Beverley. They sat like wondering children, and looked at each other without speaking, held by the majesty of silence – silence that could be felt. Then the stillness was broken by a little rattling noise, made by the diving fin connections, and the faint swirl of water, as it rushed into the tanks, and the sharply uttered "Achtung" of the leading seamen, as they answered the commands from the conning tower. Down, down we went![22]

As they approached Ireland, Casement shaved off his distinctive beard, leaving only a moustache. The U-19 arrived twenty-four hours after its projected arrival. Weisbach was under the impression that a pilot boat would help the *Aud* and the U-19 rendezvous and transport Casement to the arms ship. Devoy had agreed to a three-day window to allow for the two vessels to link up; this proved a costly over-calculation. When the *Aud* arrived into Tralee Bay there was no pilot boat, as the signallers on land had not been given prior notification of the arrival of a submarine. A combination of misunderstanding, bad luck, careless preparation and incompetence scotched the plans. Over the years blame was apportioned in various directions. In some ways all parties were at fault: Casement, Devoy, and the men on the ground in Kerry. Some columns of Volunteers as far away as Slieve Luachra had mobilised and were making their way towards Tralee to meet the shipment.

Casement was eager to get ashore and Weisbach, anxious for the safety of his crew, agreed. On Good Friday, 21 April 1916, in the hours before dawn, Casement, Monteith and Bailey emerged through the conning tower of the U-19 and boarded a small rowing boat. They took with them basic provisions: a few side arms, maps and rudimentary food. For well over an hour they battled against quite adverse seas in the darkness. At one point the boat capsized. Finally, they landed on Banna Strand, an expansive sweep of open beach where Atlantic tides roll in across the low, sandy shallows.

It is a sublime location. The landscape here is deeply associated with the life and spiritual odyssey of St Brendan, the navigator monk. On the peak of Mount Brandon, to the southwest on the Dingle peninsula, are the ruins of two roughly built cells, where St Brendan is said to have spent several years in contemplative isolation, before setting out on his voyage west in search of Hy-Brazil. It is an extremity of Ireland infused with the mysticism and mysteries associated with the land of saints and scholars. For Casement, whose life had deliberately connected to the cosmography of the early Irish saints, there was something profoundly symbolic about his landing in this place.

In a commemorative speech made near Banna Strand in August 1917, Thomas Ashe addressed a large crowd of republicans and nationalists: the first momentous gathering of sympathisers after the 1916 Rising. He commented that by landing on the Corcaguiney Peninsula (another name for the Dingle Peninsula), Casement was fulfilling an ancient prophecy in folkloric memory that related how a 'mystical liberator' would land in these parts to set Ireland free:

> Back in the years of History many an eye similar to the eyes of the old Irish speakers in numerous other countries outside of Ireland, looked on many occasions for the mystical liberator of their country to come with the sword and bayonet for their deliverance; and it's no wonder that the people of Kerry thought that the deliverer would come with an army and armaments, and he did come. The mystical man of Colcumbcille's prophecy came; he came unknown, but I tell you he is not unknown today. He is not unknown today, nor will he be unknown tomorrow. He did not bring with him that great army; he brought no great powers in his train to back up his work for Irish liberty; but he brought with him a loving heart and an undaunted spirit that will live in Ireland as long as any man will live who believes in the Irish ideals of an Irish republic.[23]

For Casement it was a homecoming, but it was one his enemies had been patiently awaiting.

Chapter Eleven

April–June 1916

Capture and Trial

When I landed in Ireland that morning (about 3 a.m.) swamped & swimming ashore on an unknown strand I was happy for the first time for over a year. Although I knew that this fate waited on me, I was for one brief spell happy and smiling once more. I cannot tell you what I felt, the sandhills were full of skylarks, rising in the dawn, the first I had heard for years – the first sound I heard through the surf was their song as I waded in through the breakers and they kept rising all the time up to the old rath at Currahane where I stayed and sent the others on. And all around were primroses and wild violets and the singing of the skylarks in the air, and I was back in Ireland again; as the day grew brighter I was quite happy for I felt all the time it was God's will that I was there.[1]

The arrival of Roger Casement on the shores of County

Kerry is commemorated today with three impressive monuments strung out along the coastal plain stretching between the village of Ballyheigue and the Romanesque cathedral at Ardfert, built on the site of a sixth century monastery founded by St Brendan. Though he spent less than thirty hours in 'the Kingdom', Roger Casement's spirit has passed indelibly into the popular memory of the southwestern corner of Munster. The precise events of those few hours would prove critical to his trial. Some witnesses to his landing with Monteith and Bailey were brought over to London for his trial and carefully cross-examined. For all of them it proved a life-transforming moment and propelled them into the epicentre of a bitter and divisive courtroom drama.

After the considerable ordeal of landing their small vessel, the three men gathered themselves as best they could before continuing on along the track skirting the wide coastal plain. As they passed along the boreen in the first light of the day, they were spotted by a local farmer praying at a holy well and by a housemaid going about her morning chores. Weak from the ordeal, Casement was left at an overgrown ring fort, or *rath*, while Monteith and Bailey continued on to see if help could be found. As he waited, Casement buried some of his possessions, including gold coins, somewhere inside the fort and spread his sodden wool overcoat out in the fresh breeze to dry.

But the local RIC had been alerted to the presence of the

suspicious strangers and the abandoned boat had been found. Around 1.20 p.m., Casement was spotted from the road and approached by two RIC constables. When asked for his name and identity, he said that he was 'Richard Morten' and that he was researching 'a life of St Brendan'. The story was plausible, but the policemen were unconvinced. Casement was arrested and transported in pony and trap via Ardfert to Tralee and held there overnight.

He spent much of that night talking to John A Kearney, a cultured RIC officer.[2] On various occasions Casement beseeched the guards to get a message through to MacNeill in Dublin to avert the Rising. News of Casement's capture had by now filtered through to the capital. Writing some years later, Margaret Pearse recalled hearing of Casement's fate while in the company of her brother Patrick at St Enda's school: 'I can remember well when the terribly tragic news came from Kerry. In the room where I am now writing, my brother Pat was sitting, silent, stricken as it were with the import of the message just received. I asked him if the tragic occurrence would make any serious difference to his plans. He replied: "Yes, a terrible difference."'[3] Efforts by local Volunteers to liberate Casement that night did not materialise.

On Saturday morning Casement was escorted from the barracks to the railway station. A train had arrived during the night with one hundred Dublin Fusiliers from Cork to reinforce the small garrison at Tralee. At Mallow they waited on the platform for a Dublin-bound connection. On arriving into Kingsbridge (Heuston) station in the early afternoon, Casement was taken the short distance by car to Arbour Hill Military Prison by an RIC sergeant, and handed over to Frederick Whittaker, the Sergeant-Major of Arbour Hill Prison. Casement later remembered: 'This fellow was a cad and shouted at me as if I were a dog.'[4] He was treated roughly, refused to give his name and was denied all requests for legal representation. By now word had reached the inner circles of power in London that they finally had caught their renegade consul.

Later that evening, the prisoner was taken in an ambulance to the port, then by overnight train to London and to a nondescript room in Scotland Yard where, over the next three days, he was interrogated by the most high-ranking intelligence chiefs in the country: Basil Thomson and Patrick Quinn from Special Branch, Admiral Reginald Hall (Naval Intelligence/Room 40) and Frank Hall of MI5g (later MI5). For Thomson and Admiral Hall, Casement's capture brought to a successful conclusion eighteen months of scheming. In early 1915, they had chartered a yacht, the *Sayonara*, to sail up and down the west of Ireland gathering information on possible landing places for armaments. They had also shared the intelligence from intercepted communications between Berlin and the IRB in the US and were aware of the details of the Rising well in advance of Easter Monday. But instead of acting on the intelligence, they had decided to allow the Rising go ahead.

There were other political complexities to Casement's interrogation. In recent years, with the partial declassification of British intelligence files, it has emerged that one of his senior interrogators from the state security service now known as MI5, Frank Hall, was a key conspirator in the Larne gunrunning operation and had served as military secretary to the Ulster Volunteers. This collusion between the British secret services and Loyalist paramilitaries would endure throughout the twentieth century.[5]

Most of what is known about Casement's interrogation derives from a transcript of the interrogation compiled by the Special Branch.[6] This document has succumbed to a life in many ways as shadowy as the soon-to-emerge Black Diaries. A century on, it should be read with a healthy dose of scepticism. Police interrogation statements are a highly contested area of relations between Irish rebels and the security state. During centuries of resistance to British rule in Ireland, there have been too many infamous instances of forced confessions, forged statements and manipulated testimony for such documents to be accepted readily at face value.

Although much of the reported conversation between the prisoner and his interrogators appears genial and even cordial at times, it is apparent that Casement was losing the last vestiges of influence within the corridors of power. His requests

to access senior Whitehall officials, such as his former Foreign Office colleague Sir William Tyrrell, were stonewalled.
Thomson, in particular, started to taunt and humiliate the
prisoner.

Casement was clearly in a nervous and anxious state. He
later recalled:

> I was dazed and absolutely incapable of thinking clear on
> any subject but the one – how in the name of God, to still
> stop the Rising without doing a mean or cowardly thing or
> giving any man away.[7]

The interrogation apparently began amiably, with assurances that what was being discussed was 'private'. Casement
later claimed that within the first quarter of an hour of
entering the room Thomson and Hall had told him that 'the
whole thing was known to them'. They 'knew of the Rising,
had already captured the steamer, knew all the leaders in
Dublin and were there with their hands on them to arrest.'[8]
Admiral Hall 'knew the day I sailed! … We were waiting for
you, Sir Roger.'[9]

'Who are you?' Thomson asked. 'Officially I am Sir Roger
Casement.' 'There are people who may be impersonating Sir
Roger Casement.' 'I don't think there are many people who
would care to impersonate me.'

Casement then inquired about the nature of the charge
against him, only to be told that he was not presently charged

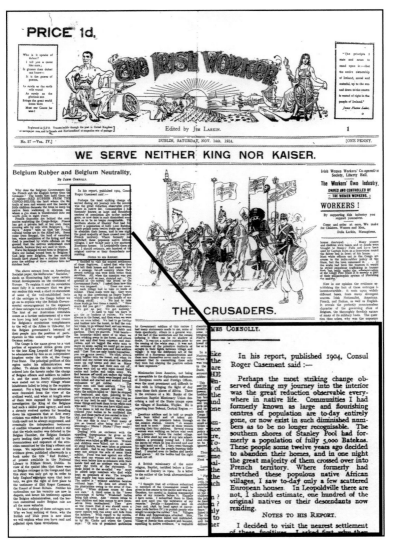

The Irish Worker published a front-page article by James Connolly on 'Belgium Rubber and Belgium Neutrality' with prominent references to Casement's revelations of the outrages committed in the name of European civilisation. The Congo Reform Association galvanised international working class solidarity in the early twentieth century.

Above left: Roger Casement (seated, right) at the Irish College, Cloghaneely, Co Donegal, (1904), with Agnes O'Farrelly (1874-1951), a founding member of Cumann na mBan and later professor of Irish at UCD, and others.

Above right: Republican activist Alice Milligan (1865-1953), who collaborated closely with Casement in the Gaelic League.

Left: Despite his Quaker background, Bulmer Hobson (1883-1969) was a key IRB organiser of the Dungannon Clubs and Na Fianna Éireann. Roger Casement supported many of his publishing ventures and they collaborated on several clandestine operations including the running of guns into Howth in July 1914.

Above: Belfast members of Na Fianna Éireann pictured outside 'Ardrigh' the home of FJ Bigger in Belfast in January 1914. Casement is at the back left. Lord Ashbourne (no. 2) and FJ Bigger (No. 3) are the kilted figures standing at the front door. Alice Stopford Green is seated on the steps.

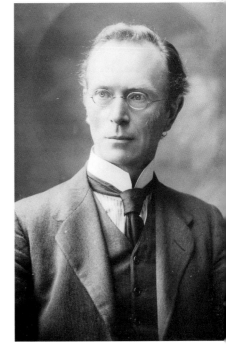

Right: Irish language scholar and revolutionary Eoin MacNeill (1867-1945) was the first Chief-of-Staff of the Irish Volunteers. On hearing of Casement's capture in County Kerry and the loss of the *Aud*, he countermanded the order for the Easter Rising.

105 Antrim Road
Belfast,
14 Augt 1912.

Dear Mr de Valera

I shmed be much obliged if you would take charge of the inclosed £5. being my contribution to the prizes at Ky or Sh End of

Left: Letter from Roger Casement to Éamon de Valera enclosing prize money for the *feis* on Tawin island in Galway Bay, where Casement and Douglas Hyde raised funds for building a new school house for Irish language speakers.

Right: Roger Casement's fund-raising efforts to improve conditions for victims of typhus in Connemara in the summer of 1913 was used as another vehicle for supporting Irish language teaching.

Reprint of a Letter published in the "Irish Independent," 18th April, 1914.

APPEAL

FOR THE

Irish School Children of Connemara,

TO PROVIDE FOOD FOR THEM IN SCHOOL AND SUPPORT FOR THE IRISH LANGUAGE.

SIR,

With reference to the Annual Report of the Congested Districts Board published in to-day's "Irish Independent," I observe it stated, with reference to the Connemara islanders, that "while exception is taken to the assertions that chronic starvation and famine existed in the year 1913, yet what has been written is well founded as to the insanitary housing and surroundings, the polluted water supply, and the comfortless habits of life of the district."

When your correspondent's reports from Gorumna, Lettermullen, and Carraroe, in May last year, excited so much public feeling in Ireland, and resulted in a considerable sum of money being raised for the immediate relief of those in distress, I pointed out that a permanent change could come only through the agency of the State, and that private efforts to relieve the often acute want there prevailing could bring about no permanent betterment.

I indicated one direction in which private goodwill could proceed with some prospect of beneficial results, namely, by providing a free meal daily for the infant children of the Carraroe National School. In response to my appeal, a sum of over £600 was received, and is now being expended in giving the large infant school at Carraroe an excellent meal of bread and hot cocoa every midday. A sufficient sum is in hand to carry this on for several years at Carraroe. But Carraroe School is not the poorest of the locality. There are others quite as poor—if not, indeed, poorer—and at which large numbers of little hungry boys and girls put in an enforced and dazed attendance of six hours daily, to imbibe a knowledge of English phrases on an empty Irish stomach.

I revisited the district two weeks ago, being accompanied by three friends, one a doctor, another a Professor of one of the Irish Universities, and the third the Editor of one of the leading papers of Germany. I went with a two-fold purpose—to see how the school children at Carraroe were getting on under the changed circumstances, since the daily meal was introduced, and if possible to see whether this daily meal could not be extended to the neighbouring schools equally in need of such help, and to let the German Editor see the conditions under which a large number of Irish people dwell, in the twentieth century, and under the rule of the most enlightened administration in the world.

The result of my journey, so far as Carraroe School is concerned, was most encouraging. There a complete transformation has been wrought since the daily meal was introduced in September last. The excellent schoolmistress (Mrs. Tulridy) presides each midday over one of the happiest schools in Ireland. The children are bright and fresh-skinned and clear-eyed, with rosy cheeks and happy smiles. Not only are they physically better—but they are mentally improved, and confidence and an air of friendship have taken the place of the former dull and listless disregard that met the visitor's eye.

My three companions were greatly struck with the atmosphere at Carraroe School, and the contrast between the children there and at the neighbouring schools of Turine (on the Carraroe mainland), of Trabane, and Drim (Gorumna), and of Lettermullen is a painful one. At Turine and Trabane the doctor, who accompanied me, declared that half the children were "half-starved," and he again and again indicated one, a boy or girl, with the most apparent proofs of physical exhaustion due to lack of sufficient nourishment. I became convinced, as the journey proceeded, that what has been attempted and done for Carraroe with such happy results, should be attempted and done for at least the four neighbouring schools of Turine, Trabane, Drim, and Lettermullen.

An outlay, say, of £25 a year per school would go far to provide a meal during the worst months of the year, when food in the home is scarcest, to these neglected and literally half-starved little Irish-speaking boys and girls, who represent at once the hope and the last of Irish-speaking Ireland.

£100 a year would bring new life into these schools, and new strength into these little bodies, and new strength into the Irish language throughout the whole of a wide region where it still prevails as the home tongue. But, like the people themselves, it is clinging to the rocks.

Above: Roger Casement and John Devoy seated together during a public procession in Philadelphia on 2 August 1914, just hours before the outbreak of the First World War.

Left: Roger Casement and Robert Monteith pictured with Captain Weisbach and the crew of the U-19 en route to Ireland in April 1916.

Left: *The Graphic,* 6 May 1916, cartoon of Roger Casement wearing a Sinn Féin sash being unceremoniously booted out of a German submarine.

FURTHER PROGRESS BY THE BRITISH NORTH OF OVILLERS

The Daily Mirror

CERTIFIED CIRCULATION LARGER THAN THAT OF ANY OTHER DAILY PICTURE PAPER

WEDNESDAY, JULY 19, 1916.

ROGER CASEMENT'S APPEAL FAILS: "HE WAS THE KING'S LIEGE WHEREVER HE MIGHT BE."

Right: News items about Casement's trial ran throughout the summer of 1916. After the collapse of his appeal on 18 July, newspapers around the world reported his imminent execution.

THE HALTER BECOMES A HALO

ENGLISH LAW HAS ITS REVENGE AND THE WORLD A NEW HERO

Above: *The Continental Times*, a Berlin-based English language newspaper published many of Casement's most seditious essays in 1915 and ran this cartoon on its front page after his execution. The names Emmet, Parnell, Pearse and Skeffington run along the lower margin of the frame.

Right: WJ Maloney's *The Forged Casement Diaries* (1936) was an early effort to explain the interaction of different British intelligence agencies involved in the co-ordinated smear campaign launched against Casement in Britain, Ireland and the US.

Below: After rumours of the Black Diaries had been used in 1916 to assassinate Casement's character, their existence was vigorously denied by the British Home Office until their publication and partial release in 1959. Controversy endures on the question of their authenticity and their relevance to Irish history.

THE FORGED CASEMENT DIARIES

From a Drawing by L. Fanto, Art Director,
State Theatre, Saxony, 1916

WILLIAM J. MALONEY, M.D., LL.D.

with anything, but that this would soon change. For the time being he was being held under the Defence of the Realm Act (1914). He was then asked to identify various documents. His interrogators made much of the short encrypted 'diary' he had kept before leaving Germany recording, in coded form, the itinerary of those last days before arriving in Ireland.

That afternoon Casement was taken to Brixton Prison and admitted under a false identity as 'Mr C.R.'. He was told that if he informed any warder of the prison who he was, the warder would be dismissed immediately.[10]

Early the following morning, as the Irish Volunteers and the Irish Citizen Army mobilised and took control of key locations in central Dublin, Casement was driven from Brixton to Scotland Yard. He recalled later that he was happy compared to the day before 'for there was not a word in the papers of any trouble in Ireland.' His interrogation ranged across a number of different areas: his identity, his time in Germany, the nature of the arms shipment. On the third and final day of his interrogation, Tuesday 25 April, Thomson began the interrogation:

> Since I saw you yesterday what we thought would happen has happened. There has been more or less a Rising in Dublin, and a good many have been killed, and that is all the good that has proceeded from your expedition.[11]

Thomson also announced that some trunks of papers had been found at Casement's old dwellings at 50 Ebury Street, a residential neighbourhood of Pimlico in central London, where Casement had resided in 1913. The interrogation transcript then recorded some rather benign dialogue about the nature of Casement's nationalism, his intentions regarding running guns into Ireland, and why he had fallen out with the German General Staff.

In the closing page of the official interrogation, Thomson announced: 'Sir Roger, your trunks are here but there are no keys.'

'Break them open,' Casement answered.

At that point Hall and Thomson brought the interrogations to an end and informed Casement that he would be taken into custody with a view to a military trial.

The news about Casement was no longer secret. London was buzzing with speculation about what was happening in Ireland; nowhere more so than in Westminster. The breaking of the news about the Easter Rising is one of the most irregular moments in the history of British parliamentary democracy. On Tuesday afternoon the House of Commons was packed. Many members were dressed in army fatigues. The benches were alive with chat and speculation. The Chief Secretary for Ireland, Augustine Birrell, announced that a state of martial law had been declared. After brief references to the disturbances, the House of Commons suddenly began to debate the need for a 'Secret Sitting'. Noel Pemberton Billing, a newly-elected MP who was waging his own campaign as a back-bencher on the amount of information that the government was letting out about the war, asked the Prime Minister if 'Sir Roger Casement has been brought to London, and can he give this house and nation an assurance that this traitor will be shot forthwith?' Asquith answered: 'I do not think this is a question which ought to be put.'[12]

Immediately following Asquith's reply there was a demand by the Speaker for all strangers to withdraw from the Strangers' Gallery, and reporters from the Press Gallery. The war's first secret session involving both chambers began. Information of what was discussed has not survived, as MPs and Peers were forbidden to either discuss or record the proceedings. A statement issued under the authority of the Speaker described one of the broader issues debated regarding amendments to the Military Service Act. It seems probable, however, that the dominant issue was the rebellion in Dublin and, quite possibly, the capture of Casement. A list has survived of those who took part in the debate: it included Sir Edward Carson, Sir John Simon, Andrew Bonar Law, Noel Pemberton Billing and Winston Churchill. The atmosphere of secrecy surrounding both the Rising and Casement's role intensified.

Following his interrogation, Casement was removed from Brixton Prison and placed in solitary confinement in the Tower of London with orders that no one was to see the prisoner. He became part of a noble lineage of prisoners held in the Tower, which included Princess Elizabeth, Sir Walter Raleigh, Guy Fawkes and the Duke of Monmouth. The director of MI5g ordered that 'all letters addressed to the state prisoner were [to be] forwarded to … the War Office.'[13] Initially, Casement was treated with some severity, watched closely and forbidden to smoke. His mail was censored and in the first days he was given little freedom to write. As tensions heightened in Dublin, surveillance was increased. He recalled later:

> On Wednesday 26 April two soldiers had been put into the room, never to leave me and to look at me all the time – & the sentry outside looking through the single pane. Three men with eyes never off me night and day – changed every hour – & electric light on full every night – so that sleep became impossible – & thought became a page of hell.[14]

His morale was so depleted that he tried unsuccessfully to take his own life by rubbing poison into a cut in his finger. On 1 May, he gave up eating altogether and began a brief hunger strike. But following an examination by the resident doctor, he was told that he would be forcibly fed if he continued to refuse food.[15] For the next two weeks he subsisted on the barest intake of bread and water.

There was still confusion at Westminster on how to proceed. On 3 May, during Question Time, Prime Minister

Asquith announced in the Commons that he had received news that morning that three of the signatories to the *Proclamation of the Republic* – PH Pearse, Thomas J Clarke and Thomas MacDonagh – had been tried by court martial, found guilty and shot. A question from the floor of the house asked 'when the man Sir Roger Casement is going to be tried. He was the forerunner of this movement.' Asquith answered: 'With the utmost expedition: as soon as the evidence is ready.'[16] Over the next nine days another twelve rebels would succumb to the same ruthless treatment, most of them known to Casement.

Behind the scenes efforts were being made on Casement's behalf. Alice Stopford Green approached several senior legal luminaries, but all refused to help. The only solicitor prepared to take on the case was George Gavan Duffy, an Irish solicitor practicing in London with open Sinn Féin sympathies. The Gavan Duffys had a long association with nationalist politics in Ireland. His father, Charles Gavan Duffy (1816-1903) was a prominent nationalist intellectual who had worked his way from humble origins as the self-educated son of a shopkeeper to become a journalist and lawyer. In 1842 he co-founded *The Nation* with Thomas Davis and John Blake Dillon and emerged as a central intellectual in the Young Ireland movement. For a time Gavan Duffy served as MP for New Ross, but in 1855 emigrated to Australia. His nationalist credentials served him well in a land where many Irish had been forcibly settled. He was elected Prime Minister of Victoria in 1871 and two years later knighted. In 1880, he retired to the South of France, and in 1882, aged 66, he fathered George Gavan Duffy. Louise Gavan Duffy, George's sister, had helped to prepare food in the GPO during Easter Week.

Gavan Duffy had written to Casement via the Governor of the Tower of London offering his services on 1 May, but it was not until 9 May and after a great deal of obstruction from different departments of state that a short meeting was granted between the prisoner and his representative.[17] At the end of their discussion, Casement wrote a brief note, 'I hereby instruct you to defend me and to employ counsel to defend my cause.'[18] Duffy later wrote of the Casement he found:

> He was suffering from acute mental strain, as a result of the rigorous confinement in which he had been kept during the previous fortnight, the interrogations to which he had (despite his appeal for independent advice) been subjected while in great distress of mind and body and the exclusion of every relative and friend. He told me that he had been allowed no change of clothing nor underclothing, and that he had worn the same garments for about four weeks, though his relations had shortly after his arrest offered in writing to supply him with everything he might need; he appeared to me to be very ill and he looked so haggard and so worn that I had difficulty persuading myself of his iden-

tity with Sir Roger Casement whom I had known some three years before.[19]

On 10 May Casement's name once again echoed through the House of Commons when the Irish Party member, John Dillon asked the Prime Minister to explain:

Why Sir Roger Casement has been brought to London, and is apparently to have a public trial before a civil tribunal, whilst comparatively obscure men whom he has been largely responsible for seducing into rebellion have been sentenced and executed in Ireland by secret military tribunal.

Prime Minister Asquith answered evasively 'this is a very serious matter, as it affects a man who is under suspicion and about to undergo his trial. I therefore think in fairness to all parties I should have a little more notice of this question.'[20] Dillon's use of the word 'seducing' is also noteworthy. The word had been adopted in the press for many months to describe Casement's endeavours to influence Irish prisoners of war to join the Irish Brigade. Over the following weeks, however, the meaning of the word would start to mutate as Casement's narrative was twisted in unforeseen directions.

Gavan Duffy had no difficulty in quickly engaging two able barristers to Casement's defence. The first was JH Morgan (1876-1955) a Professor of Constitutional Law at King's College in London and part of the inner circle of Liberal power in Britain, with considerable influence over the discussion on Home Rule. From as early as 1904, Casement and Morgan corresponded on constitutional and international affairs. In 1912, Morgan had edited a work entitled *The New Irish Constitution*, which contained contributions from leading advocates of Home Rule, including Stopford Green. The intention of this edition was to show how Home Rule could really change imperial relations for the better and should not be either feared or dismissed. In some ways, though, Morgan is the mystery man of Casement's defence counsel.

What made Morgan's presence complicated was his ongoing involvement with departments of British propaganda and his work into German atrocities. In the twelve months before taking up the Casement brief, Morgan was appointed to the adjutant-general's staff as Home Office representative with the British Expeditionary Force fighting in Europe. He had worked closely with the Bryce Committee compiling and publishing evidence on allegations of German war crimes. In 1916 he would put his name to a work entitled *German Atrocities: An Official Investigation*, an edition that rapidly ran through several printings and supplemented the Bryce report on alleged German outrages that Casement had dismissed in such accusatory terms. Even though Morgan had undertaken this official role for the government, he committed himself wholeheartedly and honourably to Casement's defence. An authority on legal aspects of both the Defence of the Realm Act and the law of treason, Morgan's expertise proved indispensible over the following months.

With Gavan Duffy's support, Morgan recruited another Welshman, Artemus Jones, a barrister with good experience of case law. Interest from the US was now gathering pace and it was decided that a US attorney, Michael Francis Doyle, should attend and report to Clan na Gael. Doyle had been introduced to Casement in the summer of 1914 and was closely linked to Devoy, McGarrity and the Irish-American leadership in the US. By now Gavan Duffy had received notice from the Director of Public Prosecutions of the Crown's intention to prosecute Casement for high treason. He visited Casement again to prepare a brief and produce some sort of narrative to explain how Casement had arrived in the predicament he now found himself.

Over his last two days in the Tower of London, Casement dictated a biographical chronology of his life in preparation for his appearance at Bow Street Magistrates' Court. As a life it is succinct and revealing as much for what it excludes as for what it includes. Casement's work in Africa and South America is reduced to a few pages and the narrative concentrates on his post-1913 story and why he went to Germany. It is informed by a clear logic justifying his actions. Casement argued that his own role in raising and arming the Irish Volunteers was justifiable in light of the language of anarchy unleashed by the failure of the government to deliver Home

Rule and the paramilitarisation of British politics initiated by the leading Unionist barristers, Edward Carson and FE Smith. Casement's intention was always to keep Ireland out of conflict.

> I had been prepared to sacrifice myself alone to achieve, if humanly possible, the keeping of Ireland out of the war; and if things should offer a chance, and this world conflagration permitted it, of going further. I had never contemplated an insurrection in Ireland when engaged in the Volunteer movement; although then I dreamed, then and before it, of a possible state of European affairs that might bring effective foreign help to Ireland – as in the days of Wolfe Tone and the Directory – if a war should ever arise and that war move westwards. But that was only a "dream", a supposition based on a study of history, on reflection over the possibilities of a sea-war between Great Britain and a rival sea power. I nursed that dream. It harmed no one as a dream kept to myself – and a day might come, in a turn of human affairs, when the dream might become a possibility. Had the war not come, the dream remained a dream.[21]

But Casement's hope to manoeuvre his trial so as to challenge the rationalisation of war and Ireland's role in it was something his prosecutors would work hard to avert. A trial is a place of metamorphosis and can facilitate the transformation of the accused into a martyr. Casement's views had so far been restricted to low circulation propaganda newspapers, and few in Britain knew why he had gone to Germany. It was important that his trial did not provide him with a platform to broaden his argument, speak his mind and question the legitimacy of Britain's justification for war.

The Crown began to prove its case immediately. At 7 a.m. on 15 May a number of police officers entered Casement's cell at the Tower of London. Inspector Parker informed the prisoner that he had a warrant for his arrest. He was then removed from the Tower of London and handed over to the civil authorities.[22] Thereby he passed from military into civil custody. Later that morning he arrived by car at Bow Street for the magisterial inquiry presided over by the chief Metropolitan Police Magistrate, Sir John Dickinson.[23]

Public curiosity in the case was immense. On the same day, *The Times* published a short article clarifying the history of the law for high treason, based on the statute of King Edward III (1351), the same law that had authorised the state trials of Charles I and James II. The paper also carried a short item announcing the choice of the prosecution and defence teams: the case for the Crown was to be conducted by the Attorney General, FE Smith (1872–1930).

Accusations of conflict of interest in the choice of Smith were inevitable. Antagonism between Casement and Smith ran deep. Since 1912, Casement's correspondence had made regular mocking asides against Smith and his role with Carson stirring up political difference in Ireland. Smith operated at the very nerve centre of Unionist power in Britain and, as a founder of the Ulster Volunteer Force, he was a remarkably inappropriate figure to lead the prosecution of his sworn political enemy. The decision to allow Smith to take the brief was indicative of how threatened the government felt by the Casement situation.

From his birth on 12 July 1872, Smith had risen quickly up the ladder of the British establishment. Elected as MP for the Walton division of Liverpool in 1906, he nurtured strategic political friendships with Winston Churchill, Lord Beaverbrook and other imperial statesmen and warriors. From 1910 he became increasingly involved in the opposition to the Home Rule Bill. In 1912, he visited Belfast and addressed an audience of Loyalists with Sir Edward Carson on the anniversary of the Battle of the Boyne. Casement was in the crowd. The following year he 'galloped for Carson' at a review of the Ulster Volunteers.

On 5 August 1914, the day after the outbreak of the war, Smith met with the War Minister, Lord Kitchener, and Churchill, First Lord of the Admiralty, and was asked to oversee an office established to supervise press censorship. On 7 August, Churchill told the Commons that the Press Bureau had been founded to ensure that 'a steady stream of trustworthy information supplied both by the War Office and the Admiralty can be given to the press.'[24] This was quickly christened by sceptics the 'Suppress Bureau' on account of the fact that it seemed more intent on censorship than publicity. But it demonstrates that Smith was in at the birth of British government propaganda strategies and would remain in that undisclosed twilight zone linking British propaganda and public opinion with both judicial and executive power. Towards the end of 1915 Smith succeeded Sir Edward Carson as Attorney General and by the summer of 1916 had worked himself into a position of broad influence in Britain.

Although strenuous efforts were made both at the time and ever since to suggest that Smith's role as Casement's prosecutor was an instance of fair justice, clearly it was not. To help build his case, Smith called upon some of the ablest legal luminaries of the day. His supporting counsel included Archibald Bodkin (1862-1957), a specialist in the prosecution of spies, and Travers Humphreys (1867-1956), who first came to public notice in the trial of Oscar Wilde. Moreover, the presence of Smith invested the case with a sense of both spectacle and sacred drama that trials of treason generally awaken. Over the three stages of the trial – the preliminary hearing (May 15-16), the trial (June 26-29) and finally the appeal (July 17-18) – Smith ruthlessly manipulated public opinion against the accused and worked his influence in the corridors of power to achieve his end: Casement's public downfall, character assassination and execution.

On the opening day of the preliminary hearing, *The Times*

reported that Casement was 'more gaunt and thin than ever' and appeared 'restless and ill at ease in body and mind. His black beard which had been shaved for the great expedition, had been allowed to grow, but is still short and scrubby. He took copious notes throughout the proceedings.'[25] Daniel Julian Bailey sat in the dock beside Casement. Monteith was still on the run and hiding in a bunker on a farm in County Limerick.

Over the next two days various witnesses were called. These included soldiers who had observed Casement's efforts to recruit Irish POWs at Limburg and individuals involved in his arrest in Kerry. Intelligence officers provided opinions about some of the items found on Casement, including the German train ticket found in his pocket. Once the statements had been heard, the two accused men were committed for trial. What is apparent from this initial stage of the trial is how the news channels were being very carefully controlled to mediate the official story. At some point during the Bow Street hearing, a photograph was illegally taken of the prisoner in the dock and syndicated to newspapers around the world. Meanwhile, in Dublin a backlash of public opinion had emerged in response to the ruthless series of secret courts martial and the executions of fifteen rebel leaders. Casement's trial was shaping up to be as much an exercise in public relations and a battle for hearts and minds as it was an instance of British war-time justice.

The accused man was now moved to Brixton Prison hospital, in the diocese of Southwark, where he was provided with the first proper meal since his arrival in London. The preliminary hearing had revived his energies and he now rose to the occasion. Over the centuries political trials had played a key role in defining relations between Britain and Ireland. The trials of Robert Emmet, Charles Stewart Parnell and Oscar Wilde endure as critically formative moments in understanding British-Irish relations. For the British government, however, the trial was not merely controversial but highly sensitive. Casement's career had turned him into an internationally respected figure. Many high-placed statesmen had campaigned and supported Casement over the years and various reputations were in varying degrees harnessed to Casement's story. Added to this was the American factor, as Britain was trying to diplomatically persuade the United States to come into the war as an ally. Casement not only had important friends in the US but his perspective and experience of the war might prove extremely damaging to this consummation of the special relationship.

On 16 May, at the morning Cabinet meeting, Sir Edward Grey circulated a confidential memorandum outlining the American point of view regarding Casement. The statement emphasised the need to prevent Casement from achieving martyrdom.

If Casement were executed it would lend dignity to an

absurd adventure which ought to have been smothered in ridicule. The way out was to commit Casement to a lunatic asylum without trial. [26]

The best course of action was to expose the protagonists of the Rising as a group of 'madmen' and deny them and their cause all intellectual justification. The memo recommended that a 'criminal lunatic asylum' was the best place for Casement and that a trial should be avoided as it would allow for 'unlimited opportunities for patriotic posturing.' The British public may have been unaware of much of the intellectual background to the Rising in terms of the Cultural Revival, but most people both at home and abroad were well aware of Casement and his laudable investigations into crimes against humanity. For that it was necessary to begin a process to close Casement down.

As soon as the hearing at Bow Street was over, Casement devoted himself to constructing a defence. He sank his energies into rallying every ally he had. Behind the scenes, Alice Stopford Green, his cousin Gertrude Bannister, the essayist and Gaelic Leaguer Robert Lynd, his wife Sylvia Dryhurst, and the journalist HW Nevinson worked hard to build support. During the latter half of May until his trial opened in the last week of June, he scribbled incessant notes to Gavan Duffy. He annotated and expanded his *Brief to Counsel*, and in the tradition of many Irish political prisoners before and afterwards, he kept a prison journal (which has not survived) and drafted and redrafted his speech from the dock. Both Alice Stopford Green and Gavan Duffy visited the prisoner frequently. But warders were always present and the content of conversations was quickly relayed to different state agencies. While Casement prepared for his last fight, his health improved.

To justify his action, Casement now sought to historically locate his treason and compare his actions to other independence struggles and freedom fighters. He had no problem whatsoever in admitting his treason. He believed that it had both an internal logic and historical precedence. What he wished to articulate was the evolution of his nationalist revolutionary trajectory and thereby vindicate his 'treason' to England by highlighting his patriotism and loyalty to Ireland. He drew up a memo *Things that Mrs Green might do for me or Robert Lynd*.[27] 'I want some striking instances from their own history,' he wrote to Mrs Green.

> What I want to establish is this – not that I did not commit high treason, because that of course I committed openly and knowingly, but that I did not act dishonourably or "treacherously". The Crown really wants to convict me not so much of the offence at law as of the mean, dastardly "betrayal of my country". I want to show that the very thing I did has been done again and again by <u>far</u> greater men, by the noblest men in history, men whom the English nation are asked to honour and praise for ever.[28]

One good example was the Italian soldier and politician, Giuseppe Garibaldi, whose story demonstrated the thin line dividing patriotism from treachery. Casement argued convincingly that his own actions and those of the other 1916 rebels were no different to the struggle of Garibaldi and the 'Young Italians'; a battle which the British government had openly supported.[29] At one point he mooted the idea of calling the historian of Garibaldi's life, GM Trevelyan, into the witness box on his behalf. In another essay, Casement dwelt at length about the hypocritical thinking of constitutional nationalists, who were prepared to defend Wolfe Tone's actions trying to 'seduce' Irishmen from their allegiance in 1798, and yet lambasted Casement's actions as reprehensible. In each of these comparative contexts, Casement demonstrated how his actions were no different to other independence struggles and how his perceived acts of treason had historical precedence, which in less inimical times had been applauded as patriotic acts. Was not William the Silent as guilty as he was in conspiring with the traditional enemy?

Was he not in deep confidence of Philip II & yet a rebel at heart & only waiting his time? Did he too not "betray his allegiance" & plan in secret beforehand while ostensibly in the King's council to free the Dutch provinces? … The present Br. Constitution is founded on an act of the basest treachery & some of the proudest names in the English peerage are derived from the act of betraying James II …

Please look up & verify the names of the leaders of the Whig Revolution of 1689 & their acts to get the Prince of Orange brought over to supplant his father-in-law.[30]

Beyond his efforts to establish historical precedent, he logically dissected the strategy adopted by his prosecutors and used this to question the very legality of proceedings against him and the hypocrisy underlying British treatment of Ireland. He wrote to Stopford Green:

They are really attacking me not on the legal charge at all – but on some thing other that the law has no cognisance of viz. my opinions. What they want to assert is that I had no right to hold certain opinions & be a public servant. That is nonsense. I was employed for my action and work & they cannot show I ever failed in that while I was a public servant. The fact that I held rebel views about Ireland is not their business – any more than if I held certain religious or atheistical views. The only thing the law has a right to assail me on is when did I translate my (well known) rebel views into action.[31]

But from an early stage it was apparent to Casement that his enemies wanted more than just a conviction. 'They want much more than the legal penalty. They want to damn my character as a man first & then hang me afterwards for the breach of law. They are welcome to my life & my body – my spirit is not theirs to hang or vilify.'[32] From his broad knowledge of Irish history, he was well aware of how the courtroom, like the prison, could be transformed into a theatre for the spectacle of resistance. Equally, the authorities were conscious that Casement would use the dock to help him to achieve the martyr's crown, and with public opinion starting to shift against the government in the wake of the execution of the other rebels, Casement's trial required careful handling.

A preoccupation for Gavan Duffy was the need to find a suitable barrister to lead the defence, as FE Smith was an intimidating opponent for anyone. Various senior barristers were approached, but each refused. On 19 May, Gavan Duffy wrote to his brother-in-law, AM Sullivan, to ask if he would take the Casement brief: 'I am particularly anxious to have an Irish barrister and there is no one but you at the Irish bar who can fit the bill,' he wrote. [33] On 24 May, Sullivan wired: 'Yes will act,' adding that he would accept the brief, but this would be no favour; he wanted professional fees for his work. 'It is obvious that I shall be at grave disadvantage in trying to adjust myself to a new atmosphere and new procedure', he predicted, adding 'I shall be useless to you with worry by the time we get to trial.'[34] The following day Sullivan was formally nominated as Counsel by the Lord Chief Justice.

The choice of Sullivan would remain a point of friction for many years. His father, also AM Sullivan, was a nationalist MP who took over editorship of *The Nation* from Charles Gavan Duffy and was one of the editors of *Speeches from the*

Dock, or Protests of Irish Patriotism, a critical work in shaping the Irish national consciousness. However, sons do not inevitably share the political sympathies of their fathers. Attaching Sullivan's name to Casement's trial may have strengthened the symbolic resonance with the Young Ireland movement, but it was a costly miscalculation. Sullivan proved to be hostile to Casement and his cause. In the years to come he went on the record several times, and on each successive occasion his antipathy to Casement became more apparent, while the justification of his own role in the trial became more defensive. His interest in the case was motivated primarily by financial gain and a desire to impress the legal fraternity. Rather than fight the case along the lines that Casement suggested – that as an Irishman he had the right to act against England – Sullivan wished to base his argument on a technical ruling against the law of treason. The problems resulting from the choice of Sullivan were further compounded by the family connection with Gavan Duffy, who was married to Sullivan's sister.

Casement and Sullivan disliked one another from the outset. On 2 June Casement drafted a long memo entitled 'Line of My Defence'. He was adamant in laying down his views on how he wished to approach the trial.

> The best defence is to admit one's full responsibility and accept all the consequences. This involves not only responsibility for the Rising in Ireland which was, without ques-

tion, based on my prior teaching, on my pro-Germanism,
on my presence in Germany and the hope of help from that
country derived from my being there …[35]

The object of the prosecution, he predicted, would be to
indict the German government and dismiss the Rising as a
'German plot'. Casement argued that in order to avoid this
it was 'essential to show that the idea, the aim, the responsibility for the rebellion arose with Irishmen, in Ireland, and
was carried to an issue by 'themselves alone', that in very
truth it was a Sinn Féin rebellion. 'For Ireland and Irishmen
throughout the world it is far better that they should realise
that this was a wholly Irish fight from start to finish.'[36] This
effort to frame the rebellion along nationalist rather than
internationalist lines, however, compromised Casement's
wider agenda for the Rising and his own intervention that
had purposely encouraged the discussion on cultural nationalism towards a discourse of anticolonial resistance. His conspiracies with other anti-imperial groups were a dimension
of his own revolutionary trajectory that he consciously suppressed within the context of his own defence.

Several leading socialist intellectuals, however, who sym-
pathised with Casement's work for international social justice and were opposed to the war spoke out in his defence.
The most important supporter in this respect was the Fabian
playwright, George Bernard Shaw. Shaw realised that the
war had presented a conflict of allegiances for the Irish. Both

Casement's trial and the Rising were a consequence of that conflict. To Shaw's mind, Casement had three possible lines of defence. He could plead insanity; he could throw himself at the mercy of the court and appeal for leniency based upon his sacrificial service for both the empire and humanity; or he could admit to what he had done and argue that it was out of a sense of duty for his country. Shaw's own sympathies had been shifted to the rebels because of the ruthless execution of the other leaders. On 5 June, Casement drafted a note for Mr Gavan Duffy about George Bernard Shaw:

> I shall be grateful if you will convey to Bernard Shaw my warmest thanks for the "defence" he wrote out & suggested and by your telling him that his view is mine ... I shall certainly dispute their jurisdiction to try an Irish rebel under an English statute by an English Court — but as they have my body they may do with it what they please — while the rest of me will remain unconvicted still.[37]

Shaw remained a vital intellectual ally of Casement over the next few months and offered sanctuary and counsel to Casement's cousin Gertrude Bannister as she boldly faced the brick wall of an unresponsive British Home Office. Casement's prison writings contain many references to Shaw and to his preface to *John Bull's Other Island*. The quite open support for Casement from British socialists, Fabians and members of the Bloomsbury group was doubtless bolstered by Shaw's defence of the Irish cause.

The decision to hire Sullivan to represent Casement did not deter the prisoner from writing copiously about his trial. This was partly done in response to aggressive strategies being implemented to control his narrative and to recapture the moral high-ground that Casement had occupied through his investigation of crimes against humanity. Casement continued to scribble furiously On 6 June, Sullivan wrote to George Gavan Duffy:

> Tell him he must stop scribbling. Papers get mislaid or over-looked or spied upon sooner or later. He has told us as much as can be of use – and everything else that is worse than useless.[38]

By early June it was apparent to the government and secret agencies of the state that Casement was preparing a coherent and measured defence. An aura of integrity had been lent to the moment by the supportive interventions of Shaw and other public intellectuals, especially Alice Stopford Green, whose leverage in the corridors of the Liberal Party in Britain remained considerable. Those few who could see through the fog of press deception and rumour-mongering could at least comprehend, if not necessarily condone, Casement's actions.

A deliberate plan was already well underway to further manipulate public opinion and alienate his intellectual followers. Most of the press was compliant with official versions of events and editors were doubtless aware of Casement's own outspoken criticisms of various organs of the press and their role as instruments of mass deception. He had already instructed Gavan Duffy to initiate proceedings against *The Graphic* for a double page illustrated story, run on 20 May 1916, describing Casement as the bungling puppet of Germany.[39] But a more insidious smear campaign was already well underway to destabilise Casement's defence council and his network of national and international support and to subvert his path to martyrdom.

In early May, Admiral Hall, the head of British Naval Intelligence, had invited a group of journalists to Whitehall to view pages from a diary allegedly found in the Casement trunks left in his former residence in Pimlico, and referenced in the last page of the interrogation transcripts. One of those journalists was Ben Allen of the Associated Press, and another was Mary Boyle O'Reilly (1873-1939), the daughter of the Fenian poet, John Boyle O'Reilly. At the start of the war, Mary O'Reilly had entered Belgium disguised as a peasant woman and had witnessed the burning of Louvain. She had significant influence among Irish-Americans and US philanthropists. On 3 June she wrote to Gavan Duffy:

> Mrs Green desires me to tell you, what I have just told her, that almost a month ago a group of important American journalists were called to Whitehall and there shown letters

and a diary of Sir Roger Casement's which proved him to be a moral offender unworthy of public sympathy.[40]

By early June the rumours had started to seriously destabilise the defence. On 8 June, Alice Stopford Green wrote to Gavan Duffy:

> I had a serious talk of an hour last night with Sir John Simon. He was perfectly horrified at the story I told him, and said that such an outrage on justice would be a dreadful slur, and that, if known to judge and jury, would have the opposite effect from what was intended. He promised me many times that he would make it his business to enquire today into the facts of the journalists' invitation and of Sir Robert Morant's warning. It impressed me that these alarms spread from two different centres. If he finds that there is truth in them he will probably let it be known in high quarters.[41]

The rumours of these secret diaries started to unhinge some of Casement's longest and most intimate friendships. On 8 June, Richard Morten and JH Morgan visited Casement and, after discussion about the trial, Morgan left the cell and left Morten alone with the prisoner. Towards the end of the conversation, Morten made reference to the rumours. Casement and Morten had known each other for almost twenty-six years and had an intimacy akin to brotherly love.

He told me that the only thing he said to R.C. of the kind
you indicated was the question at parting "What about the
other thing Roddy?" to which R.C. made no reply except
"Dick, you've upset me." M. said not a word about it being
common talk etc.[42]

Casement appears to have largely ignored the gossip and
Gavan Duffy shielded him from the rumours. Continuing
to work on his defence, on 10 June Casement wrote a four-
page 'Note for Counsel' wondering about the legality of his
prosecution in England under the Defence of the Realm
Act.[43] He went into some detail as to his handling by the
authorities and ended by saying that he would prefer to be
tried by military court.

They have put me before the High Court not to meet the
ends of justice, but to meet the ends of British World policy
by a sham trial for treason, which is really to be an impeachment of Germany & they think to have me as the instrument of impeachment.[44]

On 12 June, Casement, Gavan Duffy and Sullivan met at
Brixton and had a long meeting about the best course for
his defence. Casement was very depressed by the discussion
and the following day drafted a two-page memo on *Reasons
why Serjeant Sullivan's line must fail*. 'My objection to the line
he proposes is based on principle. He calls it "sentiment".
We are, as he says, "poles apart" … I think it is far better

therefore, since there is no counsel to support my line to do without them altogether and conduct my case myself.'[45]

Interest in the trial was attracting widespread attention in the US. The eccentric media tycoon, William Randolph Hearst, rowed in strongly behind Casement and his newspaper empire covered the story at close quarters over the following months. Michael Francis Doyle, the attorney sent to report on proceedings for Devoy and McGarrity, arrived into England on 13 June aboard the passenger steamer *St Paul*. British intelligence agencies had been forewarned of his arrival and were highly suspicious of his presence, so a plan was set in motion to manage his involvement. The legal adviser to the Home Office, Ernley Blackwell, tried to have an officer on board the *St Paul* gain Doyle's confidence, but the plot failed.[46] Casement hoped that Doyle could be used to go to Germany to pick up some papers and act as his emissary. He felt the Germans needed to be aware of how the trial was being used 'to implicate Germany in the Irish Rising' and defame Germany in the US 'as plotting to get Irishmen into trouble for her own selfish ends.'

> They may hang me – but I am going to stick up for Germany to the end & I want the German govt. to feel this, and if they help Mr Doyle as they should do in their own interests, we can convert the trial into an exposure of Shawn Bwee – and a strong defence of Ireland, Germany and the Freedom of the Seas.[47]

On his arrival in London, Doyle was taken to the Home Office and interviewed by Blackwell, who told him that he would not be allowed to travel to Germany and was expressly prohibited from discussing any such proposal with Casement. The following morning, 15 June, he went to visit Casement in Brixton Prison. His interview was conducted within the presence of the prison governor, and the planned visit to Germany was not mentioned. The refusal to allow Doyle to go to Germany was subsequently raised to suggest that the conviction had been achieved by preventing important witnesses and documentary material from being presented at the trial. Doyle cabled the *New York Times* with stories about Casement's ill-treatment at the hands of the prison authorities. In response, British secret service agencies extended their smear tactics and sent agents to work their influence in high places.

The trial took place over four days, from Monday 26 to Thursday 29 June, in the Royal Courts of Justice, a Victorian Gothic edifice at the top of the Strand on the edge of the City of London's financial district. The City was the control room of Britain's global financial power and its reputation had been greatly damaged by Casement's widely publicised investigation of the unethical role of British venture capital in the Amazon. Structural alterations were made to the court and a new dock erected in such a position to assure that Casement was in full view of the jury. The weather remained warm and sunny that week. Women wore summer gowns. Barristers looked uncomfortable in their thick woollen wigs and black robes. The packed courtroom was inadequately ventilated and stuffy.

The demand for tickets far exceeded available seating room. Gavan Duffy had difficulties finding places for the list of those who wished to attend. Casement's cohort of supporters was in court: Alice Stopford Green, Ada McNeill, Alice Milligan and Sylvia Lynd. HW Nevinson was covering the story for various news outlets. The social worker and poet, Eva Gore-Booth, the sister of the rebel leader the Countess Markievicz, attended, although she had never met Casement. Various figures from the diplomatic world discreetly slipped into watch events unfold. They included the recently widowed Argentine heiress, Grace Duggan, now engaged to the former viceroy of India, Lord Curzon; Casement's friend Nina Douglas-Hamilton, the Duchess of Hamilton and an anti-vivisection activist; and the former British ambassador to Brazil, Sir William Haggard.

As it was likely that there would be technical questions raised by the procedure of the case to do with the law of treason, this was a trial 'at bar' and held before three King's Bench judges. Presiding over the case was the Lord Chief Justice of England, Viscount Reading; beside him sat two senior judges, Mr Justice Avory and Mr Justice Horridge. There were thirty-seven objections to jury members before an exclusively male jury was agreed and the offence was read out:

> Sir Roger Casement is charged with the following offence:
> High Treason by adhering to the King's enemies elsewhere
> than in the King's realm – to wit, in the Empire of Germany
> – contrary to the Treason Act, 1351.
>
> Sir Roger Casement, Knight, on the 1st day of December
> 1914, and on divers other days thereafter, and between that
> day and the 21st April, 1916, being then – to wit, on the said
> several days – a British subject, and whilst on the said several
> days an open and public war was being prosecuted and car-
> ried on by the German Emperor and his subjects against our
> Lord the King and his subjects, then and on the said several
> days traitorously contriving and intending to aid and assist
> the said enemies of our Lord the King against our Lord the
> King and his subjects, did traitorously adhere to and aid and
> comfort the said enemies in parts beyond the seas without
> this realm of England – to wit in the Empire of Germany.

Six overt acts were then detailed. Five of them referred to
specific visits to the prison camps to address Irish POWs and
seduce them from their loyalty. The sixth charge concerned
his departure from Germany in a 'warlike and hostile expedition'. The convoluted and archaic tone of the charge did
not help clarify the complex situation faced by the jury.

Lord Reading then ruled on a number of matters that
could not be raised during proceedings. He restricted refer-

ence to the arming of the Ulster Volunteers, which some felt removed the last vestiges of fairness from the trial. If Casement's actions raising and arming the Irish Volunteers were an inevitable response to the arming of the UVF and the military mutiny at the Curragh, then the public would not be allowed to draw such conclusions. The belligerency of the Ulstermen, compounded by the refusal of the British army to protect the Home Rulers against their threats to fight, drove the Irish nationalists into a position where they had no recourse but to arm.

Another undeclared issue lingering in the background to the trial was the Marconi scandal. In the summer of 1912, just a few weeks before Casement's Putumayo report was published, senior cabinet ministers in the Liberal Party, including Lord Reading (Rufuis Isaacs), Herbert Samuel (the Home Secretary in 1916), and the future Prime Minister, David Lloyd George, were accused of insider dealing. Lord Reading, it was alleged, had influenced the mind of Samuel, the Postmaster-General, in his decision to award a lucrative government contract to install an imperial wireless chain to the American subsidiary of the Marconi Company. Isaacs' brother was managing director of Marconi. The named ministers had then all bought shares in the English Marconi Company, before the news became public and the value of the shares soared. The libel case was complicated by the decision by the cabinet ministers to employ as their defence barristers two of their most able political opponents: Edward Carson and FE Smith. While the fall-out from the Marconi scandal lingered on for many years and proved to be another nail in the coffin in the strange death of Liberal England, there were rumours that Casement's trial provided the opportunity for Lord Reading to return the legal favour to Smith. While such an allegation can only ever be speculative, the trial entered that highly combustible space where politics and justice mixed.

After the six charges of which he was accused had been read out, Sullivan then moved to quash the indictment on the ground that no offence known to the law was disclosed in the charges as framed. Despite his own wish to plead guilty, Casement eventually pleaded 'Not Guilty'.

FE Smith then opened for the prosecution. His strategy was to represent Casement's life in somewhat black and white terms by suggesting that there was no intellectual or political foundation for the treachery of the accused. Casement was regarded as a loyal public servant with impeccable credentials, whose turn towards rebellion in Ireland was fanatic, impulsive and incoherent. His support for Germany and his conspiracy against Britain were integral to his fanaticism. Gertrude Bannister's fear, expressed in advance of the trial, that her cousin would be too much associated with sympathy to Germany, proved right. Smith made much of the letter Casement wrote to Sir Edward Grey in the summer of 1911 thanking him for his knighthood. Once again the word 'seduce' echoed through the courtroom to describe efforts by the accused to persuade men to join the independence struggle.

Many of those witnesses, who over the next two days were placed under oath in the witness box, provided the evidence that ultimately condemned Casement. The words of those ordinary men, women and children of Kerry and the rank-and-file Irish soldiers of the British army were turned against the accused. Stories were elicited and used to belittle and humiliate the prisoner and his cause. Sympathetic accounts describe how Casement sat through the proceedings in a remarkably calm and detached way. Despite permission obtained from the Home Secretary, Herbert Samuel, (the man who, in an extraordinary twist of fate, had vocalised parliamentary anger against King Leopold II's regime in the Congo Free State back in 1903), Casement was not allowed visitors when the court recessed at lunchtime. Nevertheless, there was an upbeat feeling to how things were going. Half way through the trial Gavan Duffy wrote to Francis Joseph Bigger to thank him for the clothes that he had sent over from Belfast and commented 'everything is going splendidly.'[48]

At the start of the third day, the court was filled with members of the Bar interested in listening to the legal argument on the motion to quash the indictment. Sullivan looked pale and unwell, and asked if Morgan might continue the argument on his behalf. The discussion continued over the exact meaning of the law, but the Lord Chief Justice Reading eventually refused the motion to quash the indictment. Casement was then granted permission to clear up various misinformed statements – or 'abominable falsehoods', as he termed them. He categorically denied ever advising Irishmen to either fight alongside the Turks or with Germans on the Western Front (although this statement left him vulnerable to accusations of lying, because he clearly had planned for the Irish Brigade to be used in the liberation of Egypt). He took exception to the allegations that he had cut the rations of those who had refused to join the brigade or that he had sent some to punishment camps. He also rejected the rumour, spread initially in the American press, that he had accepted 'German Gold.' Finally, he completely refuted Smith's claim that Germany had financed and organised the rebellion.

Sullivan spoke next and addressed the jury at length on the issue of Irish identity, arguing that Casement was Irish and that his actions must be understood within the context of his Irishness. He claimed that Casement's work for the Empire was not in the service of England but for Ireland as part of that Empire. He went on to explain how Casement's own rebellious turn was part of the political confusion initiated with the signing of the Ulster Covenant in September 1912. But as Sullivan entered into analysis of the logic driving his political action, the Lord Chief Justice interrupted and asked him not to 'dredge up the embarrassing past.' But the moment had become too much for Sullivan, and overwhelmed by the pressure and heat of the moment he collapsed from nervous exhaustion. The case was adjourned until the fourth day.

The last day opened with an apology from the next senior barrister on Casement's counsel, Artemus Jones, apologizing for Sullivan, who could not attend court on doctor's orders. Jones then began to finish Sullivan's summing-up. He explained that Casement was really a product of the political polarisation brought about by the inability of the government to deliver Home Rule. He asked the jury to make a decision based on humanity.

It took the jury less than an hour to reach their verdict of 'Guilty' and it was then, almost as an afterthought, that Casement was allowed to have his moment.

From his personal papers released by the British Home Office in 1995, it is evident that Casement made two other drafts of his speech from the dock weeks in advance of his trial. In some respects this oration is as relevant to the justification of rebellion in 1916 as the *Proclamation of the Republic* read by Patrick Pearse from outside the GPO. In the century since its delivery, it has come to be recognised as a masterpiece of courtroom oratory. Even the most hardened opponents of Casement could not deny the power, lucidity and logic of the dialogue. Apart from its attention to style and content, the speech is full of rhetorical devices and rhythms that codify many of the intellectual struggles of his life into a single statement about rights: natural rights, sovereign rights and human rights. It resonates to the very core of discussion about universal questions to do with imperial power, national self-determination, and the relationship between law and history.

Spoken in a calm and measured voice, Casement's every word held the attention of the audience in the hot and over-crowded court room. By a calm deployment of a historical argument reaching back over five hundred years, Casement exposed the redundant nature of the law and the constitutional contradictions and tenuous foundations underpinning English rule in Ireland, where power was based upon oppression and the denial of fundamental civil rights. On another level, his speech eloquently justified his aims and actions in founding and arming the Irish Volunteers and vindicated his denunciations of the ruling elite in Britain and their policies which had resulted in a war of destruction without limits of either suffering or slaughter.

The speech built up to a resounding defence of Ireland's right to rebellion in 1914:

> We have been told, we have been asked to hope, that after this war Ireland will get Home Rule, as a reward for the lifeblood shed in a cause which, whomever else its success may benefit, can surely not benefit Ireland. And what will

Home Rule be in return for what its vague promise has taken, and still hopes to take away from Ireland? It is not necessary to climb the painful stairs of Irish history – that treadmill of a nation, whose labours are as vain for her own uplifting as the convict's exertions are for his redemption, to review the long list of British promises made only to be broken – of Irish hopes, raised only to be dashed to the ground. Home Rule, when it comes, if come it does, will find an Ireland drained of all that is vital to its very existence unless it be that unquenchable hope we build on the graves of the dead. We are told that if Irishmen go by the thousand to die, not for Ireland, but for Flanders, for Belgium, for a patch of sand in the deserts of Mesopotamia, or a rocky trench on the heights of Gallipoli, they are winning self-government for Ireland. But if they dare to lay down their lives on their native soil, if they dare to dream even that freedom can be won only at home by men resolved to fight for it there, then they are traitors to their country, and their dream and their deaths are phases of a dishonourable phantasy. But history is not so recorded in other lands. In Ireland alone, in this twentieth century, is loyalty held to be a crime. If loyalty be something less than love and more than law, then we have had enough of such loyalty for Ireland and Irishmen. If we are to be indicted as criminals, to be shot as murderers, to be imprisoned as convicts, because our offence is that we love Ireland more than we value our lives, then I do not know what virtue resides in any offer of self-government held out to brave men on such terms.

Self-government is our right, a thing born in us at birth, a thing no more to be doled out to us, or withheld from us, by another people than the right to life itself – than the right to feel the sun, or smell the flowers, or to love our kind. It is only from the convict these things are withheld, for crime committed and proven and Ireland, that has wronged no man, has injured no land, that has sought no domin-ion over others – Ireland is being treated today among the nations of the world as if she were a convicted criminal. If it be treason to fight against such an unnatural fate as this, then I am proud to be a rebel, and shall cling to my "rebel-lion" with the last drop of my blood. If there be no right of rebellion against the state of things that no savage tribe would endure without resistance, then I am sure that it is better for men to fight and die without right than to live in such a state of right as this. Where all your rights have become only an accumulated wrong, where men must beg with bated breath for leave to subsist in their own land, to think their own thoughts, to sing their own songs, to gather the fruits of their own labours, and, even while they beg, to see things inexorably withdrawn from them – then, surely, it is a braver, a saner and truer thing to be a rebel, in act and in deed, against such circumstances as these, than to tamely accept it, as the natural lot of men.[49]

Reactions to the speech were inevitably mixed. A heavily censored press was reticent in its reporting. But those who understood the symbolism of the moment would continue to speak out for many years to come. Wilfred Blunt described it as 'the finest document in patriotic history, finer than anything in Plutarch or elsewhere in Pagan literature'. When languishing as a political prisoner in the 1930s, Jawaharlal Nehru, the first prime minister of India, commented how 'it seemed to point out exactly how a subject nation should feel.' As recently as 2010, the former British Chancellor of the Exchequer, Norman Lamont (Conservative) claimed it as the greatest speech of all time.[50]

There is an assumption underpinning the working of the judiciary that law is always performed in pursuit of justice. This may be the intended ideal most of the time, but it is not always the case. It is especially difficult whenever issues to do with treason or martyrdom are in the balance. In Casement's trial, the law was clearly steered towards protecting the ruling elite and bolstering the coalition of executive power that was now determining the course of the war. Despite claims of fair play, the trial was never anything but a profoundly superficial exercise in impartiality. In time it would expose extremely disturbing dimensions of the functioning of British power and, in later years, the case was justifiably compared to a Stalinist show trial.[51] At the time, the tide of anti-German and anti-Irish feeling in England was used defiantly by the

State as an often crude exercise in propaganda and as a severe lesson to other potential traitors. In the ensuing decades the British justice system made determined efforts to cover up the murkier aspects of Casement's judicial assassination. Most of the leading players involved, including Lord Reading, FE Smith, Travers Humphreys, Artemus Jones, Basil Thomson, and AM Sullivan wrote their version of the events in volumes of memoirs intended to both obscure and clarify the different roles they had played. The moment provides lasting insight into what Lord Denning once described in his comments on the miscarriage of justice over the prosecution and conviction of the Birmingham Six as 'an appalling vista' into the ruthless workings of British State power during wartime.

Chapter Twelve

• • • • • • • •

July–August 1916

Appeal and Execution

After the trial, Casement was incarcerated in Pentonville Prison, in the Archdiocese of Westminster, to await execution. He was forced to wear convict clothing. Visits were restricted and he caught up on much-needed sleep. An announcement from Whitehall declared that he had been stripped of his CMG and degraded from knight of the realm; although he had anticipated such an eventuality and had voluntarily handed back his decorations in his letter to Sir Edward Grey in February 1915.[1]

His defense counsel immediately issued a notice of appeal based on three points. First, that the offence of high treason committed elsewhere than within the realm is not an offence within the statute of Edward III. Second, that the Lord Chief Justice was wrong in law and misdirected the jury as to the meaning of the words 'aid and comfort'. Third, that the Lord Chief Justice misdirected the jury in that he did not put the case for the defence adequately to them.[2]

Over the following days Casement studied the transcript of the trial and wrote a lengthy response: *Some of my Objections to the Lord Chief Justice of England's Charge to the Jury – 29 June 1916*.[3] It amounted to an astute critique of the law of high treason and why the charges against him were inconsistent with the facts. In his view, it was the distorting commentary in the press that had shaped the trial, along with the biased and politically-driven views of the Lord Chief Justice, and not the evidence placed before the court.

> What cannot fail to strike anyone who reads the report of my trial is the extraordinary discrepancy between the <u>facts</u>, as revealed in the evidence laid upon the Jury, and the circumstances as narrated in the public press, and so obviously present in the minds of everyone in Court.[4]

Casement took particular exception to the fact that he was being tried for his alleged acts in Germany, his landing in Ireland and for fomenting an armed insurrection. He argued that, to the contrary, he had tried to build peace and understanding between nationalists and loyalists, but had no option but to arm the Volunteers because of the lawlessness of Carson and Smith. He categorically accused Lord Reading of failing to preside over the trial with the expected level of impartiality and going 'out of his way to introduce points, not in evidence that must inflame the jury's mind against the prisoner.' In his fifteen pages of summing up, Reading had failed to make a single point in the prisoner's favour. More than this, he had stretched the meaning of treason to its limits with his suggestion that 'any act which weakens or tends to weaken the power of this country' was giving 'aid and comfort to the King's enemies' and therefore treasonable. Casement responded:

> If this be so then every conscientious objector is guilty of High Treason; many Christian Clergymen are guilty of High Treason; the Bishop of Limerick is guilty of High Treason; the workman who goes on strike is guilty of High Treason — in fact every class and calling may be guilty of High Treason and the Statute of Edward III should fill every jail and scaffold in the three kingdoms — but particularly in England for there is much more of this form of High Treason — constructive High Treason in the Realm of England than in the Realm of Ireland.[5]

Far from being 'the gravest crime known to law', as the Lord Chief Justice claimed, high treason was 'a matter of opinion' and 'a political offence to be proceeded against or not proceeded against according to the political complexion of the time, or the passion or fury of the time ... I call it the gravest piece of hypocrisy known to law.'[6]

In writing down this scathing critique of Lord Reading, Casement highlighted the presiding factor at the trial: the issue of loyalty. Beyond the prosecution of an avowed traitor, the trial was an exercise designed to test the boundaries of allegiance to both the Crown and the Empire. At 7.20 a.m. on 1 July, just two days after the trial ended, a huge mine was detonated on the Western Front at Hawthorn Ridge and the Battle of the Somme began. This convergence between Casement's conviction and the opening blasts in the Somme were integral to a new political and military offensive that would turn the course of the war. Over the following months, the Battle of the Somme resulted in a tragic loss of life, many of them Irish lives, and 1 July 1916 passed into the commemorative memory of the Ulster Volunteers as a symbol of its unyielding loyalty to the Union and the Empire. As thousands of lives were lost each day in bloody trench warfare, Casement's fate remained firmly in the balance.

Various friends argued for clemency, and campaigns to save him from the gallows were launched on several different national and international fronts. Eva Gore-Booth argued that his life should be spared because he had come to stop the Rising, an argument that was seen by many as potentially holding the most weight.[7] Behind the scenes, Alice Stopford Green used her influential network to find powerful allies, but the circumstances of the war meant that most public figures were at best reluctant and at worst hostile towards the campaigns for a reprieve. British intelligence had circulated correspondence that classified Stopford Green as 'a red hot revolutionist',[8] and her actions were closely surveillanced.

Increasingly isolated, Casement reconciled himself to his end. Despite strict restrictions, he managed to scribble a few letters in his final weeks. He wrote a chatty note to his cousins, Elizabeth and Gertrude, asking them to retrieve the books he had left behind at Brixton after his transfer to Pentonville. The safety of his papers became a major concern. In correspondence to Gavan Duffy he wrote:

> I also wish you to apply to the Home Office for the recovery of my personal effects seized by the police – and the restoration of all books and documents they may have extracted therefrom. I beg that formal application may be made for the complete restoration of all this property and its delivery to you as my legal representative. You are already acquainted with the manner in which I wish my private effects disposed of – and the whereabouts of important papers I wish to be secured after my death, and when peace comes for the custody of my heirs.
>
> I further beg of you as a last wish – or as if it be a last wish – to make absolutely clear from my letters and private papers in your hands and from the other sources of information given to you wherein I have been wrongfully and most untruthfully assailed in the course of the prosecution by the Crown witnesses. You are acquainted with the facts and I leave the vindication of my personal honour thus aspersed and falsely charged in your hands and those of my friends.[9]

Casement's awareness of the vulnerability of his archive was met by a strategy on the part of the authorities to restrict his rights to write. The prisoner was undergoing a process of silencing and those missing dimensions of state power that had colluded in his capture now engaged in taking control of the immense paper record of Casement's life. Since 1904, when Casement had first come to public attention for his report on the Congo, he had used his pen with extraordinary energy and efficacy to both describe and justify his path to rebellion. Because a considerable amount of his official work had been covert and constrained by the Official Secrets Act, there was much about his consular work that Casement was prevented from revealing, even to his closest friends. Equally, his deepening alliances with Irish republican and revolutionary causes had required great discretion when he mixed with his Foreign Office colleagues. This compartmentalising of his life had compelled Casement to become a master of dissimulation; his detractors would claim this to be evidence of a split personality, a Janus-faced Dr Jekyll and Mr Hyde. But as an Irish nationalist buttoned up inside the uniform of a British imperial official, he had spent much of his life concealing his Irish republican and anti-imperial sympathies from his superiors. Similarly, his work on behalf of the Foreign Office had required him to be extremely discreet about the nature of his official career when mixing within nationalist and republican circles.

In the last months, as he reconciled some of the deep paradoxes of his life, he encrypted comments that tried to clarify his trajectory from imperialist to rebel to revolutionary. Casement realised that this need for dissemblance in his life would render his story full of irreconcilable contradictions and very hard to tell. However, he had faith that whatever lies, silences or trickery were imposed, history would ultimately vindicate him. In a letter to Richard Morten he made a revealing reference to the deficit of public knowledge about him:

> Don't mind what anyone says about me, Dick – it is easy to pelt the man who can't reply or who is gone – but remember no story is told till we've heard all of it – and no one knows anything about mine – including those who think they know all! But I know most – and I know the reasons for everything in my own action and many of the reasons for much in the action of my friends. I have not attempted to tell my side – there is no use to begin with in trying to do what I have not liberty to do – so I must let it be, and bear the fate that came.[10]

On 17 and 18 July the appeal was heard at the Court of Criminal Appeal, once again in the Royal Courts of Justice. Casement had predicted the outcome as a forgone conclusion. 'If I had Solon for an advocate, the result, I fancy, would be the same', he wrote privately.[11] The moment brought another cohort of England's leading legal luminaries into the spotlight: Mr Justice Darling presided, supported by four other Judges of the King's Bench Division: Reginald Bray, AT Lawrence, Thomas Scrutton and James Atkin.

Most of the first day and a good part of the second were taken up with Sullivan's ponderous objection to the 1351 Treason Act. Casement's valid objection to Lord Reading's direction to the jury and the protestations about the admission of certain printed evidence by the prosecution were ignored by Sullivan. During the course of the appeal, it was revealed that Darling had visited the Public Record Office to check the original statue of 1351 with a magnifying glass to see if a comma had appeared in the critical sentence pertaining to the charge – namely, that he was 'adherent to the King's enemies in his realm giving them aid and comfort in the realm and elsewhere'. An argument was made that if a comma had appeared between 'realm' and 'giving', it would have altered the sense of the clause significantly, which gave rise to a popular view that Casement had been hanged on the strength of a non-existent comma. Darling concluded that Casement was 'the King's liege wherever he may be, and he may violate his allegiance in a foreign country just as well as he may violate it in this country.'[12] The conviction for high treason stood.

In a latter written immediately after the appeal, Casement wrote in a mocking tone about Sullivan's incompetence and his failure to address the three main points upon which the appeal had been based. Instead he had mired discussion in the legal minutiae of treason acts. The conversation confirmed Casement's view that 'were I free now I should not rest till I had committed a treason, high, low, or otherwise, that lay beyond the reach of statute, Judge or Jury – an amphibious treason that would lead me far 'beyond the venue' in a new world.'[13]

The appeal produced the most revealing (if mildly distorted) of all the contemporary interpretations of Casement's trial: Sir John Lavery's large painting entitled 'High Treason: The Court of Criminal Appeal'. Justice Darling was a friend of Lavery and permitted him to sit in the jury box with his wife Hazel and capture the moment for posterity. It would take Lavery more than twenty years to complete the work, and due to lingering embarrassments to do with Casement's trial it was never exhibited in the great reception hall of the Royal Courts of Justice as originally intended. Instead, it was placed on permanent loan to the King's Inns in Dublin, where it can still be viewed today.

The painting captured the sense of disciplined confusion in the court. Casement's face peers out from behind bars in the dock. He is deliberately positioned in the very centre of events – at the vanishing point in terms of the painting's perspective – but the attention of the crowded court is no longer focused on the prisoner. It is as if his relevance has ceased to matter. Above the prisoner's head, the hands of the clock are fixed at the Faustian hour of five to twelve. Despite capturing the moment *in situ*, Lavery took various liberties with the scene. He placed a group of unidentified women on the bench immediately in front of the accused, representing that close-knit group of female companions (such as Gertrude Bannister, Alice Stopford Green and Alice Milligan) who stood by Casement in the decades after his execution. Lord Reading, who was not present at the appeal, is also placed in the crowd immediately behind Sullivan.

The trial left a residue of bitterness and division. Gavan Duffy felt that Sullivan had mishandled the defence. Morgan wrote to Gavan Duffy, 'the fact of the matter is that our main point was never properly put to the court but we cannot say that! One can't repudiate one's own leader.'[14] Gavan Duffy wrote to Artemus Jones to defend Sullivan. Sullivan tried to excuse his own conduct by blaming Darling and he complained to Gavan Duffy that 'Darling's conduct was very bad – it was most unfair to the prisoner, and there was no occasion to make any pronouncement. I quite recognise that you had a grievance.'[15] Casement, too, was angry and wrote to Richard Morten on 28 July:

> My 'leader' Mr Sgt S. played me a sad trick at the end in dropping so important part of my appeal without a word of notice. You know what I always said of 'lawyers'! I say it now again – only more so … God deliver me, I say, from

such antiquaries as these to hang a man's life upon a comma, and throttle him with a semi-colon.[16]

Casement regretted that he had appointed Sullivan and would have preferred to have trusted in his Welshmen, Morgan and Jones. In years to come, Sullivan would do even greater disservice to Casement by making inappropriate public statements about his client and revealing information that was either fanciful or false. In two volumes of memoirs, Sullivan referred to his part in the Casement trial and made a deeply unfavourable oral statement to Casement's biographer René MacColl in the 1950s.[17] Even if the comments were true, they contravened the principles of client confidentiality. In the view of several senior members of the Irish Bar, Sullivan's indiscretions constituted 'gross and dishonourable professional conduct'. Following a vote, his name was removed from the roll of honorary benchers of the King's Inn.[18]

Beside Sullivan's untrustworthiness, the defence had a much greater problem to face: the burgeoning power of rumour. War tends to empower rumour and with so much of Casement's life shrouded in mystery, there was a rising tide of speculation to explain his path to treason. The logic of his actions was denied in the public, while the word 'madness' and 'lunacy' appeared in much private and official correspondence. US newspapers claimed Casement as a 'spy' and the secret dimensions of his life took on a life of their own. Alice Stopford Green wrote to Gertrude Bannister on

19 July from Courtown Harbour in County Wexford saying, 'He was practically unknown here. The story that he was an English spy has been spread everywhere and is believed.'[19] But it was the figment of the secret sex diaries, or Black Diaries as they are known today, that were widely deployed to destabilise his support, to foster confusion and to deny him the martyrdom he craved.

After the trial, the question of Casement's sexuality was made public mainly through the arteries of the pro-imperial press. It is fair to say that in 1916 the average British subject would have considered homosexuality to be a monstrous aberration. The liberal society of the twenty-first century and its toleration of gay lifestyles was a long way off. On 30 June 1916, *The Daily Express* commented: 'It is common knowledge that Sir Roger Casement is a man with no sense of honour or decency. His written diaries are the monuments of a foul private life. He is a moral degenerate.'[20] The following day the same paper added: 'There is no danger whatever that Ireland will ever look upon Casement as a martyr … Casement's diaries, which reveal him in the light of a moral degenerate, abandoned to the most sordid vices. They are unprintable, and their character cannot even be hinted at … Ireland does not make martyrs of such people.'[21]

The war-time propaganda machine stepped up a gear. A process intended to demonise the prisoner, similar to the wider stratagem used to dehumanise the rapacious 'Hun'

after the invasion of Belgium in 1914 – a policy that Casement had so forthrightly objected to in his essay 'The Far-
Extended Baleful Power of the Lie' [see Appendix] – swung
into action. Sexual rumours and salacious gossip were openly
used to malign the prisoner in the public imagination and
undermine his networks of support. If the British intelligence chiefs Basil Thomson and Reginald Hall had used the
rumours of the Black Diaries from early May to spin confusion and scurrilous gossip about Casement and destabilise his
defence counsel, their plan was now given a boost by a compliant press happy to vilify a condemned traitor. One rising
newspaper tycoon in particular, with a complex perception
of both history and propaganda and a vested interest in the
historical defence of the British Empire, rose to the occasion.

By the summer of 1916, *The Daily Express* was under the
controlling influence of the ambitious Canadian press baron
and Unionist MP, Max Aiken – created Lord Beaverbrook in
1917 – a close friend and political ally of FE Smith, Andrew
Bonar Law and Winston Churchill. Beaverbrook was destined to become the first Minister of Information in 1918,
when he assumed responsibility for Allied propaganda. Since
1911, he had been lending money to prop up *The Daily
Express* and its editor RD Blumenfeld, and in November
1916 he bought managing control of the paper. It is significant that Lord Beaverbrook's two flagship newspapers, *The
Daily Express* and *The Evening Standard*, and some of his lead-

ing newspapermen would emerge as central to sustaining the story of the Black Diaries and fuelling the anti-Casement campaign in the British press for several decades to come. Beyond his work as a newspaper proprietor, Beaverbrook was also a proficient historian who understood the centrality of primary sources to the writing of history. During his life he cultivated friendships with a number of leading British historians, most notably his official biographer AJP Taylor.

Between the end of the trial and Casement's execution, gossip about the Black Diaries circulated widely and confused Casement's potential supporters at the highest levels of influence. Copies were shown to King George V and John Redmond. The former missionary John Harris, Casement's colleague from the antislavery campaigns on the Congo and Putumayo, was summoned to the Home Office and used to authenticate the documents on behalf of the Archbishop of Canterbury, Dr Randall Davidson. Another voice prepared to approve the Black Diaries was the influential banker, Sir William Wiseman, recently appointed by the director of the Secret Intelligence Service (also known as MI6), Mansfield Smith-Cumming, to establish a satellite agency in New York.[22]

The Home Office did, however, admit in March 1994 that they used the diaries to engineer a smear campaign to counteract the pleas for clemency. Various arms of the British secret services at home and abroad collaborated in a co-ordinated campaign to assassinate Casement's character. Basil Thomson showed diary extracts to the US Ambassador, Walter Hines Page 'and pointed out the innocuous passages that identified the writer as well as the filthy parts.'[23] Page was another influential journalist and publisher whose pro-British stance during the war influenced President Woodrow Wilson's sympathies for the allies. Many of those individuals whose support Casement had deliberately sought out and courted over the years for his various campaigns were now harnessed to authenticate the Black Diaries in public and endorse the view that Casement was some kind of unaccep-table moral deviant.

So what did Casement know about these rumours in the last weeks of his life? One of the few surviving state-ments about Casement being aware of these documents is an undated report made by the US attorney, Michael Francis Doyle:

> When the trial was over, Gavan Duffy and I agreed we should tell Casement about this gossip. He was astounded at first and then he became bitterly indignant ... He referred to the reputed habits of certain individual Englishmen among his persecutors. But still he said he could not get it into his mind that the British would stoop to such forgery to destroy his character. It was clear to Gavan Duffy and me that the diary was not his; and he emphatically repudiated it ... he thought that they might be using some notes from his

records concerning official investigations he had conducted but that there could be nothing referring to any personal acts of perversion except what was false and malicious.[24]

On 15 July, Gavan Duffy wrote to Gertrude Bannister, who was working in the background to find out the source of the rumours:

> The suggestion that I should take any notice of the allegations about a diary belonging to Roger Casement does not commend itself to me. No such diary has the remotest connection with the case on which I am engaged and these rumours are simply spread about from the lowest and most malicious motives, a proceeding which is beneath contempt and which it would be preposterous to expect me to notice.[25]

On 18 July, a Cabinet Memorandum made the first official reference to the Black Diaries and their strategic deployment to prevent Casement from attaining martyrdom. It alleged that

> Casement's diaries and his ledger entries, covering many pages of closely typed matter, show that he has for years been addicted to the grossest sodomitical practices. Of late years he seems to have completed the full circle of sexual degeneracy, and from a pervert has become an invert – a 'woman' or pathic who derives his satisfaction from attracting men and inducing them to use him…[26]

The parallels with the trial and public humiliation of both Charles Stewart Parnell and Oscar Wilde are not hard to draw. But while Wilde privately revelled in his sexual difference, Casement was all too conscious that his reputation and the cause he stood for required him to maintain a whiter-than-white image.

In the weeks between his capture and execution the diaries successfully undermined Casement's support-base. But despite the wide circulation of rumours and a government-sponsored smear campaign, pleas for clemency reached the government from many quarters. Gertrude Bannister supplied a petition including many artists and literary figures from the Bloomsbury set.[27] Alice Milligan, who would emerge after Casement's trial as a stalwart campaigner for the rights of Irish republican prisoners, forwarded two petitions signed by 'Ulster Liberals'. Another Irish petition was organised by Colonel Maurice Moore and signed by Cardinal Logue, six Roman Catholic Bishops, twenty-three members of Parliament and forty-two representatives of Irish universities.[28] Another appeal, organised by Arthur Conan Doyle and Clement Shorter, and supported by prominent British academics, journalists, social reformers and Anglican bishops, arrived at 10 Downing Street on 26 July.[29]

Using whatever influence she could, Alice Stopford Green applied pressure at the highest level of executive and legislative power. She contacted Viscount Haldane, the former Lord

Chancellor, who spoke to his successor, Lord Buckmaster, but Haldane wrote back to say that both he and the Lord Chancellor were powerless to do anything: it was a cabinet decision.[30] In her final meeting with Casement, Stopford Green assured him that petitions had come from officials at all levels of Irish society: JPs, boards of guardians, councillors, bishops, priests and parishes had organised and appealed on Casement's behalf.[31] But it was all in vain.

On 24 July it was made public that FE Smith would not allow Casement to apply for an appeal to the House of Lords. The idea that Smith, in his position as Attorney General, should have wielded the last word in deciding the fate of his political enemy was one further perverse quirk of fate in this murky legal entanglement. A letter appeared in the *Manchester Guardian* on the same day from Mrs Hanna Sheehy-Skeffington, addressed to the Prime Minister:

> As the wife of one whose life was taken wrongfully and without trial during the recent rising, and as the victim of many wrongs yet unredressed, I feel that I have the right to approach you to ask you to prevent any further shedding of the blood of my countrymen by sparing the life of Sir Roger Casement, now under sentence of death, though he may be deemed guilty technically under British law. I hope you will exercise wisdom and humanity by seeing that in his case at least the extreme penalty is not exacted. In expressing this wish I am conscious that I am speaking in the name of my

murdered husband, who abhorred the taking of life under all circumstances and that I am voicing the sentiments of the majority of the Irish people.[32]

Further pressure was applied in the US. John Quinn organised a petition and forwarded it to the British ambassador, Cecil Spring-Rice. An impressive list of academics, newspaper editors and businessmen openly advocated a reprieve. Quinn's influence within legal circles was evident from the support of two heavy hitters: William Guthrie, leader of the American Bar, and George Wickersham, a former US Attorney General.[33] The Negro Fellowship League asked for clemency after a unanimous vote at a meeting in Chicago, stating: 'But for him the world might not have known of the barbarous cruelties practiced upon the helpless natives.'[34] In South America, a further appeal was made by the President of Colombia, where the Senate and Chamber of Deputies had each adopted resolutions demanding mercy for his humanitarian work.[35]

In the last days of July, a debate in the US Senate brought anti-British sentiments boiling to the surface.[36] On 25 July, two resolutions were passed requesting President Woodrow Wilson to ask the British Government to exercise clemency in the treatment of Irish political prisoners and to obtain commutation of the sentence of death. One senator made the point:

The same aspirations and sentiments that animated George Washington, John Adams, Sam Adams, Thomas Jefferson,

Alexander Hamilton, Benjamin Franklin, Warren at Bunker
Hill, Nathan Hale, John Stark, Anthony Wayne and Daniel
Morgan in our Revolutionary War animated and controlled
Sir Roger Casement, Patrick H. Pearse, Thomas J. Clarke
and their compatriots and coadjutors in 1916.

The debate provided an opportunity to confirm Ireland's
immense contribution to the building of modern American
democracy. But the resolutions from the Senate met with
opposition from-the Committee on Foreign Relations. On
27 July they deemed it inexpedient that the Senate should
adopt either of the resolutions. Not to be out-manoeuvred,
the Senate debated the issue again on 29 July.[37] Spring-Rice
kept Whitehall closely advised on developments. At 10.45
a.m. on 30 July, a telegram was sent to the Home Office
stating that the opposition from the Committee on Foreign
Relations had been ignored and the 'Senate has passed by
a large majority resolution requesting President to ask His
Majesty's Government to exercise clemency in treatment of
Irish political prisoners.'[38]

On 1 August a telegram from Spring-Rice was circulated at the cabinet meeting in London. It warned of 'a
great explosion of anti-British sentiment' if Casement's
execution went ahead, and a possible blockade of American
manufactured munitions destined for English ports. Finally,
he advised the British press to observe 'reserve under prov-
ocation.'[39] But the cabinet was split. It was rumoured at

Westminster that Smith had threatened to resign from the government if a reprieve was granted. Lord Lansdowne, on the other hand, who sat as Minister without Portfolio in the coalition cabinet, remained reticent. His previous support for Casement during his Congo campaign made him cautious and the Lansdowne family's long connection with Ireland and their estates in County Kerry made him hesitant to support the hardliners.

On the morning of 2 August, the cabinet met and the following statement was placed on the record:

> The greater part of the sitting was occupied in a further & final discussion of the Casement case, in view of some further materials and the urgent appeals for money from authoritative & friendly quarters in the United States. The Cabinet were of the opinion that no ground existed for a reprieve, and Edward Grey drew up a statement of reasons to be shown by Sir C. Spring Rice to Senator Lodge & others.[40]

Grey's telegram to Spring-Rice was then circulated among the cabinet ministers. It stated unequivocally that a reprieve would 'not be consistent with justice or tolerable to public opinion.' It reconfirmed the view that Casement was the leader most to blame for the Easter Rising and could not be spared when less important men had already been executed. Grey was ruthless in his ultimate condemnation: 'There is

nothing either in his public action or his private character that can be pleaded in extenuation of his action and in
favour of mitigation of the sentence.'[41]

On the afternoon of 2 August, Spring-Rice informed
the Home Office that during a conversation with Michael
Francis Doyle, he had been told privately that 'Clan na Gael
want Casement executed.'[42] John Devoy was in the process of turning openly against Casement, as he believed that
Casement's writings had contributed towards the betrayal of
secret aspects of the Rising. As yet he was unaware of just
how much of the transatlantic communication between Ireland, Germany and the US had been intercepted. It would
later emerge that it was Devoy's dispatch, sent to the German
General Staff on 16 February 1916, that had provided Admiral Hall and Basil Thomson with confirmation that a Rising
around Easter time in Ireland was planned. Was Devoy
deflecting some of his own culpability for this critical mistake by turning on Casement?

Despite Devoy's private views, efforts to save Casement
from the scaffold continued in the US. At 8.05 a.m on the
morning of Casement's execution, a telegram was placed
on the desk of the Home Secretary Herbert Samuel from
Spring-Rice:

> If Casement is executed you must be prepared for a most
> serious situation here. President is very personal and his
> attitude towards us, already changing, will become hostile

by force of circumstances and immense influence of Irish in his party. American public, which never reasons, will be inflamed against England and we may anticipate political difficulties of a serious kind, not to mention crimes like late explosions at New York. On the other hand a reprieve at President's request would strengthen his hands in dealing with his own party and place him under deep obligations to us. Publication of Casement's diary will only be looked on as an act of revenge and would only be effective if his life is spared.[43]

The prisoner whose fate was being discussed in these undisclosed diplomatic and cabinet exchanges was oblivious to the situation. For Casement, the priority of these days was to reconcile himself to his fate. Before the trial he had written to his uncle: 'Some day, a rather interesting account of my doings will come to light I hope – altho' I shall not be able to revise the proofs – but it will show a side of the picture that people now in this jaundiced time don't understand ... I have left a pretty full record.'[44] Control of this 'pretty full record' now became the critical issue for both Casement and the authorities trying to close him down.

On a legal level, Casement requested Gavan Duffy to open a correspondence with the Metropolitan Police and retrieve the papers confiscated from his rooms in Pimlico. His final letters contain several veiled, ambiguous and encrypted references and clues about how his paper trail would eventually lead to a revised and more sympathetic view of who he was and why he had chosen such a perilous path to the gallows. A presiding concern was how little was actually known of him. As much of his life had been conducted in secret, either in the service of the Foreign Office or in his subversive work for Ireland and the republican movement, it was inevitable that confusion would continue for many years to come about his relevance to the Irish rebellion. In a letter to his sister Agnes, he explained:

> It is a cruel thing to die with all men misunderstanding – misapprehending – and to be silent forever. I left a letter with a friend that will tell a great deal of the truth – not all – but part of it some day, and perhaps some of it you know already … If I could only tell you the whole story but, that too, is part of my punishment – of the strange inscrutable fate that has come to me – that I am not only being put to death in the body but that I am dead before I die – and have to be silent and silent just as if I were already dead – when a few words might save my life – and would certainly change men's view of my actions.[45]

Elsewhere, he referred to a large archive of papers left with Joe McGarrity (or 'at St Joseph's' as he put it). This tranche included many of his propaganda writings and poems, and he insisted that his political writings be published.

> I want you both to collect all my writings – the old ones

in *Irish Freedom*, *Sinn Féin* and *United Ireland* – the toothless one [presumably Bulmer Hobson] knows many of them and F.J.B. some … If I had lived I should have told the whole story – one reason they want to kill me is to destroy the evidence … of their crime.[46]

If Casement believed that his execution was largely because he knew too much about the inner workings of power, he trusted that his political writings would ultimately vindicate his action. 'Remember it is *The Crime against Europe* that is the key to all recent doings in Ireland',[47] he confided. Certainly, the essays make a strong case as to why Irishmen should not fight in defence of the Empire, the very instrument of their own oppression. Casement's letters, written in his last days, bristle with heart-felt emotion and humility. His prophetic tone is tempered by transparent sentiments of love for his family, for his friends, for Ireland, and a presiding conviction in the moral purpose of his life. This was not easily understood in the context of an all-consuming war. His belief in the righteousness of his cause and of the rebels against the Empire remained unshaken.

The vacuum in the wider public understanding of Casement in Ireland was filled with a short biographical pamphlet, published in July 1916, by LG Redmond Howard, a nephew of John Redmond. Considering the circumstances in which it appeared, this provided a comparatively balanced and thoughtful assessment of this most enigmatic and complex of men, written between his trial and execution. Casement was upheld as:

> a man with a mission – a philosopher of history, a prophet, and his allegiance was to his vision, and to nothing and no one else; indeed, if anything he had to convert the whole Irish race to a new conception of themselves in world politics.'[48]

By adopting words associated with religious commitment such as 'mission', 'prophet', 'vision' and 'convert', Redmond Howard grasped that sense of zeal driving Casement from an early point in his life. Casement aspired towards a utopian future for independent Ireland built upon a new moral order and based on a genuine sense of compassion, humanity, grace and justice. For the most part his views were moderate and not those of an extremist. In the twenty-first century – an age when martyrdom is often associated with fanaticism, and the majority find it hard to even protest for a cause, let alone die for one – the sacrifice of the 1916 rebels is sometimes challenging to comprehend and is easily dismissed as a pointless act by men and women of violence. But many of the ideals encoded in the *Proclamation of the Republic* were progressive for their day and armed insurrection was to become the dominant mode of anti-imperialist activism throughout the twentieth century.

The configuration of the Rising with the cycle of sacrifice

and resurrection celebrated each year in the Christian calendar was symbolism close to Casement's heart and soul. A spirit of self-sacrifice had endured as a defining dynamic of his life. Though he would turn towards the Catholic Church in his last days, his faith cannot be reduced to mere support for institutional religion. Written fragments and sacred artefacts provide evidence of his engagement with different hallowed dimensions, including the esoteric and supernatural. Among the few possessions he distributed among his friends at the very end of his life were a crucifix, rosary beads, and devotional scapular. When Eva Gore-Booth wrote in her obituary 'how the long years of selfless devotion and affectionate friendships had brought him into harmony with the unseen purposes of the universe, and very near to the Divine meaning of human life'[49] she touched on a mystical side of Casement that in a post-faith age is difficult to grasp.

His personal concept of humanism extended from traditional nineteenth-century missionary philanthropy, although this had gradually transformed into something that is more akin to an empathy and compassion evident in the teachings of Christ in line with its later manifestation in liberation theology. His critique of the system was mediated through the suffering of the victims and he believed fervently that the church had a role to play in the collective liberation of oppressed peoples from social, economic and political injustice. In Africa, he had grown close to many of the leading missionaries who had helped to pioneer the interior in the name of Christianity. The Congo Reform Association in its early years had a strong ecumenical appeal to unite Catholic, Protestant, Non-Conformist and Dissenter in a shared higher purpose. Furthermore, both the Pope and the Archbishop of Canterbury had recognised and supported his work in Africa and South America.

In July 1911, he wrote to Alice Green a comment that was deeply humanist, expressing his belief that the conscientious citizen or subject held a responsibility to improving the world:

> Life is more beautiful than death – and the world we live in and should work for more lovely than all the plains of heaven. There can be no heaven if we don't find it and make it here and I won't barter this sphere of duty for a hundred spheres and praying wheels elsewhere.[50]

His writings on South America identified the role of the missionary tradition in delivering some level of protection to the Indians. His work to raise money and organise a Franciscan mission in the Putumayo had helped bring some improvement to the region. In Germany, he had identified the need for the religious requirements of the prisoners of war to be catered for. As his own spirits and hopes were depleted, he had found solace also in his friendships with these Catholic priests, who helped him intensify his belief.

In spite of his commitment to the spirit of Catholicism, his instinct remained ecumenical. Throughout his life there is evidence of a spirituality that transcended denominational difference and was rooted in a personal interpretation of the teachings and example of Christ. The fact that he was baptised into both the Church of Ireland and Catholic faiths is significant. Indeed, that religious divide that came to define the cultural difference in Ireland was reconciled within his being and example. Towards the end, his unequivocal rejection of Anglicanism and the King James Bible was entangled with his wider denunciation of the British Empire and its instruments of propaganda.

On another level, part of Casement's self-invention was conceived through the prism of saintliness. In his most personal correspondence to Gertrude, he makes quite regular (if humorous and self-deprecating) reference to his life and work as a latter-day saint.[51] He had a particular regard for the navigator monk St Brendan and the early church fathers. On the last day of his trial he left a life of St Columbanus, which he had perused as his sentence was delivered, in the dock. The books he read in prison were distributed after his death by Alice Stopford Green; they included an annotated copy of St Thomas a Kempis's *The Imitation of Christ,* a life of St Augustine and the devotional poetry of Aubrey de Vere among other religious tracts and works.

The path leading to his conversion to the Roman Catholic faith in the hours before his execution was not an easy one. Doubt beguiled him in those last weeks. He wrote in a letter in July to Father Murnane:

> I don't want to jump, or rush or do anything hastily just because time is short. It must be my deliberate act, unwavering and confirmed by all my intelligence. And alas! to-day it is not so. It is still I find, only my heart that prompts from love, from affection for others, from associations of ideas and ideals, and not yet my full intellect. For if it were thus the doubts would not beset me so vigorously as they do. I am not on a rock – but on a bed of thorns.[52]

Having grappled with the logic of such a decision, Casement eventually converted. But this proved not to be straightforward. Cardinal Francis Bourne, the Archbishop of Westminster, demanded he renounce the treason of his actions and confess the error of his ways. Casement refused. Defiant and unrepentant to the end, he wrote in his final letter to his cousins on the eve of his execution a letter that boldly connected Christ's teaching to the cause of Irish freedom and coupled the divinity of Christ to the divinity of the nation:

> God will surely give freedom to Ireland.
>
> Irishmen, live unselfishly and die faithfully and fearlessly for Ireland, as the men of 1916 have done, and no power of Man or Empire of Gold can withhold freedom from men so vowed. What was attempted so valiantly this year by a

handful of young men is the <u>only</u> episode of this war that should survive in history. The rest is either mistaken slaughter of brave men or plotting to destroy an enemy by hate for motives of greed and dominion. I cast no stone at the millions of brave dead men throughout Europe – God rest their souls in peace – but the cause it is alone that justifies the end, and the cause of all the great combatants is essentially selfish and greedy.

Ireland alone went forth to assail evil, as David Goliath, unarmed, save with a pebble, and she has slain, I pray to God, the power and boast and pride of Empire. That is the achievement of the boys of 1916, and on it the living shall build a sterner purpose, and bring it to a greater end.

If I die tomorrow bury me in Ireland, and I shall die in the Catholic Faith, for I accept it fully now. It tells me what my heart sought long in vain – in Protestant coldness I could not find it – but I saw it in the faces of the Irish. Now I know what it was I loved in them – the chivalry of Christ speaking through human eyes – it is from that source the lovable things come, for Christ was the first Knight. And now my beloved ones goodbye – this is my last letter from the condemned cell. I write it always with hope – hope that God will be with me to the end and that all my faults and failures and errors will be blotted out of the Divine Knight – the Divine Nationalist.[53]

This final paragraph in his final letter to his beloved cousins was also repeated and extended in a statement made to the Scottish priest, Father James McCarroll, who attended him in his last hours. Casement asked if the statement could be circulated widely to the people of Ireland. It fed into the long Irish revolutionary martyrology in the fight for Irish freedom:

Think of the long succession of the dead who died for Ireland – and it is a great death. Oh! That I may support it bravely. If it be said I shed tears, remember they come not from cowardice but from sorrow – and brave men are not ashamed to weep sometimes …

It is a strange, strange fate, and now, as I stand face to face with death I feel just as if they were going to kill a boy. For I feel like a boy – and my hands so free from blood and my heart always so compassionate and pitiful that I cannot comprehend how anyone wants to hang me …

It is they – not I – who are the traitors, filled with a lust of blood – of hatred of their fellows.

These artificial and unnatural wars, prompted by greed of power, are the source of all misery now destroying mankind …

Alas, so much of the story dies with me – the old, old story – yet, in spite of all – the truth and right lives on in the hearts of the brave and lowly. It is better that I die thus – on the scaffold …

It is a glorious death for Ireland's sake with Allen, Larkin and O'Brien and Robert Emmet – and the men of '98 and

William Orr – all for the same cause – all in the same way.

Surely it is the most glorious cause in history.

Ever defeated – yet undefeated.[54]

A direct witness statement regarding Casement's last hours appeared many years later: the pacifist and anti-imperialist, Archibald Fenner Brockway, when serving time in Pentonville for distributing anti-conscription leaflets, recalled a final glimpse of the prisoner the night before his execution:

> I was in my cell and I heard steps outside. I stood on my stool and looked from the window. There was Sir Roger Casement, in the only place of loveliness in that prison, a little garden of hollyhocks and other flowers, looking at the sunset for the last time. As he did it, one could see that his spirit and his personality became united with the infinite beauty of that scene. In my view, when this country executed Sir Roger Casement the next morning it was committing a crime against the very deepest things of the spirit, whatever his reputation may have been.[55]

At her house in Grosvenor Road on the Thames embankment, Alice Stopford Green gathered her closest friends together for an all-night vigil. The eminent war correspondent, Henry Nevinson was present and wrote a moving account:

> We sat with Mrs. Green through the night, and while he in

his cell was watching for the dawn of his death, she continued to speak to us of life and of death with a courage and
a wisdom beyond all that I have known. It was as though
we were listening to the discourse of Socrates in the hours
before his own execution. So profoundly wise she was, so
cheerful and humorous through it all.[56]

Father Thomas Carey, a Catholic priest who attended to
the prisoner in the hours before his execution, wrote:

He died with all the faith and piety of an Irish peasant
woman, and had, as far as I could judge, all the dispositions,
faith, hope, charity and contrition, resignation to God's will
etc. to meet his Creator. I gave him the Holy Father's bless-
ing with Plenary Indulgence attached shortly before his
execution and for half an hour before he followed me in
fervent and earnest prayer.'[57]

At 7.30 on the morning of his execution, mass was said
in the prison chapel and Casement received his first Holy
Communion, which was also his *viaticum* (last rites). After
this he refused to eat, and prayed until the escort arrived to
take him to the scaffold.

Casement died shortly after 9 a.m. on 3 August 1916. At
six minutes past nine, the bell tolled to announce his death.
A photograph has survived of the crowd gathered outside
the gate of Pentonville in Caledonian Road, many of them
munitions workers from a local factory. The expression on

most of the faces is difficult to read and it is hard to tell whether they had come to celebrate or to protest. In a side street adjoining the prison, some of Casement's closest companions knelt down to pray.

After a highly invasive autopsy Casement's body was dumped unceremoniously into an unmarked grave and covered with lime to hasten the disintegration of his flesh and bones.[58] It would be forty-nine years before his bleached remains were finally brought back to Ireland, not to Murlough Bay, as he wished, but to Glasnevin cemetery in Dublin, where his grave can be visited today.

In Ireland, Casement's death provoked different reactions. The future IRA hunger striker, Terence McSwiney, who would die in Brixton prison in October 1920, decided to begin his diary on the morning of the execution. 'I think no day is better for a beginning than this 3rd August which will be forever memorable as the day on which Casement died.'[59] Some years later, the literary critic Clement Shorter claimed that his wife, the poet Dora Sigerson Shorter, 'never recovered from the torture of that execution'; she died of a broken heart in 1918.[60] Casement's brother Charlie lapsed into a state of deep depression for many months, and his sister Nina suffered from bouts of hysteria for the rest of her life.

But there were other reactions. Several of Casement's allies and comrades, fearing for their own safety, distanced themselves from the disgraced traitor. 'FJB [Francis Joseph Bigger]

is in an awful fright, as you know, for fear he should be connected with him', Gertrude Bannister wrote to Gavan Duffy,
a few weeks after the execution.[61] For many years afterwards,
the mention of Roddie's name in the Casement ancestral
home, Magherintemple, was strictly forbidden. But his closest friends and family never forgot. Those loyal companions
touched by his life cherished his memory and passed their
stories on fondly to the next generation. In the following
decades, moving personal memoirs were written and stowed
away, or privately circulated until such time as the fog of war
had cleared and the climate of understanding had changed.

In the ancient tradition of martyrdom, Casement rose
above bitter hatred and public humiliation. Instead, he found
an immense amount of forgiveness and love in his heart in
those final days. He ignored the squalid political bartering of
reputations in the background to his trial and the manipulative antics of his enemies and traducers. The word, 'martyr'
means 'witness' and the first martyrs were those who bore
witness to their times and were often executed for their testimonies. More than perhaps any figure of his day, Casement
witnessed and described the excesses and violent impact of
empires. But if his enemies believed that his death would
bring an end to his story they were very much mistaken; if
anything, it brought about a new beginning. Roger Casement proved to be even more minacious dead than he had
been alive.

He had placed the Irish struggle in a broader context, transcending national boundaries and religious divisions. Though he lived simply and frugally, he was a complex man and his legacy is even more complicated. Both his achievement and appeal lie in how he crosses boundaries without having compromised his values: thus he can be the subject of an Irish nationalist's poem or the novel of a Peruvian Nobel Laureate; he is both the monastic aesthete and the gay icon; he can appeal to the Congolese anti-imperialist or the British socialist; he is a source of fascination for the Spanish diplomat or the Irish republican prisoner. Put simply, Casement overrides narrow and restrictive identities to speak to all those with a concern for rights and freedom.

Chapter Thirteen

1916-2016

History as Mystery:
An Inside Story

Of the estimated nine million lives lost in the catastrophic bloodbath of the First World War, the death of Roger Casement, from a political and cultural perspective, was one of the more portentous and ultimately menacing. The troubling transformation of the fêted and decorated agent of the Foreign Office into a reviled conspirator, hell-bent on the overthrow of the British Empire, was a story that would inevitably intrigue people for generations to come. It had involved a web of interconnecting conspiracies linking the highest agencies of state power. On the road to the scaffold, Casement had revealed nefarious dimensions of European imperialism and the ruthless, terrorising capacity of the British Empire. He also highlighted a tradition of administrative corruption in the English governance of Ireland. In his capacity as a consul in Africa and South America, Casement learnt to speak truth to both power and the powerless, but when he turned his voice on his former paymasters, his fate was sealed.

His political writings had forthrightly accused leading politicians of the age, including Sir Edward Grey, Winston Churchill and James Bryce, of instigating a deliberate strategy to deceive the British people and of involving the world in a war that was the consequence of a decade of democratically unaccountable secret diplomacy. Britain's justification for declaring war in defence of small nations was merely a mask for the protection of British economic and imperial interests. In attacking Churchill and Bryce, he attacked not merely two statesmen, but two of the most accomplished historians of the age and key architects of the Anglo-American 'special relationship'. For both Bryce and Churchill, defending the history, destiny and integrity of the British Empire was a sacred duty: their story of triumph and progress was religiously upheld and never to be compromised by accusations of duplicity and systemic violence.

Casement's investigations into slavery and crimes against humanity in the Congo and Amazon had set in motion bitter wars of representation upon which hung the long-term reputations of empires, nations, markets and individuals. His official writings left on the record evidence of an immeasurable interlinking ethnocide, driven by the insatiable demand for rubber, and a financial system unregulated by any sense of moral responsibility to either humanity or the living environment. Today, a century on from the resource wars inaugurated by the extractive rubber industry, the interiors of central Africa and the Amazon are still in a process of recovery from the trauma wrought by the brutal violation of their rainforest worlds. When analysed together, his investigations of the hugely profitable transatlantic rubber trade had laid bare the destructive capacity of venture capital and the violently oppressive force of colonial power. While the horrors of the First World War temporarily obscured these atrocities, the people of central Africa and the Amazon had memories and histories too. Casement lived on as a symbolic champion of the oppressed. His history would prove difficult to contain.

But Casement's transition from memory into history would not be straightforward. Throughout his life he had lived dangerously between two paradigmatically-opposed spaces of secrecy: the British Foreign Office and Irish revolutionary resistance. By its very nature, secrecy unsettles and even defies historical certainties. Casement's end had involved clandestine collusion between leading Liberal imperialists, Unionist statesmen, senior judges and intelligence chiefs. Many different reputations and histories were interrelated with Casement's story.

His intervention in the intellectual build-up to the Rising had helped to reveal troubling dimensions in the administration of Ireland. His contribution to the revolutionary project was to develop, along with Alice Stopford Green and other cosmopolitan nationalists, an integrated, international dimension for Ireland within Europe and the wider world. He aspired to the hope that Ireland would develop an alternative cultural space, driven by a sense of humanity and compassion, justice and equality. In the final statement, dictated to Father McCarroll before his execution, he confided: 'My dominating thought was to keep Ireland out of the war. England has no claim on us, in Law or Morality or Right. Ireland should not sell her soul for any mess of Empire.'[1]

Once Casement's treason had been identified, the challenge to the British authorities was intricately bound up with controlling his narrative. In the century that has passed since his death, it is evident that an internal policy was evolved whereby Casement's story was framed and manipulated for public consumption. Through a mix of officially agreed deception, the engineering of his archive, and the maintenance of a policy of confusion, his history was shaped in a manner that was amenable to a retreating British Empire and a partitioned Ireland. A series of memoirs and biographies were published that intended to fill the silences left by the uncertainties born of secrecy and to entrench the myths of Casement as a deviant Pro-Germanist and 'fanatic' Irish nationalist. Such interpretations were critical to preventing him attaining martyrdom and to deny his revolutionary turn the logic that he believed would one day vindicate his action.

Historians have delineated the intellectual confrontation between Ireland and England going back to Gerald of Wales. Both the British Empire and the tradition of Irish nationality had been established upon mythologising tendencies of their distinct pasts. In his incarnations as both British official and Irish rebel, Casement had deployed history for his own ends. He had left on record a substantial interlinking record that proved to be his most enduring and indelible act of subversion. It provided a resource for those who wished to interrogate the colonial encounter and to map the conspiratorial rationale for his virulent turn against the empire. The challenge for his enemies was to hold that narrative in check.

On one level the British authorities held the advantage in that the significant part of Casement's story was ineradicably tied up in the National Archives (UK), now housed near the Royal Botanic Gardens at Kew in London. That part of the narrative could be diplomatically managed through sanitisation and selective access. But from his own experience in imperial affairs, Casement was well aware of how the art of official deception and the manipulation of public opinion was a key weapon in the waging of war and the winning of peace. His writings that repeatedly return to how revealing such deceptive practices challenged the right of states and kings to use and abuse information, news, and ultimately history for their own ends. During the First World War, Britain pioneered intricate propaganda techniques to justify their actions far in advance of any other nation.

Family and friends closest to Casement realised at the time of the trial that the narrative emerging from official British sources did not configure with how they understood Casement. Gertrude Bannister persisted in her endeavours to extract more information from the Home Office, but her efforts were in vain, although she realised that the story was in a process of being 'doctored.' In 1917 she wrote:

> They have at least disgorged 8 trunks full of stuff chiefly concerned with the Putumayo – and in my examination of them, I have come across letters concerning the diary … These letters show without a doubt that his diary, sent to them by himself was in their hands in 1913 … and that it contained extracts useful to prove the terrible state of affairs he had witnessed …The diary has I have no doubt been doctored to make it fit in with the use they wished to make of it...[2]

What Bannister identified was how the state had set about taking control of Casement's historical reputation in terms of his official career. As far back as 1905, Casement had predicted how his legacy was even then caught in a vicious cycle of propaganda. In Germany, conscious of his own vulnerability to deliberate acts of historical manipulation, he prepared for the war over his reputation by leaving complex instructions for the publication of his papers.

The defeat of Germany and the bitter legacy of the War of Independence in Ireland meant that Casement's relevance was drowned out by the continuing blast of guns and the deepening sectarian and class divisions defining British and Irish relations. Beyond Casement's German and Irish sympathies, a belligerent Secret Intelligence Service also targeted his relevance to the nascent socialist discussion on foreign policy. A year after Casement's execution, ED Morel, his collaborator in Congo reform, was imprisoned for a technical breach of the Defence of the Realm Act. He never properly recovered from his harsh prison experience. After the war, Morel was selected to contest a parliamentary seat for the Independent Labour Party and defeated Winston Churchill in a bitterly fought campaign for Dundee. An indication of his feelings for Churchill was made clear in a comment during his campaign: 'I look upon Churchill as such a personal force for evil that I would take up the fight against him with a whole heart.' But Morel's political career was cut short by his death in 1924, at the very moment when it was mooted he would become the next British foreign secretary.

Only in the last decade or so, with the release of official files of the intelligence services, can we better understand how the relationship between the judiciary and intelligence agencies resulted in an often heavy-handed suppression of dissent. The war on Casement and Morel was part of a hard-nosed and ruthless targeting by Britain's secret state of all forms of dissent from socialists, internationalists, Irish republicans, feminists, pacifists and homosexuals.

While his status within British memory as an enemy of empire could be gently discarded into the dustbin of history, Casement's negotiation in Ireland was more recondite. Furthermore, the full telling of his story required some unsettling questions to be asked about the collusion between a hawkish Unionist/Tory Right in Britain and their entanglement with Loyalist political and paramilitary forces in the North of Ireland. Control of his story depended on a deliberate suppression of the role of that group of Belfast and Antrim-based nationalists – Alice Milligan, Eoin MacNeill, Jack White, Bulmer Hobson and FJ Bigger – whose work had been critical in the move towards 1916, but whose narratives upset the blood sacrifice interpretation of 1916. MacNeill's countermanding order was doubtless contingent upon Casement's wish to stop the Rising, and was upheld as a primary reason why the rebellion had failed. That broader, inclusive and transnational nationalism that Casement and Stopford Green promoted, which placed Ulster at the heart of a thirty-two county United Ireland, cut against the grain of the two-nation history written in defence of partition. Within Irish-American circles, Casement became a scapegoat and was blamed as the weak link in the revolutionary chain of command.

But whatever he represented to the histories of the British Empire or the sectarian differences that would define the two Irish states, Casement endured as a powerfully symbolic figure within Irish republican circles. Exactly a year after his execution, Thomas Ashe delivered an oration at the rath where Casement had been arrested. Thousands of Irish citizens walked and cycled to listen to him speak. It was the largest single gathering of nationalists since the 1916 Rising, and Alice Stopford Green paid for the printing of a small pamphlet containing Ashe's emotive words. The occasion showed the continuing belief in Casement's principles. Within weeks, Ashe was on the run and his death while on hunger strike later that year would be the first of a succession of such sacrifices in Ireland.

The spirit unleashed by 1916 could not be contained.

In 1922, Churchill commented how, after the floodwaters of the war had subsided and the boundaries of many countries re-drawn, the dreary steeples of Fermanagh and Tyrone reappeared and the integrity of the Irish struggle returned into view. In late 1921, as media outlets around the world reverberated with news on the emerging treaty negotiations for Irish independence, Casement's German diary was published in a small edition in Munich.[3] This was an important step in helping to explain some of the circumstances of his treason, but there was still a vacuum in general understanding. What the press did not pick up on was the significant contingencies between his trial and the treaty negotiations.

Two of Casement's most strident political opponents, FE Smith, by now Lord Chancellor, and Winston Churchill, then Secretary of State for the Colonies, were both signatories of the treaty. On the Irish side, George Gavan Duffy and Erskine Childers were part of the Irish negotiating team led by Michael Collins. Within weeks of the transference of power at Dublin Castle, there was a peculiar new development in the Casement saga. In February 1922, Collins and another Irish treaty delegate, Eamon Duggan, met FE Smith at the House of Lords to examine the Black Diaries. On returning to Dublin, Collins opened a file in the Department of the Taoiseach called 'Alleged Casement Diaries' and wrote a letter to Tom Casement about 'a matter that I cannot write about – or at least is so lengthy as to make it difficult for me to write about it.'[4] Did the veiled and indirect comment hint at the fact that Collins had been required to authenticate the Black Diaries as part of some secret agreement made in the background to the Irish Free State treaty? If so, was it a decision determined by Churchill and Smith?

This hypothesis might help to explain why subsequent Irish leaders and governments had such an ambivalent view of Casement and why the controversy over the Black Diaries remained an unresolved issue at a government level. After 1922, Gavan Duffy took no further part in the Casement controversy. Had he, too, been a party to the Collins-Smith secret accord? In the aftermath of partition, Casement's

nationalism, which placed Ulster at the heart of the independence project, became a form of nationalism against the
Free State. It prioritised the place and role of Ulster, the very
province that was ultimately largely excluded. On his arrival
into power in 1932, de Valera was immediately confronted by
the Casement affair and a project to make a Hollywood film
about his life. He opposed the plans, claiming that outsiders
could not begin to understand Casement and his contribution to the Irish rebellion, but that his reputation was safe in
the hearts of the Irish people. This proved not to be the case.
In private de Valera ambiguously stated that a further period
of time must elapse before the full extent of Casement's sacrifice could be understood.[5]

The early thirties saw the publication of four biographies
on Casement, two in English, one in Italian and another in
German. The first major public dispute erupted with the
publication of William Maloney's *The Forged Casement Diaries* (1936). Maloney's book was an early effort to explain
and expose the role and links between different intelligence
agencies and operatives in the overthrow of Casement. The
book stands as one of the first studies of British intelligence
operations during the First World War. But there were many
inaccuracies and several arguments of a somewhat speculative nature. Maloney's book provoked an intervention from
George Bernard Shaw and inspired WB Yeats to write his
poem *The Ghost of Roger Casement*, which introduced the

trope of haunting into the dispute. Casement was transformed into a ghostly presence within Irish history. If he
had been a victim of an agreed lie at the time of the signing
of the treaty, then his spectre would return perpetually to
remind the governments in both Westminster and Dublin of
their betrayal of him.

A volume of memoirs written by Casement's defence barrister, Artemus Jones, captured the situation well:

> Roger Casement was not the ghoulish monster or the
> monument of human villainy depicted at the time in the
> pages of certain sections of the press. What the verdict of
> history may be, no one save a seer can foretell – the flight
> of time is inexorable and the merciful hands of oblivion are
> always at work.[6]

In the early 1950s, with Churchill back in power, it became
all the more imperative to influence the verdict of history.
Financially bankrupted by the defeat of the Nazis and with
the winds of change about to blow through Whitehall, Britain engaged in messy conflicts of decolonisation. Propaganda
would play an even greater part in this retreat from imperial
outposts; the production of a positive history was vital to the
Empire in retreat. Casement's intellectual relevance to the
anti-colonial struggle had inspired a number of anticolonial
leaders. These included Kwame Nkrumah in sub-Saharan
Africa and Jawaharlal Nehru in India. Likewise in Northern

Ireland, Casement was symbolically resurrected as a rallying point for nationalist sentiment. In 1953 the GAA stadium in West Belfast – Páirc Mhic Easmainn – was inaugurated in Casement's honour. This was followed a few weeks later by an impromptu cross-border visit by de Valera with two former Chiefs of Staff of the IRA, Seán MacBride and Frank Aiken, to deliver an oration to a large gathering in Murlough Bay, where Casement had expressly wished to be buried.

In response to this rallying to Casement's memory, the Orange hand of Lord Beaverbrook once more came into play and he strategically deployed his political influence and newspaper empire to actively revive the campaign against the rebel-traitor. In 1956, one of his senior reporters, René MacColl, a former Ministry of Information operative, published a deeply hostile popular biography – *Roger Casement: A New Judgement* – giving credence to several unsubstantiated stories and to some untrustworthy and ideologically hostile witnesses. Another newspaperman, Peter Singleton-Gates, made various interventions in the diaries dispute from 1925 and was largely responsible for the publication of *The Black Diaries* in 1959. In 1995, it was revealed that Singleton-Gates worked for Beaverbrook's *Evening Standard* as an embedded journalist for the Special Branch, where he developed close links with Basil Thomson. The third man in the ring was the Unionist MP, lawyer and historian, HH Montgomery Hyde, who was deployed to aggravate the issue at a parliamentary level and to obfuscate the murky role of the British justice system involved in Casement's overthrow.[7] The historian AJP Taylor, a confidant of Lord Beaverbrook, made a veiled reference to the conspiratorial relationship of British statesmen between the wars; in his book surveying the tradition of dissent in British Foreign Policy, *The Troublemakers*, he wrote how:

> Asquith and Balfour, Lloyd George and Bonar Law, Churchill and FE Smith, passed many an evening together; and they successfully hushed up scandals which far outdid the *Letters of Junius* or the satirical imaginings of Hilaire Belloc.[8]

While this is not a direct reference by Taylor to the Casement scandal, it alludes to an informal dynamic of executive power that is covert, unaccountable and entangled with conspiracy and the protection of political reputations. In the early 1960s the on-going acrimonious exchange in the letters page of the *Irish Times* over Casement's treatment at the hand of propagandists led to direct and legitimate accusations about Montgomery Hyde's direct links with MI6.[9] Officially, the British government neither confirmed nor denied knowledge of its secret services.

Negotiations had been on-going for years about the return of Casement's bones to Ireland, and they intensified in the early 1960s. The leader of the Labour Party, Harold Wilson, invoked Casement's name to his Liverpool constituents during his election campaign at the end of 1964. Supporters of Irish origin, and others who favourably remembered the campaign of the Congo Reform Association, were promised that Casement's body would be returned to Ireland in the event of a Labour Party victory. True to his promise, communiqués between Dublin and London intensified after Wilson became Prime Minister. The British Ambassador in Dublin, Geofroy Tory, was instrumental in facilitating the discussion.[10]

The negotiations leading to the release of Casement's physical remains from the unmarked grave in Pentonville were not finalised until the day of Churchill's state funeral. Immediately after the procession, Wilson and Ireland's Minister for External Affairs, Frank Aiken, met for a private conversation at No. 10 Downing Street. A few weeks later, the bones were exhumed under the cover of darkness and behind specially-erected screens. Casement's bleached skull and lime-scaled bones were identified by one of the Department of External Affairs most able ambassadors, Sean Ronan, and then flown back to Baldonnell Airport (later renamed Casement Aerodrome). As Casement's remains crossed the Irish Sea at 20,000 feet, co-ordinated statements about his repatriation were made in the British House of Commons and Dáil Éireann. The moment was used to symbolise a new climate of co-operation between Northern Ireland and the Republic of Ireland. After lying in state in Arbour Hill beside the mass grave of fourteen of the other executed

1916 leaders, Casement was given his own state funeral and buried (contrary to his last wishes, it must be said) in Glasnevin cemetery.

Ever since Casement had openly chastised Churchill for his defence of 'terminological inexactitude', in other words, lying (for the public good), Churchill had turned historical distortion into a literary art form. Many anecdotes might be conjured to illustrate this, but one will suffice. During a disagreement with Prime Minister Stanley Baldwin in the House of Commons in the 1930s, Churchill turned on him and remarked that he was confident that history would find him wrong 'because I shall write that history.' The debunking of Churchill's imperial historiography is on-going, but enough is already known to vindicate Casement's concerns about the political use of lying and to provide a critical motive as to why Britain's secret state went to such extravagant ends to demonise Casement and manage his traitorous meaning.

In the early 1990s, public demands in Britain grew louder for transparency and accountability in the wake of further revelations about Britain's apparatus of state secrecy. The Black Diaries were fully released under the Open Government Initiative. Since 1959, researchers had to obtain permission from the Home Secretary to see the documents; from 1994 access was unrestricted. Eighteen months later, Casement's prison writings and several hundred associated Home Office and Prison Commission files were declassified. Over the next decade, further staggered releases of intelligence files cast new light on how Casement had been prioritised by the intelligence services in the counter-insurgency war. Cabinet minutes revealed the fact that all decisions about Casement had been dealt with at the highest level of executive power in both London and Dublin.

However, despite concerted efforts to control his meaning, various cultural factors turned the tide of historical understanding. In 1993, the decriminalising of homosexuality in Ireland resulting from amendments to the Sexual Offences Act, precipitated a different kind of evaluation about the role of the Black Diaries in Casement's interpretation. The question of Casement's sexuality was no longer *the* issue and potentially could be decoupled from the enduring controversy over the authenticity of the Black Diaries.

Casement's political writings were also undergoing a process of re-evaluation. New research into such hitherto obscure subjects as the role of 'black' propaganda by the secret state, the use of an embedded press, and the construction of an official version of history became recognised dimensions of how Britain pioneered and finessed the business of modern warfare and governance. Casement's stand against secret diplomacy, the arms industry, and his pessimistic view of the Anglo-Saxon alliance could no longer be dismissed out of hand as the mutterings of a 'mad man' and 'fanatic.' They were in fact a thoughtful response by a sensitive, humanist observer confronted by a horror that defied definition. Casement's treason was principally a stand against a ruling class in Britain determined at all costs to hold on to redundant and unrepresentative formations of power.

The last century has produced a host of studies on the causes of the First World War that endorse several of Casement's opinions and arguments articulated in *The Crime Against Europe* and other political essays. Obviously many different factors determined Britain's decision to go to war in 1914. But those reasons identified by Casement, such as the culture of secrecy, the political bungling by Grey, the crisis in Ireland and the ascendancy of a hawkish imperialist and Unionist elite, are now widely accepted as integral to that complexity of causes. While a view persists that this was a 'war to unite us all', the argument can be made that the First World War was a deliberate counter-revolutionary strike by reactionary ruling elements in Europe against democratic trends advocating social justice, equality and less centralised government. The execution of the sixteen leaders of the Rising is evidence of such a motive.

If it has taken a century for the archive to be opened and for the fog of war to partially lift in order to understand Casement's relatively moderate views, it has similarly required different cultural conditions in Ireland. At the *feis* in the Glens of Antrim in 1904 those language teachers, scholars, civil servants and social reformers realised the need for cross-community understanding. Their vision aspired towards a common good where Presbyterian, Catholic, Protestant, Unionist, National-ist, Republican and Non-Conformist could work towards a common and mutually beneficial future. Their Ireland was an inclusive Ireland, an Ireland of shared histories and recipro-cally-respected remembrances. But it was not until the end of the twentieth century that such a discourse would return to favour in the light of the Good Friday Agreement and the need to build a dialogue of peace.

Assessment of Casement's global stature has necessitated the writing of alternative histories that transcend national preconceptions and deal with universal problems enabling other perspectives to be interpretatively considered. In *The Book of Laughter and Forgetting*, Milan Kundera wrote how 'the struggle of man against power is the struggle of memory against forgetting.' By the mid-1920s there was a deliberate official wish to forget Casement and all he stood for. After the First World War, in line with a desire in Brit-ain to obviate understanding of the role of Ireland in the shaping of both national and international affairs pre-1914, the significance of Casement, Morel and Stopford Green was disremembered. There was little appetite to recall the new slaveries that lay in the shadows of imperial expansion and how those controversies had contributed to redefin-ing political allegiances. Britain's justification for going to war in defence of Belgium (and small nations) rendered its earlier campaign for reform in the Congo Free State highly inconvenient.

The work of Casement, Stopford Green and Morel, so important to the recalibration of colonial power relations, was appropriated, forgotten or confused. The African Society, founded by Stopford Green, was rebranded the Royal African Society and continues to this day enjoying royal rather than republican patronage. In 1946, George Orwell described Morel as 'This heroic but rather forgotten man'.[11] The steady stream of biographical studies between 1956 and 2008 accommodated Casement's paradoxes and conflicts into a comprehensible whole, but this was done by silencing some parts of his story and either downplaying or omitting vital aspects of his political writings as well as the unsettling dynamic of conspiracy. The most influential of these biographies, by the historian and TV journalist Brian Inglis, built consensus on the question of both Casement's sexuality and the authenticity of the Black Diaries, but this was done by avoiding all reference to Casement's Amazon journal and dismissing his political writings as little more than the ravings of a paranoid and feverish imagination. Casement's involvement with British intelligence remained the vital missing dimension of his interpretation and did not become a subject of discussion until the 1990s, when intelligence history was recognised as a sub-discipline of modern historical study.

Likewise, Belgium historiography adopted a position that remained cautious on the question of its colonial legacy and demonised Casement and Morel as unreliable exaggerators. Official archives were destroyed or remained hard to access. Only when a former Belgian diplomat, Jules Marchal self-published volumes of documents about the colonial outrages did a revised interpretation reclaim the Congo Reform Association as a necessary and positive intervention.[12] The Black Diaries continued to be deployed to subvert Casement's moral authority and his denunciation of the system by locking public understanding inside a futile discussion on his sexuality.

As new methods of research deconstructed the politics of historical writing and memory, different questions came to the fore. In 1998, the publication of *King Leopold's Ghost* claimed the Congo Reform Association as a bridge linking nineteenth-century humanitarian endeavour with twentieth-century human rights advocacy.[13] In the light of recent releases and alternative approaches to the past, Casement's official career and his intellectual relevance to the Irish revolution were interrogated in different ways. In 1997, conflicting versions of Casement's 1910 diary appeared. The ensuing controversy defined the central riddle concerning the Black Diaries: why would a man conducting a highly incriminating investigation into crimes against humanity maintain two parallel diaries for the same seventy-five day period: one version self-incriminating, the other version critically revealing of the injustice of the system?[14]

Increasingly, Casement's writings were relevant to a new generation and could be scrutinised for what they revealed about contemporary concerns for environmental protection, fair trade and corporate responsibility. In 2009, the historian Jordan Goodman situated Casement's investigation in South America at the source of twentieth-century human rights discourse.[15] Casement and Morel were retrieved as able activists who had unselfishly challenged the excesses of imperial power and exposed an appalling crime against humanity. John Tully, in his social history of rubber, *The Devil's Milk*, dedicated the book to Casement and other campaigners who were prepared to sacrifice their lives in order to take on the forces of transnational business in defence of indigenous and environmental rights.[16]

The new dilemma presented by the Casement conundrum, however, and one that must inevitably be confronted in this telling of his story, are its implications: what does it tell us about the use and abuse of history and historical production? In his life Casement held a mirror up to western hegemony and asked extremely unsettling questions about power and how both the past and present interact. A century on, he continues to make us confront that 'nightmare of history' from which Stephen Dedalus, in James Joyce's *Ulysses*, was trying to awake.

The last word in this brief reconstruction of an intricate life that defies orthodox biographical treatment should go to Alice Stopford Green, whose imagination more than any other helped to shape Ireland's historical consciousness in the decade before 1916, although she too has fallen victim to the neglect of history. After the Rising and Casement's painful end, Green left her home on the Thames Embankment in central London and lived out the last years of her life in a house overlooking St Stephen's Green. Her closest friends thought she would write the life of Casement, but her work for Irish independence kept her busy. In 1922 she stood as an independent candidate and was elected as the first woman to the Seanad Éireann. Conscious of the historical importance of the occasion, Stopford Green commissioned an exquisitely crafted casket – the Cranwill casket – to hold the scroll listing the names of those who sat in the first senate.[17] Her dedication would have appealed to her great friend and collaborator Roger Casement. It reads:

> No real history of Ireland has yet been written. When the true story is finally worked out – one not wholly occupied with the many and insatiable plunderers – it will give us a noble and reconciling vision of Irish nationality. Silence and neglect will no longer hide the fame of honourable men.

Appendix:
The Far-Extended Baleful
Power of the Lie

This war is essentially a world war.

Not only are all the great Powers of the world, save one, actively engaged in it, but the bulk of the human race are now employed in trying to kill each other.

Of European States all the great Powers and four of the smaller States are actively involved, representing a population of some 430,000,000 engaged in war, as against some 56,000,000 still neutral.

In Asia, China alone is not engaged; for the war has already reached in some degree Persia and Afghanistan. Fully 400,000,000 Asiatics are now in the war field, and with the exception of Turkey and parts of Arabia, all are on the side of 'the Allies'.

Practically the whole continent of Africa, all except Abyssinia; all Australasia and half of North America are in the field and need-less to say almost wholly on the same side.

Even South America has its representatives – British and French Guiana.

Counting by heads, the Germans, Austro-Hungarians and Turks are fighting in the proportion of one against six; counting by hearts, they are something more than equal.

The question, therefore, is whether the head or the heart is going to prevail in this great conflict?

The 'Allies' place their reliance on the things that appeal to the head: their opponents on the things that come from the heart.

The decision is not yet in sight, but we may begin to assess the relative value of the factors that make for success.

England, as was to be expected, easily leads in the things that belong to the head. She is confident that with innumerable weapons she wields, directed by this lofty but cold seat of human intelligence, she must in the end prevail over those whose armament is derived from warm blood.

Chief of the weapons she relies on is that once described by Mr Winston Churchill, in a facetious moment of parliamentary repartee, as a 'terminological inexactitude'.

Let us therefore deal with this chief weapon. Let us inspect the lie to see what elements of success it confers on those who alone are capable of handling it with conviction, with sincerity and with that complete assurance that comes from long experience of its utility in the field of human endeavour.

A lie, rightly wielded, has before this shattered empires, emptied thrones and dispossessed entire peoples. Directed with judgment and exposed at the right moment, the lie is the 'white weapon' *par excellence*, that takes the edge off the bayonet and blunts the bravest sword. A fine art cannot be acquired in a day. It has taken British statesmanship (and British journalism) a very long study, and a most assiduous application to perfect an art acquired in the strenuous days when Great Britain was only a small island in the North Sea, and not the focus of an imperial system on which the truth never rose.

From the many examples this world war furnishes, I will take one as being, perhaps the most striking illustration of the lie the widespread conflict offers.

I take the report of the Committee dealing with the 'German atrocities in Belgium' presided over by the Right Honourable Lord Bryce – let us for short call them 'the Belgian Atrocities'. The name has a familiar ring. I knew something in former days of Belgian atrocities not committed, it is true, in Belgium or by Germans, but in another field where Lord Bryce was one of my supporters. When I first met Lord Bryce, then plain Mr Bryce, at Delagoa Bay in the autumn of 1895, neither of us thought that one of the principal tasks the future should hold for us would be to deal with my report upon 'Belgian atrocities'. In my case they were investigated on the spot at some little pains and danger to myself.

In Lord Bryce's case they were not encountered upon earth but fell, as it were from heaven, and had to be inspected with a very long telescope. It was not until three years after I first met Mr Bryce in 1898 that I proceeded to the Congo State, and not until 1903 that I revisited the upper Congo and investigated in the great centres of rubber demoralisation the innumerable charges preferred by the Congolese natives against the administration of the late King Leopold.

In 1895 when he visited me at Delagoa Bay Mr Bryce had ceased to be a Minister of the Crown and was then engaged in a holiday tour round Africa, by mail steamer, on the strength of which brief journey he founded a book dealing with South African Affairs. His holiday endured until 1905 when, on the resignation of Mr Balfour, a Liberal Ministry returned to office under the leadership of Sir Henry Campbell-Bannerman, and Mr Bryce became Chief Secretary for Ireland. He had been a 'Home Ruler' in Mr Gladstone's last Cabinet, and was believed to have the cause of Irish 'Autonomy' at heart.

As Chief Secretary for Ireland Mr Bryce was not a success. Whether his convictions were stronger than those of his colleagues, or his courage weaker than his convictions, I cannot say. I met him more than once during his brief tenure of this thankless and forbidding office and while I felt that he remained probably a 'Home Ruler' at heart it was clear that he lacked the necessary strength of character to insist on the charges called for from a Ministry pledged not only to undo great wrongs, but to effect a great return.

After a short and unsuccessful stay at the Irish Office, Mr Bryce was appointed British Ambassador at Washington.

The appointment in itself was unique, probably the first instance in English history when a member of the Government was sent direct from the Cabinet to represent his country in an embassy abroad. In America the arrival of Mr Bryce was greeted with a chorus of welcome.

Not only had it the 'democratic touch' in that he was not a peer but a very simple plain man, but Americans were flattered that a member of the Cabinet should be selected to represent Great Britain in their midst and they saw too, in Mr Bryce a distinguished scholar, and one whose able work on the 'American Commonwealth' commended him to intellectual circles as a very friendly critic.

I think it was in 1907 that Mr Bryce went to Washington. His tenure of the post of British Ambassador there certainly did much to cement the ties of something more than intimacy, or even friendship whose manifestations we witness with interest today.

Like his successor, Sir Cecil Spring-Rice, Lord Bryce is an Irishman or it would be much more correct to say that he was born in Ireland. The accident of birthplace does not necessarily impart the stamp of nationality and both Lord Bryce and Sir Cecil Spring-Rice would be greatly shocked if I presumed to claim them as my fellow-countrymen.

It was during his occupancy of the British Embassy at Washington, that I again met Mr Bryce. He had not yet then received the title.

Coming from an investigation of the crimes of the London Rubber Co., called the Peruvian Amazon Co., committed upon the defenceless Indian population of the upper Amazon, I decided to seek to interest the United States Government in the fate of these unfortunate human beings. Accordingly, on getting down to the mouth of the Amazon in December 1911, I set out for Washington instead of for London, in the hope that a personal appeal to President Taft might convince the Administration of the need for supporting diplomatically at Lima the action I had already taken on the spot, in the heart of the Amazon forests. On this brief visit to Washington (January 1912), I had to thank Mr Bryce for much courtesy and assistance, and in large measure for the success of my self-imposed mission.

Mr Bryce cordially supported my personal representations to the President, and manifested an active interest in the fate of the Indian population who had been for years the victims of a callous system of exploitation and outrage, devised it is true, in South America, but maintained and directed from London.

I think it was in 1913 that Mr Bryce retired from the British Embassy at Washington and returning to England, was raised to the peerage, and received, if I mistake not, the very singular distinction of the Order of Merit. Had his public career terminated at this point, his friends and admirers would have felt less difficulty to-day in recognizing the service he rendered in the past to the enlightenment of contemporary opinion.

His charming work, the *Holy Roman Empire*, will always claim the attention of English readers; while his study of American conditions has passed, I think, into a text-book for transatlantic students of their own institution. Unhappily for Mr Bryce or as I should now call him, Lord Bryce, his retirement from active service, was cut short by the present unholy war. Had he been permitted to remain in the seclusion of his study, we might still have hoped for some final manifestation of that charm and simplicity of style, directed to the realm of the past, that render the *Holy Roman Empire* one of the most interesting portrayals in the English language, of a great period of European sovereignty. But, the claims of the present could not spare this veteran from the service of his country. Since it was necessary to muster all her forces for the work in hand, England called upon the ex-Ambassador, Cabinet Minister and scholar to undertake a task for which I believe, in all justice to Lord Bryce, he was singularly unfitted. But his name carried weight and particularly in America.

It was there that the particular form of attack upon Germany he was selected to lead, was designed to have its fullest effect.

The *New York Sun* in reviewing the work he undertook stated that if there was one man whose veracity Americans believed in it was Lord Bryce. It was in that belief the British Government appointed him to preside over the committee nominated to enquire into and report upon the press charges brought against the German troops in Belgium.

American sympathies with the cause of Belgium were honest, sincere and universal. The American people, overborne from the first with the heavy discharge of British ordnance were deposed to regard Belgium and the Belgian people as victims of a wanton act of German aggression. The German side of the case they never heard. They perceived only that Belgium, a small neutral State, was invaded by the overpowering army of a country that had guaranteed its independence and neutrality, its armies dispersed, its King a fugitive and its people reduced to a state of what was represented as extreme privation and misery.

These facts were sufficient to enlist the sympathy of American citizens on the side of the little country and the weaker people. But the necessities of England demanded more than active sympathy for the Belgians: hatred and horror of the Germans were essential to the English cause, if America was to be made actively useful to it. It was not enough that American generosity should feed and clothe the starving and homeless; American animosity must be excited against those who were responsible for the act of invasion, and whom England was assailing for quite other reasons. Hence it became necessary to establish against Germany much more than the violation of Belgian neutrality. Other violations were needed. It became essential that 'the Hun' should be revealed in all his horror to the American people, just as he was portrayed in the *Daily Mail* to the London mob. To effect this, it was necessary that the lie should be well staged, and presented in a more imposing garb than any that Fleet Street industries could furnish.

Such efforts as the following, culled at random from the *Daily Mail* were good enough for the man in the street at home; but something nearer the Law Courts style was necessary if the conscience of mankind was to be aroused.

> Carpers do not realise that so long as fresh packs of these predatory humans, these beasts with brains, can reinforce the falling and replace the fallen, so long as a new and vast generation of them is growing up under the same tutelage, with a Satanic Majesty of hate as its autocrat, to carry on the ravening career of crime, the necessity of their extinction will exist, and that it is a question not only of the survival of the fittest, but of the most numerous.

> (Beatrice Heron-Maxwell, "the well-known novelist and thinker", in an article in the *Daily Mail*, 13th July 1915, urging facilities for war marriages).

This might aid the output of war babies at home, as the lady intended it do to, but it would not aid the output of those other things abroad on which English success abroad depended if 'the Hun' was to be finally overcome. Fleet Street could deal with him at home, but he must be got into a Court of some sort, if he was to be exposed abroad. The Law Courts could not yet be invoked against him, for until victory came no English writ could run east of the Rhine; but a quasi-judicial verdict might be obtained by haling him before one of those high moral tribunals so frequently constituted to pass judgment on any phase of foreign activity obnoxious to English interests.

I have investigated more bona fide atrocities at close hand than possibly any other living man. But unlike Lord Bryce, I investigated them on the spot, from the lips of those who had suffered, in the very places where the crimes were perpetrated, where the evidence could be sifted and the accusation brought by the victim could be rebutted by the accused; and in each case my finding was confirmed by the Courts of Justice of the very States whose citizens I had indicted.

Had Lord Bryce refused the commission assigned him to defame the German character by a pretended investigation in England of things alleged to have been done in Belgium, he would have done his country a far nobler service than by lending the weight of his name to a committee, that no one knew better than he, was disqualified from establishing facts.

How could it be otherwise?

The enquiry took place in England, not in Belgium. The 'witnesses' cited were largely British soldiers, those charged with crimes were not heard. From first to last the whole thing partook of the character of O'Connell's famous gibe at an earlier English indictment of a whole people when he compared the reference of the case of Ireland to the London Parliament 'as referring the question of Lent to a jury of butchers'.

Lord Bryce was appointed to preside over a jury of butchers, whose part was to see that their Lenten victim, the fame of the absent German army, was handsomely slaughtered, cut up and disposed of at a good price abroad.

It is the findings of such a body as this, controlled by the dire need of the Government that set it up and directed to one and only purpose, the blackening of the character of those with whom England was at war, that are given out to the world of neutral peoples as the pronouncement of an impartial court seeking only to discover and reveal the truth.

The document produced by this method and published by HM Stationery Office as a Government publication, was issued on the 19th May at a "popular price" and scattered broadcast in every neutral country. By a return of the Stationery Office issued in July it is shown that already in some two months' time 'over 1,000,000 copies of the Bryce Report' on the German atrocities in Belgium has been printed and distributed throughout the world at the expense of the British taxpayer.

Was there ever in history a more shockingly conceived attempt at the moral assassination of a people? I know of none, at least outside the circuit of English dealings with Ireland. There we have had this sort of thing for centuries. When we turn to Lord Bryce's summing up of the 'evidence' laid before his committee and on which he founds his judgment against the German army we perceive that it is not the jurist, not the scholar, not the historian who speaks. We need only to turn to Lord Byce's own works, when he wrote as a historian and not as a hireling, to expose the untruth of the charge he brings against the German army in Belgium.

Dealing with the German invasion, Lord Bryce thus writes in the preface to the body of the Report:

'Murder, lust and pillage prevailed over many parts of Belgium on a scale unparalleled in any war between civilised nations during the last three centuries', and we are further assured 'that it is proved' that charges of fiendish cruelty were established.

Appendix: The Far-Extended Baleful Power of the Lie

It is only necessary to turn to James Bryce the historian, to convict Lord Bryce the partisan. And I will preface the quotation from the historian by pointing out that the German army accused by the partisan was in a hostile land, fighting a hostile army, charged by the historian, was an integral part of its own dominions, attacking an unarmed population, its own fellow subjects. Speaking of the army of General Lake, the British Commander-in-Chief in Ireland in 1798, Mr James Bryce the historian thus asserts:

> Under Lake's sway the tranquil country was converted into a place of tyranny, torture and outrage, with homesteads on fire, provision destroyed, families ruined and all the atrocities which licentious ruffians living at free quarters could inflict on human beings.
>
> Death by strangulation or the bullet was common; but it was a merciful fate compared to the fearful floggings, often a thousand lashes, which tore off skin and muscles. To compel confessions, the son was compelled to kneel under his father, and the father under his son, while the blood fell hot on them from the lash. Half-hanging was a common form of torture, picketing another; when the victim strung up by an arm could only rest the weight of his body with bare foot on a pointed base. Hot pitch was poured into canvas caps and pressed on the head, not to be removed from the inflamed and blistered surface without tearing off the hair and skin.

(*Two Centuries of Irish History*, by James Bryce, DCL)

No crime I charged against the rubber tyrants on the Congo or Amazon, committed, be it remembered, against a savage and distant people inhabiting a wild and barbarous region, exceed in infamy or horror the acts of the officers and soldiers of the English army in Ireland, acting as the agents of the English sovereign in dealing with his own subjects at home.

And Lord Bryce issues his Report against the German army in Belgium as he asserts 'to rouse the conscience of mankind'!

Lord Bryce is a historian. He knows the record of English armies in the field in other countries besides Ireland. It was not alone in Ireland the troops of King George III distinguished themselves in their dealings with friendly and defenceless people in the domain of 'murder, lust and pillage'. It is true that in Ireland their own Generals denounced the crimes of their own soldiery in terms Lord Bryce is very familiar with.

Sir James Abercrombie and Sir John Moore, two high-minded English officers, resigned their commands in Ireland rather than lead the forces their sovereign entrusted to them for the terrorisation of his Irish subjects. A near friend of Lord Bryce's, the English historian John Richard Green, in the house of whose widow I have met him, thus supports Lord Bryce's indictment of the English army in Ireland.

The soldiers marched all over the country, torturing, scourging, robbing, ravaging and murdering. Their outrages were sanctioned by a Bill of Indemnity.

This was in Ireland, not Belgium, in 1796 and 1797, well within 'the last three centuries'. A hundred years ago – 1809-1914 – the English army was in Spain defending their allies the Spaniards from the 'Huns' of that day, the French.

Here is how their Commander-in-Chief, the Duke of Wellington, deals with their treatment of those they came to protect. He asserted that he commanded "the scum of the earth, who were never out of sight of their officers without committing every kind of outrage upon a people who had always treated them well."

Sir William Napier, the historian of the Peninsular War, described in these terms the operations of Lord Wellington's army at the siege of Badajoz, a friendly Spanish city they came to 'relieve':

> the shameless rapacity, brutal, intemperate, savage lust, cruelty and murder, shrieks and piteous lamentations: groans, shouts, imprecations, the hissing of fire, the bursting of doors and windows, and the reports of muskets used in violence, resounded for two days and nights in the streets of Badajoz. All the dreadful passions of human nature were displayed. On the third day, when the city was sacked, when the soldiers were exhausted by their own excesses, the tumult rather subsided than was quelled. (Napier, Vol. II, p. 122)

Is it necessary to prolong the list, or to cite more instances? ... say the evidence of Sir Robert Hart on the conduct of the Christian armies on the march to and sack of Peking? I think enough is quoted to establish the reputation of the British army in the field of 'murder, lust and pillage' and to disestablish the reputation of Lord Bryce as an honest witness against the German army.

Unlike Lord Bryce I have been in Belgium since the war began. I was there within a few weeks of the passing of the great wave of invasion. I saw the wrecked and ruined houses; I passed through some of the stormed and battered cities Namur, Liege, Dinant; I conversed with Belgians in the streets of those terrorised towns and I formed a judgment of my own, not derived from hearsay in another land or the lips of fugitives afar, but from the scenes and spots and human wreckage I passed through.

While wrong exists in the world wrong will be done by man to man – in war a thousandfold more than in peace. Wrongs there were undoubtedly committed in Belgium, but they were not all committed by Germans upon Belgians.

The conviction I drew from what I saw while the occurrences were still recent, while the houses were still burnt and charred and the roar of the great guns had not long since passed south-wards over the dark ridges of the Ardennes, was that, if a million of invaders had passed here, fighting every foot of the way, the wreckage left behind was that which a sea in storm hurls upon the shore, and not the puny work of mere human wreckers.

Those responsible for raising that storm, to sweep across the peaceful plains of Belgium, are the true authors of 'Belgian atrocities' and not the brave armies that contended heart to heart and breast to breast, each in equal degree striving to defend their country.

The English, having called up the storm for their own ends, left their victims to the deluge. And now, when the waves have subsided, again for their own ends, their paid and ennobled beach combers go out to scavenge amid the wreckage cast up on distant shores, in the hope of finding enough to soil the honour of those they ran away from.

It is not German barbarity which distinguishes this war from all others that have preceded it. It is not the colossal numbers of men engaged; the vast holocausts of slain; the enormous waste of human energy and wealth. It is that, above all other contests between nations and men, this war has revealed the baleful power of the Lie.

That has been the chief weapon, the chief power displayed by the foremost of the belligerents.

Lord Bryce's name will be associated not with that Holy Roman Empire he sought to recall by scholarly research, but with that unholy Empire he sought to sustain in the greatest of its crimes by lending the weight of a great name, and prostituting great attain-ments to an official campaign of slander, defamation and calumny conducted on a scale unparalleled in any war between civilised nations during the last three centuries.

Originally published in *The Continental Times*,

3 November 1915.

Bibliography

ARCHIVES:

Ireland:

Central Library, Belfast (CLB)

Farmleigh House, Dublin (FH)

National Library of Ireland (NLI)

National Archives of Ireland (NAI)

Public Record Office, Northern Ireland, Belfast (PRONI)

Royal Irish Academy, Dublin (RIA)

Trinity College Dublin (TCD)

University College Dublin (UCD)

University of Limerick (UL)

England:

Antislavery International, London

British Library (BL)

University of Oxford, Bodleian Library and Rhodes House

British Library of Political and Economic Science (BLPES)

Regent's Park College, Oxford

The National Archives (UK), Kew (TNA)

Wellcome Library, London

Scotland:

National Library of Scotland

National Register of Archives, Scotland

US

New York Public Library

Boston College

University of Notre Dame

NEWSPAPERS AND PERIODICALS

Catholic Bulletin

Fortnightly Review

Freeman's Journal

Saoirse

Sinn Féin

The Belfast Telegraph

The Contemporary Review

The Continental Times

The Gaelic American

The Guardian

The Irish Times

The Irish Volunteer

The Irish Worker

The Nation

The Outlook

The United Irishman

Times

Uladh

PUBLISHED WRITINGS OF ROGER CASEMENT

Bannister, Gertrude, *Some Poems of Roger Casement* (Dublin, 1918)

Curry, Charles E., *Sir Roger Casement's Diaries: His Mission to Germany and the Findlay Affair* (Munich, 1922)

Doerries, Reinhard, *Prelude to the Easter Rising: Sir Roger Casement in Imperial Germany* (London, 2000)

Mackey, H.O. (ed.), *The Crime Against Europe: Writings and Poems of Roger Casement* (Dublin, 1958.

Mitchell, Angus (ed.), *The Amazon Journal of Roger Casement* (Dublin & London, 1997) Mitchell, Angus (ed.), *Sir Roger Casement's Heart of Darkness: the 1911 Documents* (Dublin, 2003).

Mitchell, Angus (ed.) 'My Journey to the German Headquarters at Charleville' and 'A Last Page of my Diary', *Field Day Review*, 8 (Dublin, 2012).

Ó Síocháin, Séamas & O'Sullivan, Michael, *The Eyes of Another Race: Roger Casement's Congo Report and the 1903 Black Diary* (Dublin, 2003)

Note on published books and articles about Casement

Published material on Casement and related subjects is extensive. This includes biographies, memoirs, academic articles, volumes of edited documents, letters to the editor, fiction, plays and films. The most comprehensive listing of secondary material is to be found in Séamas Ó Síocháin, *Roger Casement: Imperialist, Rebel, Revolutionary* (Dublin, 2008). For the literature relating to his Amazon investigations see Jordan Goodman, *The Devil and Mr Casement: One Man's Fight for Human Rights in South America's Heart of Darkness* (London, 2009). Other relevant works are included in the section of endnotes.

Endnotes

Abbreviations:

BLPES: British Library of Political and Economic Science

BL: British Library

CAB: Cabinet

CAE: Herbert Mackey (ed.), *The Crime against Europe: Writings and Poems of Roger Casement* (Dublin, 1958)

DT: Department of the Taoiseach

FO: Foreign Office

HO: Home Office

NAI: National Archives of Ireland

NLI: National Library of Ireland

NYPL: New York Public Library

PRONI: Public Record Office of Northern Ireland

RAMT: Royal Africa Museum, Tervuren, Belgium

SRCHD: Angus Mitchell (ed.), *Sir Roger Casement's Heart of Darkness: The 1911 Documents* (Dublin, 2003)

TNA: The National Archive (UK); (FO: Foreign Office, HD: Historical Documents)

Introduction

1 Shaw Desmond, *The Drama of Sinn Fein* (New York, 1923), 165.

2 NAI, DT, 7804, E. de Valera to Julius Klein, 11 October 1934.

3 Feicreanach, 'Roger Casement: The Man they had to Kill', *The Irish Democrat*, August 1975.

4 Brian Inglis, *Roger Casement* (London, 1973); Benjamin Reid, *The Many Lives of Roger Casement* (New Haven, 1976), Roger Sawyer, *The Flawed Hero* (London, 1984), Séamas Ó Síocháin, *Roger Casement: Imperialist, Rebel, Revolutionary* (Dublin, 2008).

5 *New York Review of Books*, 25 Oct 2012, LIX: 16, 35-37.

Chapter One: 1864-1883 (Nomadic Upbringing)

1 Dónall Ó Luanaigh, 'Roger Casement, senior, and the siege of Paris (1870)', *The Irish Sword*, XV, 58, Summer 1982, 33-35.

2 Agnes Newman, 'Life of Roger Casement: Martyr in Ireland's Cause', serialised in *The Irish Press*, Philadelphia, December 1919-March 1920.

3 NLI MS 10,880, Notes on Irish Language, RC to Eoin MacNeill.

4 Ibid.

5 NLI MS 9932.

6 Margaret O'Callaghan, '"With the Eyes of another race, of a people once hunted themselves": Casement, Colonialism and a Remembered Past', in Mary E. Daly (ed.), *Roger Casement in Irish and World History* (Dublin, 2005), 46-63.

7 CAE, poem dated 5 July 1883.

8 RC to ED Morel, 8 April 1911, SRCHD, 215.

9 NLI MS 13,082 (4), Lecture by Roger Casement on the Irish language

10 Ada MacNeill, *Recollections of Roger Casement*, Oliver McMullan Papers, Cushendall, Co. Antrim (n/d).

11 Gertrude Bannister (ed.), *Some Poems of Roger Casement* (Dublin, 1918), ix-x.

Chapter Two: 1884-1898 (African Roots)

1 TNA FO 10/815, RC to the Marquess of Lansdowne, 9 October 1905.

2 RAMT, HM Stanley Archive, Inventory Nos. 59.29.43. and 61.1.139.

3 TNA FO 10/807, RC memorandum, 14 January 1904.

4 Dorothy Middleton (ed.), *The Diary of A.J. Mounteney-Jephson: Emin Pasha Relief Expedition 1887-1889* (Cambridge, 1969), 87-93.

5 NLI, Sanford Collection. Box 22, folder 5, RC to General Sanford, 27 August, 1888.

6 Regent's Park Collge, Oxford, Angus Library, Baptist Missionary Society, A 31/4, W.H. Bentley to A.H. Baynes, 26 Feb. 1889.

7 Ibid., Bentley to Baynes, 29 April 1889.

8 NLI MS 13,074 (1/i), RC to Gertrude Bannister, 6 May 1890.

9 The Casement-Wellcome correspondence is held in the Wellcome Library, London.

10 Marcel Luwel, 'Roger Casement a Henry Morton Stanley: Un rapport sur la situation au Congo en 1890', in *Africa-Tervuren* vol. XIV, 4, (1968), 85-92. RC's letter to Stanley is dated 28 June 1890.

11 Wellcome Library, RC to Henry Wellcome, 2 August 1890.

12 See Robert Kimborough (ed.), *Heart of Darkness: An authoritative text back grounds and sources criticism* (New York, 1963), 110.

13 C.T. Watts (ed.), *Joseph Conrad's letters to R.B. Cunninghame Graham* (Cambridge, 1969), 149.

14 Frederick Karl & Laurence Davies (eds), *The collected letters of Joseph Conrad 1912-16,* vol. 5, (Cambridge, 1996), 596-7.

15 BLPES MP 5/17, RC to ED Morel, 15 March 1905.

16 For RC's maps of the Niger Delta see *History Ireland*, 14:4, July/August 2006, 50-54.

17 BL, Add. Ms. 46912, RC to HR Fox Bourne, 7 January, 1894. The letter is reproduced as an appendix in HO Mackey, *Roger Casement: A Guide to the Forged Diaries* (Dublin, 1962), 173-6.

18 Ibid.

19 NLI MS 10,764 (1), RC 'Brief to Counsel'.

20 The National Archive (UK) contains the largest body of Casement's writings relevant to Lorenzo Marques. For Delagoa Bay Railway company, FO 403/223; FO 403/231; FO 403/232; FO 403/247; FO 403/257; FO 403/266; FO 403/276. FO 63/1297. For main correspondence see TNA: FO 63/1315-1318 and FO 63/1336. For other relevant material regarding his posting, see CO 537/510 for memorandum on Katembe concession.

21 *The Memoirs of Prince Blücher: A moving record of Anglo-German friendship 1865-1931* (London: John Murray, 1932) contains a valuable chapter on life among this expatriate community in Lorenzo Marques and South Africa.

22 *Report on the Port and Railway of Lorenzo Marques* (1896), Foreign Office, Miscellaneous series [C.7920–19].

23 NLI MS 27,453 (a), RC to Henry Foley, 3 April 1896.

24 Ibid.

25 TNA FO 63/1316, RC to Foreign Office, 16 June 1896.

26 *Morning Post*, 31 December 1903.

27 NLI MS 13,074 (1/i), Roger Casement to Gertrude Bannister, March 1898.

Chapter Three: 1899-1902 (Congo Consulate)

1 TNA FO 63/1365, RC to Marquess of Salisbury, 1 September 1899, Consular No. 37. The report was printed as *Portugal, Diplomatic and Consular reports, Trade of Angola for the years 1897 and 1898* [2363].

2 *Minutes of Evidence, Fifth Report of the Royal Commission on the Civil Service*, PP 1914-16 (Cd 7749) Q. 38,495.

3 TNA FO 2/368, RC to Marquess of Salisbury, 1 March 1899.

4 NLI MS 13,089 (3), *Private and Confidential memo on Mr Casement's Special Mission to Lourenço Marques Jan-March 1900*, 7 June 1900.

5 2/368 RC to Marquess of Salisbury, 1 March 1900.

6 Ibid.

7 Ibid.

8 TNA HD 3/118, Joseph Chamberlain to Sir Alfred Milner, 11 p.m. 6 April 1900. No. 2.

9 Ibid. Sir Alfred Milner to Joseph Chamberlain, 25 April 1900.

10 NLI MS 10,764, George Gavan Duffy Papers, RC's 'Brief to Counsel'.

11 TNA FO 2/368, RC to Sir Martin Gosselin, 30 April 1900.

12 Ibid.

13 TNA FO 2/336 contains two lengthy memoranda by RC describing his meetings with King Leopold II.

14 TNA FO 10/739, RC to the Marquess of Salisbury, 17 October 1900.

15 NLI MS 36,199/2, RC to Richard Morten, 16 March 1901.

16 NLI MS 36,201/1, RC to Francis Cowper, 9 March 1901.

17 TNA FO 2/626, RC to Marquess of Lansdowne, 23 February 1902 and 24 July 1902.

18 TNA FO 403/305, RC to Marquess of Lansdowne, 28 June 1901.

19 TNA FO 10/751, RC to Marquess of Lansdowne, 13 November 1901.

20 TNA FO 629/9, RC to Sir Eric Barrington, 28 April 1902.

21 Ibid.

22 TNA HO 144/1636/311643/33, *Rex v. Roger Casement*, 190.

23 TNA FO 629/9, RC to Sir Eric Barrington, 28 April 1902.

24 TNA FO 629/12, 18 July 1902, RC to Marquess of Lansdowne, Africa No. 10, 20.

25 TNA FO 2/626, RC to Marquess of Lansdowne, 8 July, 1902.

26 NLI MS 36,201/2, RC to F.H. Cowper, 27 June 1902.

27 TNA FO 629/9, RC to Marquess of Lansdowne, 29 June 1902, Africa No. 5.

28 Lowell J. Satre, *Chocolate on Trial: Slavery, Politics & the Ethics of Buisness* (Athens, 2005)

Chapter Four: 1903-1904 (Heart of Darkness)

1 TNA FO 10/804, RC to Marquess of Lansdowne, 29 June 1903.

2 Ibid. RC to Marquess of Lansdowne, 11 June 1903, Africa 13

3 'The Causes of the War and the Foundations of Peace', in CAE, 3.

4 TNA FO 10/805, RC to Marquess of Lansdowne, 3 August 1903.

5 *Correspondence and Report from His Majesty's Consul at Boma respecting the Administration of the Independent State of the Congo*, [Cd. 1933] 1904, 9.

6 Ibid. 23.

7 NLI MS 10,464 (2), RC to Alice Stopford Green, 24 February 1905. The reference to a passage in his diary entry for 4 September 1903 makes this letter of special interest.

8 TNA FO 10/806, RC to Marquess of Lansdowne, 30 September 1903, Africa 38.

9 Ibid. RC to Marquess of Lansdowne, 30 September 1903, Enclosure 1.

10 Ibid. RC to Marquess of Lansdowne, 7 October 1903, Africa 39.

11 BLPES Morel Papers F8/16, Casement to Morel, 23 October 1903.

Chapter Five: 1904-1913 (The Congo Reform Association)

1 NLI MS 13,080 (1/i) RC to Poultney Bigelow, 13 December 1903.

2 Angus Library, BMS Papers, A/21/12 (i), RC to George Grenfell, 22 October 1903.

3 TNA FO 10/806, RC to Harry Farnall, 4 December 1903.

4 TNA FO 10/808, RC to Harry Farnall, 20 February 1904.

5 W.R. Louis & J. Stengers (eds.), *E.D. Morel's History of the Congo Reform Movement* (Oxford, 1968) 160-1.

6 BLPES, MP F8/16, RC to ED Morel, 25 January 1904.

7 RH Antislavery papers, S22/G261 vol. II. RC to Sir Charles Dilke, 17

February 1904.

8 RC to Wilfrid Blunt, 12 May 1914, in Wilfrid Scawen Blunt, *My Diaries: being a personal narrative of events, 1888-1914* (London, 1919-20), vol. II, 455-7.

9 Quoted in ED Morel, *King Leopold's Rule in Africa* (London, 1904), 351. Conrad's letters to Casement are held in the National Library of Ireland.

10 Africa No. 7 (1904) *Further Correspondence respecting the Administration of the Independent State of the Congo* [In continuation of Africa No. 1 (1904)] [Cd. 2097].

11 TNA FO 10/811, RC Memorandum, 10 September 1904.

12 See ED Morel, *King Leopold's Rule in Africa* (London, 1904); another important outlet was The *West African Mail.*

13 ED Morel, *King Leopold's Rule in Africa* (London, 1904), xv.

14 BLPES MP F8/17, RC to Morel, 13 December 1904.

15 Mark Twain, *King Leopold's Soliloquy: A Defence of his Congo Rule* (London, 1907) 24.

16 TNA FO 10/815, RC to Marquess of Lansdowne, 9 October 1905.

17 TNA FO 10/815, RC to Sir Eric Barrington, 10 October 1905.

18 BLPES MP F5/3, "Tiger" Casement to "Bulldog" Morel, Exchange Hotel, Liverpool, 8 April 1911.

19 James Connolly, 'Belgium Rubber and Belgium Neutrality', *The Irish Worker*, 14 November 1914.

20 BLPES MP, F8/25, Casement to Morel, 5 June 1913.

Chapter Six: 1906-1913 (South America)

1 NLI MS 13,074 (6/i), RC to Gertrude Bannister, 1 September 1909, Rio de Janeiro.

2 Ibid.

3 Angus Mitchell (ed.), *The Amazon Journal of Roger Casement* (London & Dublin, 1997) 310

4 *Diplomatic and Consular Reports, Brazil. Report for the years 1905-06 on the Trade of Santos.* No 3952 [Cd. 3727-35].

5 *Diplomatic and Consular Reports, Brazil, Report for the year 1907 and previous years on the trade of the Consular district of Pará,* No 4111 [Cd.3727-194]

6 Ibid.

7 TNA FO 128/324, RC to Cheetham, 11 May 1908.

8 For RC's notes on his readings of books on South America, see NLI MS 13,087.

9 The Anthropology Archive at the National Museum of Ireland contains a number of artefacts collected from sub-Saharan Africa and the Amazon.

10 See SRCHD, 601-2.

11 The Natural History Museum of Ireland has the collection of butterflies. For an interesting reference to the collection see Rebecca Solnit, *A Book of Migrations: some passages in Ireland* (London, 1997), 28-43.

12 Sheila Pim, *The Wood and the Trees: A biography of Augustine Henry* (London, 1966) and Seamus O'Brien, *In the Footsteps of Augustine Henry* (Suffolk, 2011).

13 NLI MS 13,087 (31), *Rough notes on the timber of the Amazon valley*

14 For the text of the essay see the on-line, open access journal *Irish Migrations Studies in Latin America*, 4:3, July 2006, 157-165.

15 Dora Sigerson Shorter, 'I have been to Hy-Brasail', in *Ballads and Poems* (London, 1899), 62-63. Ethna Carbery, *The Four Winds of Eirinn: Twenty Fifth Anniversary Edition* (Dublin, 1927), 54.

16 BLPES, RC to ED Morel, 15 September 1909.

17 See Angus Mitchell (ed.) *The Amazon Journal of Roger Casement* (London: & Dublin, 1997).

18 Ibid, 497-8.

19 Casement's album of Amazon photos and captions is reproduced with accompanying text in the Spanish translation of the Amazon journal by Sonia Fernández Ordás, *Diario de la Amazonía* (La Coruña, 2011).

20 *Correspondence respecting the treatment of British colonial subjects and native Indians employed in the collection of rubber in the Putumayo district* (London, 1912).

21 US Department of State, *Slavery in Peru: Message from the President of the United States, Transmitting Reports of the Secretary of State, with Accompanying papers concerning the Alleged Existence of Slavery in Peru*, (Washington DC, 1913)

22 For the best account of the Vatican's involvement see Francesco Turvasi,

Giovanni Genocchi and the Indians of South America (1911-1913), (Rome, 1988).

23 Roger Casement 'The Putumayo Indians', *The Contemporary Review*, September 1912, 561.

24 The correspondence between RC and Roberts is held among the Antislavery papers at Rhodes House, University of Oxford Mss Brit. Emp S22. The key letter regarding the Amazon journal was written on 27 January 1913.

25 Mensaje del Presidente de la República Juan Manuel Santos, en la celebración del Día de la Raza, Bogotá, 12 Octubre, 2012.

26 Raul Teteye Ugeche, Rector del Colegio Indígena Casa del Conocimento, *Memorias del Etnocidio Cauchero*.

27 Carta de Benedicto XVI a los Indígenas Colombianos, 15 June 2012.

28 *Roger Casement en Iberoamérica: El caucho, la Amazonía y el mundo atlántico, 1884-1916* (Madrid, 2012)

Chapter Seven: 1905-13 (Building an Irish Network)

1 TNA HO 144/1636/311643/33, Rex v. Sir Roger Casement, 17.

2 *Some Poems of Roger Casement* (Dublin, 1918), x-xi.

3 See Brian P. Murphy, *Patrick Pearse and the Lost Republican Ideal* (Dublin, 1991).

4 Eamon Phoenix, Pádraic Ó Cléireacháin, Eileen McAuley & Nuala McSparran (eds.), *Feis na nGleann: A Century of Gaelic Culture in the Antrim Glens* (Stair Uladh, 2005).

5 *The United Irishman*, 9 July 1904.

6 See Marnie Hay, *Bulmer Hobson and the Nationalist Movement in Twentieth-Century Ireland* (Manchester, 2009).

7 'The Language of the Outlaw', *The United Irishman*, 17 February 1906. Reproduced in CAE, 112-15.

8 Ibid.

9 For a recent appraisal of Milligan's life see Catherine Morris, *Alice Milligan and the Irish Cultural Revival* (Dublin, 2012).

10 *Catholic Bulletin*, vol. VI, October 1916.

11 SRCHD, 134.

12 NAI DT/S7805 B.

13 James Connolly, *Labour and Irish History* (Dublin. 1914), iii.

14 NLI MS 10,464 (3), RC to A Stopford Green, 24 April 1904.

15 NLI MS 10,464 (3), RC to A Stopford Green, 25 Feb 1905.

16 NLI MS 10,464 (3), RC to A Stopford Green, 20 April 1907.

17 For my efforts to identify Casement's pseudonymous writings see 'John Bull's other empire: Roger Casement and the Press 1898-1916', in Simon J. Potter, *Newspapers and Empire in Ireland and Britain: Reporting the British Empire c. 1857-1921* (Dublin: Four Courts: 2004) 217-233.

18 UCD LA 11/A/1 WP Ryan Papers, unpublished memoir, 111.

Chapter Eight: 1913–14 (Raising and Arming the Irish Volunteers)

1 See Angus Mitchell, 'An Irish Putumayo: Roger Casement's Humanitarian Relief campaign among the Connemara Islanders, 1913-14, *Irish Economic and Social History*, 31: 2004, 41-60.

2 *Financial Times*, 30 May 1913.

3 TNA CO 904/195, Ireland – Sir Roger Casement, 1913-20.

4 'Why I went to Germany', in CAE, 144.

5 Ibid.

6 *Ulster Guardian*, 14 May 1913, in CAE, 92.

7 *The Nation*, 11 October 1913, 'The Irishry of Ulster'.

8 Ibid.

9 The speeches by the various contributors were subsequently collected and published by A Stopford Green in *A Protestant Protest*, 16.

10 Ibid., 34.

11 NLI MS 10,764 (1), RC 'Brief to Counsel', 9.

12 *Times* (London), 26 October 1913.

13 *Times* (London), 31 October 1913.

14 JR White, *Misfit* (Dublin, 2005), 164.

15 *Fortnightly Review*, 1 November 1913, 806.

16 *An Claidheamh Soluis,* 1 November 1913, 6.

17 Bulmer Hobson, *Ireland Yesterday and Tomorrow* (Tralee, 1968), 44.

18 NLI MacNeill Papers, MacNeill to RC, 25 November 1913 [Acc. 4902 (23)].

19 Bulmer Hobson, *A short history of the Irish Volunteers* (Dublin, 1918), 23.

20 NLI D4645, RC to Horgan, 16 February 1914.

21 The articles appeared in the February, March and April 1914 editions of *The Irish Review*.

22 See Thomas Toomey, *The War of Independence in Limerick 1912-1921* (Limerick, 2009).

23 *Limerick Leader*, 26 January 1914.

24 The Madge Daly Papers, University of Limerick, Folder 47, Tom Clarke to John Daly, 26 January 1914.

25 *Irish Volunteer*, 1:8, 28 March 1914.

26 This story took many years to become public knowledge. It was eventually written up in Sean Cronin *The McGarrity Papers* (Tralee, 1972) and more extensively in Leon Ó Broin, *The Prime Informer: a suppressed scandal* (Sidwick and Jackson, 1971).

27 Kevin McMahon, 'The "Crossmaglen Conspiracy" Case', *Journal of the Armagh Diocesan Historical Society*, 6:2, 251-286.

28 *Irish Independent*, 28 March 1914; reprinted in *The Irish Volunteer*, 11 April 1914.

29 Sheila Johnston, *Alice: A Life of Alice Milligan* (Omagh, 1994), 122-3.

30 'Why I went to Germany', in CAE, 146.

31 Darrell Figgis, *Recollections of the Irish War* (London, 1927), 16-58.

32 NLI MS 5611, RC to Daniel Enright, 25 May 1914.

33 NLI MS 10,464 (3), RC to ASG, 20 June 1914.

34 NLI MS 13,074 (9/1), RC to Gertrude Bannister, 6 January 1914.

Chapter Nine: 1914 (America)

1 Dr Charles Curry (ed.), *Sir Roger Casement's Diaries* (Munich, 1922), 21.

2 Michael Keogh, *With Casement's Irish Brigade* (Drogheda, 2010).

3 Dr Charles Curry (ed.), *Sir Roger Casement's Diaries* (Munich, 1922), 27.

4 *Gaelic American*, 8 August 1914.

5 *Documents Relative to the Sinn Féin Movement* (1921).

6 Diarmuid Lynch, *The I.R.B. and the 1916 Insurrection* (Cork, 1957).

7 NLI 49,154/14, RC to Gertrude Bannister, 30 July 1916.

8 CAE, 'The Keeper of the seas', 22.

9 CAE, 'The Balance of Power', 36.

10 CAE, 'The Elsewhere Empire', 83.

11 CAE, 'The Freedom of the Seas', 64.

12 Ibid.

13 NLI MS 10,464, RC to A. Stopford Green, 14 September 1914.

14 CAE, The Elsewhere Empire', 86-7

15 Political Archive of the German Foreign Office, R 21153, 42 ff.

16 NYPL, Quinn Papers, RC to Quinn, 21 September 1914.

17 NLI 4902 (2), RC to Richard Morten, 15 October 1914.

Chapter Ten: October 1914–April 1916 (Imperial Germany)

1 TNA FO 95/776, M. Findlay to Edward Grey, 31 October 1914.

2 TNA HO 144/1637/311643/140 contains these statements. They are all dated July 1916 and were gathered by Basil Thomson's agents at Special Branch.

3 C. Andrew, *The Defence of the Realm: The Authorised History of MI5* (London, 2009), 105.

4 TNA FO 337/107.

5 For the diary kept by RC during his journey to the Western Front see *Field Day Review* 8 (Dublin, 2012), 23-44.

6 Reinhard Doerries, *Prelude to the Easter Rising* (London 2000), 61.

7 Clare County Archives, RC to Countess Blücher, 1 February 1916.

8 NLI MS 29,064.

9 'My journey to the German Headquarters at Charleville', *Field Day Review*, 8 (Dublin, 2012), 42.

10 NLI MS 29,064, ff. 45, John Quincy Emerson (Casement) to Editor of *Continental Times*, 6 October 1915.

11 *The Continental Times*, 30 July 1915; manuscript version held in NLI MS 29,064.

12 Reinhard Doerries, *Prelude to the Easter Rising* (Frank Cass,

London 2000) 73.

13 Ibid., 166-168.

14 TNA FO 337/107.

15 NLI MS 1689 & 1690, RC German Diary, 27 November 1914.

16 See Honor O Brolchain, *Joseph Plunkett* (Dublin, 2012).

17 Clare County Archive, RC to von Blücher, 9 February 1916.

18 'A Last Page of my Diary', *Field Day Review* 8 (2012) 45-83.

19 Ibid. 71.

20 NLI MS 49,154/9/1.

21 Correspondence is held in NLI MSS 17,026 & 17,027.

22 Quoted in Xander Clayton, *Aud* (Privately Printed, 2007), 145.

23 Oration delivered by Commandant Thomas Ashe at Casement's Fort, Ardfert, County Kerry, on Sunday, 5 August, 1917.

Chapter Eleven: April–June 1916 (Capture and Trial)

1 NLI Acc. 4902 (18) RC to Agnes Newman, 25 July 1916; a typed copy is held in NLI 13,600 Acc 2427.

2 For a detailed account of Casement's arrest see Donal O'Sullivan, *District Inspector, John A. Kearney*, (Tralee, 2005).

3 Margaret Pearse, 'St Enda's', *Capuchin Annual*, 1942, 227.

4 The story of RC's experiences at Arbour Hill Military Prison are described in NLI MS 10,764, Notes to Counsel, 68.

5 See Jeff Dudgeon, *Roger Casement, The Black Diaries with a study of his background, sexuality, and Irish political life* (Belfast, 2002), 481–86. On the question of collusion see the report by Sir Desmond de Silva QC (2012).

6 TNA HO 144/1636/311643/3A contains the interrogation transcripts.

7 NLI MS 10,764, Typed Notes to Counsel, 20.

8 NLI MS 13,088 (4/iv) Brixton Jail, 23 May 1916, Points for Counsel.

9 NLI MS 10,764, Notes to Counsel.

10 NLI MS 10,764, Notes to Counsel, 10 June 1916.

11 TNA HO 144/1636/311643/3A.

12 Parliamentary Debates, (Commons), LXXXI., 25 April 1916, 2462.

13 TNA WO 141/3/3.

14 NLI MS 10,764, Typed Notes to Counsel, 21 (manuscript insertion).

15 NLI MS 10,764, Typed Notes to Counsel, 22.

16 Parliamentary Debates (Commons), LXXXII, 3 May 1916, 31.

17 NLI MS 13,088 (2).

18 NLI MS 10,764, RC to George Gavan Duffy, 9 May 1916.

19 NLI MS 13,088 (1/viia) Affidavit read by George Gavan Duffy.

20 Parliamentary debates, (Commons), LXXXII, 10 May 1916, 632-634.

21 NLI 49,154/11/1, Brief to Counsel.

22 TNA WO 94/104.

23 A typed copy of the Depositions is held in MS 13,088 (1/v) this includes a transcript of the shorthand notes of the opening speech by the Attorney General.

24 Hansard, 5th series (Commons), vol. 65, col.2155, 7 August 1914.

25 *Times* (London), 27 June 1916.

26 PRO CAB 37/147/33, Confidential memorandum, 13 May 1916 and signed E.P. (?) possibly E.B. (Ernley Blackwell).

27 NLI MS 10,464 (16), Two closely written pages of double-sided foolscap.

28 NLI MS 10,464 (16).

29 TNA HO 144/1636/ 331643/32A.

30 NLI MS 10,464 (16).

31 Ibid.

32 Ibid.

33 NLI MS 10,763 (3), Gavan Duffy to AM Sullivan, 19 May 1916.

34 Ibid.

35 Ibid.

36 NLI MS 10,764, Line of My Defence, 2 June 1916.

37 NLI MS 10,764, Notes for Counsel, Brixton Jail, 5 June 1916.

38 NLI MS 10,763 (7), Sullivan to Gavan Duffy, 6 June 1916.

39 NLI MS 13,088 (1/xxix) includes the Contempt of Court proceedings opened by Gavan Duffy against *The Graphic*.

40 NLI MS 10,763 (6), Mary Boyle O'Reilly of Newspaper Enterprise Association, 3 June 1916.

41 NLI MS 10,763 (7), A Stopford Green to George Gavan Duffy, 8 June 1916.

42 NLI MS 10,763 (9) JH Morgan to George Gavan Duffy.

43 NLI MS 10,764, Notes to Defence.

44 NLI MS 10,764, Notes to Defence, 10 June 1916.

45 NLI MS 10,764 (iii).

46 TNA HO 144/1636/311643/18, Ernley Blackwell, 6 June 1916.

47 NLI MS 10,764, Notes for Counsel, 'What I should like Mr Doyle to do', 5 June 1916.

48 NLI MS 21,535, Gavan Duffy to Bigger, 28 June 1916.

49 TNA HO 144/1636/311643/33, Rex v. Roger Casement.

50 *New Statesman*, 1 March 2010.

51 Brian Inglis, *Roger Casement* (London, 1973), 349.

Chapter Twelve: July–August 1916 (Appeal and Execution)

1 TNA HO 144/1636/311643/5.

2 NLI MS 13,088 (1/xxv), Notice of Appeal, 29 June 1916.

3 NLI MS 49,154/11/2.

4 Ibid.

5 Ibid.

6 Ibid.

7 TNA HO 144/311643/46.

8 TNA HO 144/1636/ ref. 20261, Letter from Patrick Quinn, 8 July 1915.

9 NLI MS 10,763, RC to Gavan Duffy, 30 June 1916.

10 NLI Acc. 4902 (3), RC to Richard Morten, 8 July 1916.

11 Quoted in HH Montgomery Hyde, *The Trial of Roger Casement* (London, 1964), 128.

12 TNA HO 144/1636/311643/33, Rex v. Roger Casement.

13 NLI MS 49,154/12/1, RC to Gertrude Bannister, 18 July 1916.

14 NLI MS 10,763 (18), Morgan to Gavan Duffy, 25 July 1916.

15 NLI MS 10,763 (19), Sullivan to Gavan Duffy, 31 July 1916.

16 NLI MS 17,044, RC to Richard Morten, 28 July 1916.

17 René MacColl, *Roger Casement: A new judgment* (London, 1956), 283.

18 *Dictionary of Irish Biography* (Dublin, 2010).

19 NLI MS 13,075 (2/i), A Stopford Green to Gertrude Bannister, 19 July 1916.

20 *Daily Express*, 30 June 1916.

21 *Daily Express*, 1 July 1916.

22 TNA HO 144/23454.

23 TNA HO 144/1637/311643/140, Basil Thomson to Ernley Blackwell, 26 July 1916.

24 NLI MS 5388. In 1995 it emerged that Doyle visited the American Embassy on 8 July 1916 to persuade the US ambassador to send a letter via the diplomatic bag to 'a friend of President Wilson' which contained a statement that 'the British Government had been circulating false reports about Casement's vices'. See HO 144/1636/311643/44, Notes sent from Basil Thomson to Sir Ernley Blackwell on 10 July.

25 NLI MS 10,763 (16), Gavan Duffy to Gertrude Bannister, 15 July 1916.

26 TNA HO 144/1636/311643/3A, Cabinet Memorandum dated 15 July and circulated at cabinet meeting on 18 July.

27 TNA HO 144 1636/311643/62-180 contains a series of files with petitions and letters from members of the public requesting clemency.

28 TNA HO 144 1636/311643/70.

29 TNA HO 144/ 1636/ 311643/ 79 and 85.

30 Haldane's letters of 24 and 31 July 1916 to A Stopford Green are held in photocopied format in NLI MS 13,600.

30 The Herbert Asquith papers held in the Bodleian Library, Oxford contain a series of petitions collected by councils and local bodies in Ireland.

31 *Manchester Guardian*, 24 July 1916.

32 TNA HO 144/1637/311643/104.

33 TNA FO 371/2798, United States Files.

34 TNA FO 144/1636/311643/141.

35 Congressional Record, 25 July 1916, 13317-13324.

36 Congressional Record, 29 July 1916, 13624-13633.

37 TNA HO 144/1637/311643/104 & FO 371/2798.

38 TNA CAB 37/153/6, 1 August 1916.

39 TNA CAB 37/153/11, 2 August 1916.

40 TNA CAB 37/153/13, 2 August 1916.

41 TNA HO 144/1637/311643/154, Sir C. Spring-Rice to HO. Received in HO 4.20 p.m, 2 August 1916.

42 TNA HO 144/1637/311643/150.

43 PRONI T/3787/19/1, RC to John Casement, 6 June 1916.

44 NLI MS Acc. 4902 (18), RC to Agnes Newman, 25 July 1916,

45 NLI MS 49,154/14, RC to Elizabeth and Gertrude Bannister, 30 July 1916.

46 Ibid.

47 LG Redmond Howard, *Sir Roger Casement: A Character Sketch without Prejudice* (Dublin, 1916).

48 Eva Gore-Booth, 'For God and Kathleen ni Houlihan', in *Catholic Bulletin,* May 1918, 230-234.

49 RC to A Stopford Green, 13 July 1911, quoted in SRCHD, 472.

50 For example, see NLI MS 49,154/7, RC to 'My dearest children of the well', 2 September 1906.

51 Denis Gwynn 'Roger Casement's Last Weeks', in *Studies,* Spring 1965, 63-73.

52 NLI MS 49,154/12/4, Roger Casement to Gertrude and Elizabeth Bannister, 2 August 1916. A typed copy of excerpts from this letter is to be found in NLI MS 17,046. Some passages have been marked in a blue crayon and at the bottom a note reads 'Marked by Censor. Not for Publication.'

53 CAE, 225-27.

54 Parliamentary Debates (Commons), 564, 6 February 1957, 503-5. A Fenner Brockway.

55 Henry W Nevinson, *More Changes More Chances* (New York, 1925), 296.

56 NLI MS 10,763 (20) Father Thomas Carey to Gavan Duffy, 5 August 1916.

57 TNA HO 144/1637/311643/141 ref 20261, Percy Mander to H. Samuel, 3 August 1916. Samuel had specifically requested for an anal autopsy to be carried out on Casement's body. For discussion of this matter see *Times Literary Supplement*, 5624, 14 January 2011.

58 Typescript of Terence McSwiney's diary held in Cork County Museum.

59 NLI MS 13,075 (2/ii), Clement Shorter to Gertrude Bannister, 6 January 1918.

60 NLI MS 10,763 (23) Gertrude Bannister to Gavan Duffy, 19 August 1916.

Chapter Thirteen: 1916-2016 (History as Mystery: The Inside Story)

1 CAE, 225.

2 Adam's auction catalogue, 20 April 2010.

3 Charles Curry (ed.), *Diaries of Sir Roger Casement: His Mission to Germany and the Findlay Affair* (Munich, 1922).

4 NAI DT S9606, Alleged Casement Diaries.

5 For a fuller discussion of this see my essay 'Phases of a Dishonourable Phantasy', *Field Day Review* 8 (2012), 85-124.

6 Artemus Jones, *Without my wig* (Liverpool, 1944),166.

7 See *Field Day Review* 8 (2012), 85-124.

8 AJP Taylor, *The Troublemakers* (London, 1969), 90.

9 The correspondence ran regularly during the last months of 1964 in both the *Irish Times* and *Irish Press*. Montgomery Hyde did serve with MI6 during the war.

10 Tory had worked closely with Churchill during the Battle of Britain, and later retired to Ireland where he died in 2012, a few days short of his 100th birthday. His obituary in *The Daily Telegraph*, 11 October 2012, included various photographs of Casement.

11 *Observer*, 6 January 1946, 'Far Away and Long Ago'.

12 Jules Marchal, *E.D. Morel contre Léopold II: L'Histoire de Congo 1900-1910*, 2 vols, (Paris, 1996).

13 Adam Hochschild, *King Leopold's Ghost: A Story of Greed and Heroism in Central Africa* (Oxford, 2006)

14 See *Field Day Review* 8 (2012), 65-124.

15 Jordan Goodman, *The Devil and Mr Casement: One Man's Struggle for Human Rights in South America's Heart of Darkness* (London, 2009).

16 John Tully, *The Devil's Milk: A Social History of Rubber* (New York, 2011).

17 Correspondence about the casket is held in NLI MS 15,129. The actual object is presently held in the Royal Irish Academy.

Index